FROM BILLY GRAHAM TO SARAH PALIN

From Billy Graham to Sarah Palin

Evangelicals and the Betrayal
of American Conservatism

———◦◦◦———

D. G. HART

WILLIAM B. EERDMANS PUBLISHING COMPANY
GRAND RAPIDS, MICHIGAN / CAMBRIDGE, U.K.

Published 2011 by
Wm. B. Eerdmans Publishing Co.
2140 Oak Industrial Drive N.E., Grand Rapids, Michigan 49505 /
P.O. Box 163, Cambridge CB3 9PU U.K.

Printed in the United States of America

17 16 15 14 13 12 11   7 6 5 4 3 2 1

Library of Congress Cataloging-in-Publication Data

Hart, D. G. (Darryl G.)
From Billy Graham to Sarah Palin: evangelicals and the betrayal of
American conservatism / Darryl G. Hart.
p.   cm.
Includes bibliographical references.
ISBN 978-0-8028-6628-8 (cloth: alk. paper)
1. Evangelicalism — United States — History — 20th century.
2. Conservatism — Religious aspects — Christianity — History — 20th century.
3. United States — Church history — 20th century.
4. Evangelicalism — United States — History — 21st century.
5. Conservatism — Religious aspects — Christianity — History — 21st century.
6. United States — Church history — 21st century.   I. Title.

BR1642.U5H3745   2011
261.7 — dc22

2011008307

www.eerdmans.com

To Jeremy Beer, Jeff Cain, and Mark Henrie,
who welcomed me into their little platoon

Contents

———◦∿◦———

Irreconcilable Differences?
Evangelicals and American Conservatives

———~《⁂》~———

For over twenty-five years an axiom of American politics has been that evangelical Protestantism is politically conservative. This notion involves the assumption that conservative religion and conservative politics go hand in hand. Prior to the 1970s, of course, evangelicals were known more for an other-worldly faith that made them more concerned with saving souls for the world to come than with turning out voters to decide on matters of the here and now. That is why evangelicals prior to the Reagan revolution had the reputation for being politically passive.

The word *reputation* needs to be emphasized because most evangelicals, like my parents, who did not have a television and so carted my brother and me over to our uncle's to see a Goldwater-Johnson debate during the 1964 presidential campaign, cared about their nation and voted in ways that students of American religion and politics back then rarely noticed. During the 1960s no one really knew about the "God vote" except when Protestants pulled levers and punched chads for candidates who were not Roman Catholic. What is accurate to say of twentieth-century evangelicalism is that from World War II until the rise of the Moral Majority, the Christian Coalition, and Focus on the Family, born-again Protestants lacked notable religious or political leaders or institutions that could rally them as an electoral bloc. Since Ronald Reagan's victory in 1980, however, evangelicalism has been a vocal and visible member of the political coalition identified as conservative.

In point of fact, this axiom of American electoral politics is looking less certain as the years pass. Figures such as Pat Robertson and James Dobson still preside over their parachurch fiefdoms and are capable of marshaling supporters to call congressional delegates or vote for specific candidates. But these evangelical leaders are old (since I began working on this book, Jerry Falwell and D. James Kennedy have died) and the ones who are filling the void are not inclined to identify themselves as conservative. Indeed, a transition is underway in which the born-again Greatest Generation is giving way to a generation of evangelical baby-boomers every bit as unpredictable as their secular, Roman Catholic, or mainline Protestant counterparts. This generational succession suggests that the days of goodwill and harmonious relations between evangelicals and conservatives may be coming to an end. Whether the final break will be on the order of an ugly divorce or simply a mutually-agreed-upon decision just to be friends, the tensions surfacing between evangelicals and the Right are reaching the threshold of irreconcilable differences.

The Religious Right in the Age of Obama

The recent leftward drift of evangelical Protestants, not to mention the uneasy alliance between born-again religion and political conservatism since 1980, may sound farfetched at a time when the two most popular evangelicals in contemporary American politics are Rick Warren and Sarah Palin, both of whom tap social convictions that drive liberals crazy. But as much as evangelicals like Warren and Palin may cause indigestion among Americans left of center, these evangelicals' ideas and behavior also create considerable discomfort for conservatives. In fact, the disparity between evangelicalism and conservatism was fully on display between Palin's nomination in September 2008 as John McCain's vice-presidential running mate and Warren's participation in the January 2009 inauguration of President Barack Obama.

Palin initially gave McCain a ratings boost by energizing the evangelical base, the very outcome for which the advisors to the Republicans' top candidate had hoped. Not only was Palin an evangelical — though few knew the exact variety — but she had recently given birth to a baby with Down syndrome who typically would have been screened and recommended for abortion. Adding to the appeal was her status as a governor of Alaska; she brought some executive credibility to a ticket that needed it. Just as important was her anti-establishment rhetoric and apparent independence from entrenched interests within either the GOP or the Washington Beltway. Almost as soon as her name surfaced as McCain's pick, Palin became the fulfillment of those hoping for an evangelical Mrs. Smith who would go to Washington and provide even more straight talk than her running mate — in part because she could speak in the cadence of conservative Christianity.

But within a week of the Republican national convention, the wheels began to wobble on the Palin bandwagon. Reporters explored the nature of her convictions and unearthed the fact that as governor she had signed a proclamation that honored Christian Heritage Week in Alaska. They also discovered that Palin had remarked that creationism should be part of the discussion in public school classrooms about human origins. Reports circulated that the governor had invoked God in prayers for the construction of a natural gas pipeline and for American soldiers in the Iraq war. This caught the McCain campaign off guard, and campaign officials refused to comment on Palin's beliefs. A McCain spokeswoman told one reporter, "I think talking about where [Palin] worships today and how she characterizes herself speaks for itself about where she is today."[1] For some Republicans, Palin was clearly a breath of fresh air precisely *because* of her faith; according to former House Majority Leader Tom DeLay, "It's obvious that's a woman with a world view. I could see it in the way she looked at her family. I could see it in the discussion around her child. It's obvious her faith is her foundation."[2] But evangelical spokesmen, arguably with the most to lose from an embarrassing vice-presidential candi-

---

1. Quotation from http://blog.christianitytoday.com/ctpolitics/2008/09/sarah _palins_re.html.

2. DeLay quotation from http://blog.christianitytoday.com/ctpolitics/2008/09/ tom_delay_on_pa.html.

date, were cautious. Tony Perkins of the Family Research Council responded to a question about how Palin's beliefs would translate into policy: "There's not a lot of evidence in Alaska other than, you know, she's conservative. . . . [Y]ou can't point to a lot of policies that people say [she adopted] because she's a conservative evangelical."[3]

Then came the infamous interview on prime-time television with Katie Couric. The CBS anchor asked Palin about hot-button issues in the culture wars regarding global warming, abortion, contraception, evolution, and homosexuality. Palin clearly sensed that Couric was highlighting positions that would alienate moderates. For instance, on contraception Palin said, "Well, I am all for contraception. And I am all for preventative measures that are legal and safe, and should be taken, but Katie, again, I am one to believe that life starts at the moment of conception." On evolution Palin told Couric, "I think it should be taught as an accepted principle." She credited her daughter's science teacher with instilling "a respect for science." Palin admitted that she saw the hand of God in "this beautiful creation that is Earth" but denied that she had inserted God into the Alaska science curriculum: "Science should be taught in science class."[4] A month later, when Focus on the Family's James Dobson interviewed Palin, she felt freer than with Couric to highlight her socially conservative positions. "This is a strong platform built around the planks in this platform that respect life and respect the entrepreneurial spirit of this great country and those things, back to the social issues that are what Republicans, at least in the past, had articulated and tried to stand on," she explained. "Now, finally, we have very solid planks in the platform that will allow us to build an even stronger foundation for our country."[5]

Sentiments like those, however, were not sufficiently persuasive to move enough evangelicals to vote in the November election for the Republican ticket. Although born-again Protestants again voted over-

3. Perkins quotation from http://blog.christianitytoday.com/ctpolitics/2008/09/belief_barrier.html.

4. Transcript of the Palin/Couric interview from http://blog.christianitytoday.com/ctpolitics/2008/09/palin_speaks_to.html.

5. Interview available at http://blog.christianitytoday.com/ctpolitics/2008/10/james_dobson_in.html.

whelmingly for a Republican presidential candidate according to tabulations by the Pew Research Center — McCain received seventy-three percent of the evangelical vote — this was down from the 2004 election, when Bush had received seventy-nine percent in his race against John Kerry. To be sure, a variety of factors, especially fatigue from the Iraq war and worries about the economy, were responsible for McCain's defeat. But Palin's performance failed to generate the evangelical votes necessary for Republican victory. In fact, her quirky combination of faith and social conservatism alienated many Americans and some born-again Protestants looking for regime change.

Rick Warren's contributions to the 2008 presidential contest and outcome were more ambiguous than Palin's but also indicated the drift of evangelical baby boomers away from the Right. On August 16, 2008, Warren bolstered his status as a public figure by hosting a forum at his Saddleback Church in which he asked questions of McCain and Obama about the nation and its affairs. McCain appeared to emerge from this event with a significant edge over Obama in the evangelical sweepstakes by answering questions about abortion in ways that affirmed born-again convictions. When McCain said that human rights begin at conception and that he would be a pro-life president, he delighted the evangelical audience. Meanwhile, when Obama answered with the infelicitous line that answers to these questions were "above my pay grade," observers wondered if Warren had suckered the Democratic nominee into a gaffe that could cost the election.

Throughout the rest of the fall Warren kept a low profile. He did appear with Sean Hannity and Alan Colmes on their Fox News show after the election to discuss McCain's defeat. When Colmes asked the Southern California pastor about McCain's loss of votes among evangelicals, the co-host was raising a legitimate question, since Warren's own humanitarian activities pointed to the dawning of a new evangelical electorate, one more willing to fight against global warming and HIV/AIDS than to oppose such perennial bogeymen as abortion and gay marriage. Colmes asked whether Darfur and the environment were responsible for Obama's gaining more votes from evangelicals than John Kerry had in 2004. Warren responded: "Actually, I think, Alan, in this particular election, the economy trumped literally everything else. People were worried about the bread and butter issues." Colmes followed with a question about the effects of the forum at Saddleback Church: "Do you think your forum with both candidates had any effect on what happened during this election?" Warren replied, "I don't know." He added, "I don't think evangelicals have changed on any of their core issues at all, not at all. But I do think that, in this particular election, that the economy came up at the top."[6]

But that was not the last word from Warren. Approximately six weeks after the election, the president-elect invited Warren to give the invocation at the January inauguration. The reaction from Obama's base was intense and formidable, particularly because of Warren's initial support for Proposition 8, a ballot initiative that prohibited the legalization of gay marriage in California. One blogger announced that Obama had chosen "Prop 8 Homophobe" Warren and in so doing had offended gays and lesbians who had mustered unprecedented support and votes for the president-elect.[7] In point of fact, Warren had waffled on the measure, first supporting it and then backtracking during a televised interview with Larry King. Meanwhile, Warren drew flack from evangelicals who could not understand how the purpose-driven pastor could endorse the new president by giving God's blessing, or how he could appear in the same program with Gene Robinson, the gay Episcopal bishop who would also be part of the ceremonies. Franklin Graham and Pat Robertson did defend Warren's decision. The latter said, "All he's been asked to do is give an invocation. He isn't asked to endorse Obama. He's going to stand up there on the steps of the Capitol and he's going to say, God, please bless this country. And he will do that very well."[8] The Episcopalian Robinson, however, was not so charitable: "I'm all for Rick Warren being at the table but we're not talking about a discussion, we're talking about putting someone up front and center at what will be the most watched

6. Transcript of interview available at http://www.realclearpolitics.com/articles/2008/11/pastor_rick_warren_on_hannity.html.

7. Quotation from http://blog.christianitytoday.com/ctpolitics/2008/12/obama_defends_r.html.

8. Graham and Robertson quotations from http://blog.christianitytoday.com/ctpolitics/2008/12/rick_warren_rem.html.

inauguration in history, and asking his blessing on the nation. And the God that he's praying to is not the God that I know."[9]

As the 2008 campaign ended and the Obama administration began, Warren had the last evangelical word. In his invocation, he prayed:

> Help us, O God, to remember that we are Americans, united not by race, or religion, or blood, but to our commitment to freedom and justice for all. When we focus on ourselves, when we fight each other, when we forget you, forgive us. When we presume that our greatness and our prosperity is ours alone, forgive us. When we fail to treat our fellow human beings and all the earth with the respect that they deserve, forgive us. And as we face these difficult days ahead, may we have a new birth of clarity in our aims, responsibility in our actions, humility in our approaches, and civility in our attitudes, even when we differ.
>
> Help us to share, to serve and to seek the common good of all. May all people of goodwill today join together to work for a more just, a more healthy and a more prosperous nation and a peaceful planet. And may we never forget that one day all nations and all people will stand accountable before you. We now commit our new president and his wife, Michelle, and his daughters, Malia and Sasha, into your loving care.[10]

These were petitions that resonated with remarks that Warren made to *Christianity Today* during an interview a few days before the inauguration: "President-elect Obama has again demonstrated his genuine commitment to bringing all Americans of goodwill together in search of common ground. I applaud his desire to be the president of every citizen." (Warren failed to clarify whether Obama was presiding over the citizens of the United States or the occupants of planet Earth, since his vision in the invocation was not national but global.)

What is striking about these two figures who dominated coverage

---

9. Robinson quotation from http://blog.christianitytoday.com/ctpolitics/2009/01/warren_applauds.html.

10. Text available at http://blog.christianitytoday.com/ctpolitics/2009/01/rick_warrens_in.html.

of evangelicals during the 2008 election and beyond is their common convictions and differing styles. For both Palin and Warren, the issues of sex, marriage, and family are of great importance. Each taps well the primary concerns that mark evangelicals as social conservatives. Yet Warren and Palin also reveal a growing divide among evangelicals. Some, like Palin, are still willing to identify with political conservatism, even if they don't necessarily understand its subtleties or appreciate its underlying philosophy. Others, like Warren, are looking for a less abrasive public reputation and so are inclined to expand their moral convictions beyond the realm of sex and marriage to the environment, war, poverty, and human rights. Obviously, Palin carries on the tradition of Falwell, Robertson, and Dobson, those evangelical leaders who funneled born-again Protestants into the Reagan coalition. In contrast, Warren echoes figures like Mark Hatfield and Jim Wallis, evangelicals motivated by Christian morality but who care little for a conservative outlook that might shape such ethical concerns.

No matter what Palin or Warren might indicate about the political direction of evangelicals in the era of Obama, their recent performance confirms an important point of this book, namely, that after thirty years of laboring with and supposedly listening to political conservatives, evangelicals have not expanded their intellectual repertoire significantly beyond the moral imperatives of the Bible. In fact, born-again Protestants show no more capacity to think conservatively than they did in the age of Billy Graham's greatest popularity. They do not know how to yell "stop" to the engines of modernity the way that conservatives typically have. They have not learned to be wary of concentrations of power and wealth, frustrated with mass society and popular culture's distraction from "permanent things," or skeptical about any humanitarian plan to end human misery. Instead, evangelicals are more likely to support political plans to improve society, grow the economy, and expand the United States' global presence as long as doctors are not performing abortions and ministers are not presiding over the marriages of gay couples.

The star power of Warren and Palin, along with the limits of Red-State-Blue State analysis, have obscured this disparity between evangelicalism and conservatism. To be sure, many evangelicals in the pews continue to vote consistently for the Republican Party, but their reasons for doing so are morally thick and politically thin. This is not to say that the GOP itself is the arbiter of political conservatism properly understood. In fact, the close identification of conservatives with Republicans has obscured the supposition, articulated over a half century ago by conservative writers like Russell Kirk, the author of *The Conservative Mind* (1953), that culture is more important and more basic than elections and legislation, that politics is merely a reflection of a culture's health. Still, whether like Palin, who tried to align her convictions with McCain's platform, or Warren, who tried to find a *via media* between Obama and McCain, evangelicals do not think or act like conservatives. This failure stems from the odd combination of certainty about morals and indifference to first-order political considerations about legitimate authority, national sovereignty, freedom, the common good, civic virtue, and the best conditions for human flourishing.

Separate Paths to the Reagan Revolution

Evangelicalism's discomfort with conservatism has been evident for some time, even if the elasticity of the Reagan coalition hid this reality. One way to illustrate the point is to examine the landmark history of modern American conservatism, George H. Nash's *The Conservative Intellectual Movement in America since 1945*. Judging a book by its index has its limitations, of course, but it can be revealing. Glancing through Nash's index yields no trouble in finding such conservative luminaries as Russell Kirk, the so-called father of modern American conservatism, or William F. Buckley Jr., the founder of *The National Review,* or Frederick A. Hayek, whose book *The Road to Serfdom* alerted Americans to the perils of big government and economic planning whether in Moscow or Washington, D.C., or Frank S. Meyer, a regular contributor to *National Review* who popularized conservative ideas, or Brent Bozell, the ghost writer for Barry Goldwater's *Conscience of a Conservative* (1960), or Wilmore Kendall, one of Buckley's professors at Yale in political science whom the student recruited to be a founding editor of *National Review.* Much harder to find — impossible, in fact — is a reference to any evangelical in the post–World War II movement that launched Fuller Seminary, *Christianity Today,* or the Billy Graham Evangelistic Association.

This may have been an oversight by Nash, an indication that he was defining modern conservatism too narrowly or was ignorant of the born-again Protestant world. But in the second edition of the book, published in 1996, evangelicalism was still a cipher. Nash did devote three pages to evangelical Protestants as part of the Reagan coalition and conceded that they shared worries with political conservatives about the health of the United States. But he also identified an important difficulty that would take some time to play out. "Whereas the traditionalists of the 1940s and 1950s had largely been academics in revolt *against* secularized, mass society," Nash clarified, evangelical support for Reagan was "a revolt *by* the 'masses' against the secular virus and its aggressive carriers in the nation's elites."[11] Nash saw that, unlike conservatives, evangelicals were oblivious to the structural problems of mass society that went deeper than abortion, gay marriage, or pornography. Although he did not say so explicitly, Nash intuited that evangelicalism was a form of Christianity essentially uncritical of modernity, since as a mass movement itself born-again Protestantism depended for its very well-being upon social forces such as mass communication, political and economic centralization, and cultural homogeneity that sustained the social and cultural ills evangelicals lamented. These Protestants could readily identify specific sins but lacked the capacity to account for the social patterns that nurtured such evils.

To be sure, the idea that evangelical Protestants are not politically conservative is implausible if the only alternative is liberalism. Aside from sectional disputes that always made southern evangelicals wary of Republicans — unless the Democratic alternative was Roman Catholic — American evangelicals generally supported the GOP throughout the twentieth century. An important factor was ambivalence about the big government programs associated with twentieth-century liberalism in the form of either FDR's New Deal or LBJ's Great Society. Also, evangelicals' patriotism made them receptive to conser-

11. George H. Nash, *The Conservative Intellectual Movement in America* (1976; Wilmington, Del.: ISI Books, 1996), 334.

vative defenses of the integrity and sovereignty of the United States. Furthermore, because evangelicals affirmed the sinfulness of human nature and feared the corrupting influence of power, they were often suspicious of government programs (especially Democratic ones) to end suffering or engineer the good society. For born-again Protestants, sin was so intractable that not policy but the gospel was the only remedy. So, if the options were between liberty or tyranny, free markets or state planning, rewarding responsible behavior or providing welfare for those capable of work, strong national defense or negotiating with hostile regimes, preserving private property or increasing the federal budget, evangelicals chose from the conservative column.

Nevertheless, the Protestants responsible for the post–World War II evangelical resurgence were bystanders to the arguments and institutions that came to define American conservatism. As Nash explains, postwar conservatism emerged from three significant concerns. Some conservatives, including traditionalists like Richard Weaver (the author of *Ideas Have Consequences*) and Russell Kirk, recognized the importance of cultural conventions handed down by previous generations, the imaginative and spiritual capacities of the human person reflected in the West's literary and philosophical contribution, and the genuine pleasures derived from ordinary human experience. Others came to a conservative position on a path trod by the likes of Whittaker Chambers, whose book *Witness* exposed not only the conspiratorial treachery of communism but also its inherently spiritual declaration of independence for human beings from the revealed truths of their creator. For these anti-communists, the Cold War was more than a political rivalry between NATO and the Soviet Union; it was a metaphysical contest between faith and unbelief. Still another strand of conservative arguments came from libertarians such as Hayek and Meyer who feared the economic, political, and cultural consequences of socialism. State planning carried out by either democratic or Communist governments was at odds with spontaneous order and political liberty. By no means did traditionalists, anti-Communists, and libertarians add up to a coherent intellectual synthesis. But in the pages of *National Review* and *Modern Age*, conservatives debated and reaffirmed the value of limited government, the sanctity of human life in its social and individual dimensions, private property, and the Augustinian suspicion of political schemes designed to end human suffering.

Evangelicalism — a form of Protestantism distinct from the mainline or liberal denominations — arose in the same years as modern American conservatism, and yet despite supplying voters for conservative politicians, the born-again faith added nothing to the conservative mind. At the beginning of the twentieth century America's largest Protestant denominations were generally unified in their understanding of the churches' responsibilities for the social order and national purpose. This outlook combined both evangelism and social activism, also known as the Social Gospel. But the fundamentalist controversy of the 1920s split American Protestants into religiously conservative and liberal camps. Evangelicals retained the convictions that nurtured evangelism and foreign missions; liberals kept alive the notion that the church had responsibility for a just society. Those Protestants who identify as evangelical generally descend from believers who were known in the 1920s as fundamentalists. Rather than trying to adapt Christianity to new intellectual and social realities for the sake of a socially and intellectually engaged faith as liberal Protestants did, evangelicals were committed to forms of ministry and devotion forged during the revivals of the Second Great Awakening.

The National Association of Evangelicals, founded in 1942, was the first of several organizations designed to create a distinct identity as well as a more unified outlet for the variety of independent congregations, small denominations, Bible schools, and missions agencies that lacked a national voice. The NAE's purpose was not simply to avoid duplication and coordinate common endeavors, but also to cultivate a warmer and more winsome image than the acerbic reputation from which fundamentalism suffered. Other evangelical initiatives soon capitalized on this new and improved version of conservative Protestantism. Billy Graham, who was closely linked to the networks that consolidated around the NAE, became a national spokesman in the late 1940s and early 1950s when he emerged as the twentieth century's greatest evangelist. In 1956 evangelicals secured a regular publishing vehicle for their concerns with the creation of the magazine *Christianity Today.* Meanwhile, the NAE established a presence in

Washington, D.C., to coordinate relations with the federal government for missionaries, military chaplains, and religious broadcasters; it eventually added the task of lobbying the federal government on public policy. Although committed to the spiritual value of evangelism and missions, these conservative Protestants also saw these activities as essential for the health and well-being of the nation, just as the proponents of the Second Great Awakening had during the antebellum era.

Despite the generally conservative American assumption that faith is essential to a good society, and despite such conservative openness to traditional Christianity, evangelicals did not identify with political conservatism until the late 1970s, with the emergence of the Religious Right and the presidency of Ronald Reagan. Indeed, after *Newsweek* declared 1976 the "Year of the Evangelical," conservative Protestants suddenly went from political anonymity to electoral celebrity. Jerry Falwell's Moral Majority was the first outlet for distinctly evangelical political motivation and action; Pat Robertson would soon follow with the Christian Coalition. These organizations did not have direct ties to post–World War II evangelical institutions like the NAE. But because practically every Protestant thought to be conservative in belief was lumped together by the media, groups as distinct as the NAE and the Moral Majority were stuffed into the broad and electorally significant constituency of *evangelical.* By then evangelicals had earned the moniker "New Christian Right" or "Religious Right." But their outlook was several steps removed from the political Right. Evangelicals had been too busy worrying about the United States' identity as a Christian nation to take notice of conservative debates about the United States' political identity and order.

Definitions and the Scope of the Book

Despite historical and religious affinities, evangelicalism and conservatism did not overlap either intellectually or demographically for some very important reasons. Perhaps most prominently, most of the leading conservatives were Roman Catholics or would convert to Rome, and in the 1950s and 1960s most American Protestants labored under a long-standing suspicion of Roman Catholicism. To have overcome this hostility for the sake of shared political theory was as unthinkable as it was anachronistic.

Additional factors prevented born-again Protestants from recognizing the emergence of American conservatism as a welcome development that could buttress their own efforts to restore America's moral standards. One important difference between political conservatism and evangelical Protestantism is the populist character of evangelical piety. Born-again Protestantism has always been more comfortable in the vernacular of mass forms of communication than the learned or formal expressions that characterized the conservative intellectual movement; evangelicalism was and continues to be primarily a popular as opposed to an intellectual phenomenon. While they may not have agreed on all points of policy or theory, political conservatives sponsored a number of high-level debates about the state, human nature, freedom, and virtue that nurtured intellectual rigor. In contrast, pastors and parachurch leaders with inspirational and therapeutic appeal dominated evangelicalism. In their institutions and publications, evangelical leaders by and large discouraged intellectual debates, especially on hot-button issues, lest such differences split the movement.

Consequently, while evangelicalism and conservatism elude simple definition, the latter has been easier to identify than the former thanks to the kind of institutions and publications that have sustained political conservatism. For some, being conservative is little more than support for small government and free markets. One challenge for this brand of conservatism is that it is usually synonymous with a large and centralized military-industrial complex that sustains the United States not as a diversely federated republic, but as a global superpower. For others, conservatism is a set of intuitions about human relations, the created order, and humanity's place on earth from which proceed ideas about the scale of government, the rule of law, the inviolability of private property, and the importance of families, neighborhoods, and community organizations. Still others conceive of conservatism as an effort to maintain and defend so-called traditional morality; this morality, accordingly, is not merely old but timeless by virtue of being derived from transcendent truth. The source of these truths can be either the natural order or sacred writings, depending on whether these conservatives are Roman Catholic or Protestant.

The faith and piety of evangelical Protestantism have no direct or obvious tie to political conservatism. To insist upon a conversion experience or new birth, to regard the Bible as the sole source of truth, to emphasize the personal nature of Christ's saving work, and to look for evidence of true faith in a life devoted to godly or holy living — these evangelical attributes are hardly foundational for an account of a good, ordered, and free society. Actually, political historians from the ethno-cultural school have detected parallels between the revivals and reforms of the Second Great Awakening (1810-1850) and the understanding of the United States that first the Whig and then the Republican parties embraced. Unlike Democrats of the time, who advocated a limited, populist government that did not legislate social behavior but rather gave room for the expression of self-interest and local autonomy, Republicans trusted government to enact laws based on eternal truths that would nurture virtuous citizens and build a righteous society. Generally speaking, since 1830 Anglo-American Protestants who supported revivals have been more comfortable with a state that promotes Christian norms as national standards than with a political order that cultivates religious diversity and the integrity of mediating institutions.

In fact, at bottom, evangelical moral idealism may actually be at odds with political conservatism, as odd as that may sound. If conservatism were simply about public morality and virtues, then the habit of pundits and scholars referring to born-again Protestants as "social conservatives" would make sense. But such conservatism did not characterize the Right prior to the Reagan coalition. Indeed, a plausible perspective on post-1950 conservatism is that evangelicals were interlopers within the American Right because they knew so little about the concerns of conservatives. To be sure, evangelicals spoke the language of limited government and free markets, not only to gain a hearing but also because such ideas are part of the traditional fabric of American politics. Nevertheless, evangelicals' moral idealism was alien to American conservatism. In fact, a moral idealism divorced from prior political or philosophical considerations leads inevitably to the kind of radicalism and social engineering that conservatives have historically opposed. Yet the rub for evangelicals is that to insist that public morality needs to be grounded in philosophical or political considerations is to deny the priority of faith to all aspects of human existence; it is to suggest that Christ or the prophet Amos needs to take notes from lectures by Aristotle, John Locke, or James Madison.

What follows is primarily a historical account of evangelical political reflection since World War II with an eye toward evangelical arguments about the American state and the health of its society. The literary evidence in the following pages reveals that evangelical political thought developed independently from the debates that shaped modern conservatism. Instead of relying on conservative insights about order, liberty, and the health of civil society, evangelicals habitually resorted to their Bibles. Indeed, for evangelicals, Scripture was a better guide to the affairs of the United States than the demands of republicanism, constitutionalism, federalism, or the balance of powers.

This means that interpreters of evangelical Protestant politics need to look beyond voting data and consider the reasons that representative born-again Protestant academics and pastors give for political participation, their understanding of the good society, or the value of the American polity. Those interpreters will see that the historical voting data and the philosophy behind it do not necessarily point to the same future. Rank-and-file evangelicals did vote overwhelmingly for Republicans in 2008, and the attraction of "Tea Party" candidates for born-again voters in the 2010 midterm contests is another apparent indication of an affinity between conservatism and evangelicalism. But even while many ordinary evangelicals continue to balk at the Democratic Party and its candidates, the evangelical intelligentsia is tracking toward the political Left and away from conservative politics and the Republican Party. These left-leaning Protestants are the ones writing books, teaching at Christian colleges, and training future evangelical pastors at seminaries. Their understanding of United States politics and biblical teaching on a good society (they will invariably speak of such goodness in terms of "doing justice") is leading them farther and farther away from the arguments, assumptions, and dispositions of conservative writers and thinkers.

Readers may object that evaluating evangelicals by the standards of American conservatism is unfair. Such a reaction is understandable if it relies upon a suspicion that the author himself is a conservative and is faulting evangelicals for not measuring up to his own political outlook. Indeed, this book is based on the conviction that modern American conservatism, as it emerged during the 1950s in the debates among traditionalists, libertarians, and anti-communists, has much to teach evangelicals and all Americans about the polity of the United States and the implications of the nation's subsequent development from a federated republic to an international superpower. Conservative wariness about progress, efficiency, wealth, concentrated power, and mass culture is hardly reactionary but redolent with wisdom about human nature, social relations, and even the meaning of the United States. But aside from the outlook that informs this book, judging evangelicals by conservative standards is fitting if born-again Protestants themselves *claim* to be conservative. If the assumptions and aims of evangelicals are at odds with conservatism, then concluding that born-again Protestantism is not conservative is not only fair, but correct. A narrative revealing this tension may well be valuable if only to help evangelicals and conservatives adjust their expectations of each other.

Aside from facilitating a better understanding of differences between evangelicals and conservatives, this book may also help evangelicals who want to be conservative but do not know how. On the one hand, evangelicals will need to see that the way they understand morality, civil society, and the function of government is actually more compatible with the idealism of the Left than with the realism of the Right. In fact, one of the great ironies of the Religious Right is that its promotion of a biblically informed and faith-based politics cleared the way for a swath of evangelical writers who are now clearly opposed to conservatism and inclined to identify with the Left. At one point in the narrative that follows, an evangelical Left looked like the way forward for born-again Protestant politics more than support for the Right. The contemporary dominance of evangelical authors and activists on the liberal side of the political spectrum may very well be a return to the natural state of born-again politics.

On the other hand, if evangelicals want to be classically conservative, they will need to reconsider the way that faith relates to politics, especially within the polity of the United States. This reconsideration will involve the recovery of an older Augustinian view of the relationship between the City of God and the City of Man, in which the ultimate purposes of history are not located in the rise and fall of empires or republics but in the church of Jesus Christ. This religious reorientation is closely related to the political transformation evangelicals will need to undergo. Rather than looking at the American nation as a divinely instituted polity to make straight the way of the Lord, evangelicals will need to take counsel from conservatives on the relative unimportance of the nation-state for securing the truly human goods of the created order. Born-again Protestants will also need to consider the ways in which the American form of government places limits on the central political institutions for the sake of human institutions that do a better job of generating real community and cultivating responsible persons. In other words, evangelicals will need to learn from conservatives that the United States is valuable less for what it says about religion than for its specific understanding of the state and the need to keep branches of government, as well as national and local authorities, in check so that the other agencies may discharge their appropriate responsibilities.

If evangelicals can come to the realization that the United States is the more superior the less it is a religious juggernaut or a military hyperpower, they may actually become truly conservative. This change of outlook will not be easy. Then again, evangelicals are a people of profound death-to-life experiences; radical transformation is part of their genetic code. To help the conservative medicine go down, familiarity with the way that evangelicals have reflected on the United States may function as the needed spoonful of sugar.

ONE

Silent Minority

—⟨⟨⟨⟨∅⟩⟩⟩⟩—

I n 1940 white American Protestants appeared to have only two
options for religious identity. Either they could belong to one of
the older and larger denominations that constituted the Protestant Establishment or they could side with the critical dissidents,
also known as fundamentalists, who believed that the established
denominations had abandoned the true faith. The Protestant mainline possessed significant resources and a measure of institutional
coherence in such organizations as the Federal Council of Churches
(renamed in 1951 the National Council of Churches). Fundamentalists were disorganized at the national level, even if individual pastors or schools had a following that extended well beyond local networks.

Fundamentalists also had little standing among the academics
and journalists who shaped public perception of American Protestantism. At the popular level, journalists such as H. L. Mencken regularly
issued witty epigrams that indicated the distance between fundamentalism and popular opinion. The Baltimore journalist popularized the
notion that fundamentalism was the "basic religion of the American
clod-hopper." He also opined that "Homo boobiens is a fundamentalist for the precise reason that he is uneducated." To add insult to in-
jury, Mencken asserted that fundamentalists "constituted, perhaps,
the most ignorant class of teachers ever set up to lead a civilized peo-

ple; they are even more ignorant than the county superintendents of schools."[1]

In the academy fundamentalism fared no better. In his article for the *Encyclopedia of Social Science,* H. Richard Niebuhr established the standard and patronizing notion that fundamentalism was simply a product of backward social conditions. He wrote that this form of Protestantism was "closely related to the conflict between rural and urban cultures in America. . . . its rise coincided with the depression of agricultural values after the world war; it achieved little strength in the urban and industrial sections of the country but was active in many rural states." In sum, in its most vigorous forms, fundamentalism was "prevalent in those isolated communities in which the traditions of pioneer society had been most effectively preserved and which were least subject to the influence of modern science and industrial civilization."[2]

For some conservative Protestants, the way out of fundamentalism's black hole was through the construction of a new label — one that would still be traditional but not as backward or belligerent as *fundamentalist.* The word that stuck was *evangelical.* On April 7, 1942, 150 delegates gathered in St. Louis for the first meeting of the National Association of Evangelicals. In addition to rallying Protestants outside the mainline for cooperation in evangelistic and other religious aims, the NAE hoped to create for conservative Protestants an identity different from fundamentalism. If Protestant conservatives were going to restore Christianity in America, they would have to find a more positive and attractive rationale than the one forged during the 1920s by critics of liberal Protestantism. As Stephen W. Paine, president of Houghton College, said at the NAE's first conference, "many sincere Christians are impelled to united action by negative motives." But without genuinely "*cohesive* qualities . . . constructively-minded Christians" hesitated joining associations based simply on shared opposition.[3]

1. H. L. Mencken, "The Collapse of Protestantism," in *A Mencken Chrestomathy* (1925; New York: Alfred A. Knopf, 1949), 79.

2. H. Richard Niebuhr, "Fundamentalism," in *Encyclopedia of Social Sciences* (New York: Macmillan Co., 1937) 6:526-27.

3. Stephen W. Paine, "The Possibility of United Action," in Executive Committee

The founding of an organization for conservative Protestants who were somewhere between theological liberals and fundamentalists was mainly religious in motivation, but it had important implications for evangelical political involvement. In fact, the NAE was a rival organization to the American Council of Christian Churches, founded a year earlier by Carl McIntire, a fundamentalist Presbyterian who was gaining a reputation for opposition to Soviet communism and any whiff of socialism in the United States. The leaders of the NAE decided that McIntire's organization was too militant and too political — in other words, it retained all of fundamentalism's defects. So by repudiating fundamentalism, the new evangelicals were putting some distance between themselves and a variety of religious agitators who were prone to conspiracy theories, millennial hysteria, and rhetorical bombast.

Nevertheless, this new breed of evangelicalism would not go in the other direction and endorse the Social Gospel of the mainline churches. The new evangelicals wanted to Christianize the social order without abandoning the proposition that Christianity was first and foremost a religion that renovated individuals rather than institutions. These were white American Protestants, after all, for whom the republican ideals of the Founding Fathers were uncontested. They believed that a free society depended on a virtuous citizenry and that such virtue could only be produced by religion. The Protestants who joined and supported the NAE assumed that America was a Christian (read: Protestant) nation and that individual pastors and church members should do all in their power to preserve the United States' cultural heritage. The result was a Protestant constituency that was wary of government but not directly engaged either in policy or electoral politics. They were generally content to remain silent, choose from the candidates nominated by the political parties, and delight whenever one of their own rubbed elbows with the leader of the free world.

---

of the NAE, *Evangelical Action! A Report of the Organization of the National Association of Evangelicals for United Action* (Boston: United Action Press, 1942), 54, 56.

Old Christian Right

Before the rise of a centrist, conciliating form of evangelicalism in the 1940s, conservative Protestant politics were associated invariably with the social activism of fundamentalists. One of the ironies of fundamentalism's reputation is that this form of Protestantism regularly receives criticism for being uninterested in earthly affairs, including the health and order of society. At the same time, critics faulted fundamentalists for promoting naive, nativist, and divisive political crusades. This was the classic case of being damned if you don't, and damned if you do. Fundamentalists clearly made the eternal destiny of men and women, boys and girls, a priority ahead of government or the economy. But they were also patriotic Americans who cared deeply about the health of their nation. Consequently, they had little trouble entering the public square, even if their presence lacked the manners and good graces of other occupants.

Fundamentalism was a movement among American Protestants to rid the church and society of theological modernism. It prompted a culture war on two fronts, one in the churches and one in the courtrooms. The first unleashed denominational battles among northern Presbyterians and Baptists that had no direct bearing on American politics. It did rearrange the chairs in the parlor of America's Protestant denominations, but these controversies did little to undermine the prestige or clout of the so-called Protestant Establishment. The second front involved the infamous showdown in Dayton, Tennessee, between William Jennings Bryan and Clarence Darrow at the Scopes Trial. The latter episode demonstrates that the evangelistic priorities of conservative Protestants allowed plenty of room for political involvement. And when fundamentalists did rally for the good of their society, they drew on an incongruous mixture of egalitarian populism, middle-class domesticity, and American exceptionalism.

Fundamentalist opposition to evolution was widespread after World War I but did not find a political outlet until legislatures in southern states, Tennessee among them, passed laws that prohibited the teaching of Darwinism in public schools. In the minds of many conservative Protestants, evolution undermined biblical morality and reduced human motivation to animalistic self-preservation. Furthermore, the source of America's superiority was biblical religion, according to fundamentalists, and to preserve this foundation opposition to evolution was essential. Darwinism was especially worrisome for what it could do to young people: a rising generation reared on godless science portended disaster for the United States — much in the same way, fundamentalists believed, as it had for Germany in the First World War.

Although various fundamentalists and related organizations opposed evolution, William Jennings Bryan almost single-handedly turned it into a political cause. He was convinced that the acceptance of Darwinism had already unleashed barbarism in Europe and would undermine Christian civilization in the United States. In 1921 Bryan devoted his energies to refuting evolution. In syndicated newspaper columns, speeches (he was a hugely popular speaker on the Chautauqua circuit), and books, the retired politician attacked the degraded view of humanity implied by the Darwinian account of man's descent from apes. Moved by the arguments from Bryan's bully pulpit, several southern states in 1922 and 1923 passed legislation that prohibited the teaching of evolution in public schools. Although the trial of John T. Scopes, the biology teacher in Dayton, Tennessee, who became the test case for that state's anti-evolution legislation, exposed the simplistic elements of Bryan's campaign, his arguments tapped mainstream political ideals in the United States. Clarence Darrow, attorney for the defense, was able to turn Bryan's own testimony on the stand into a risible expression of biblical literalism. But Bryan's case against Darwinism was not simply that it was at odds with the creation narrative in Genesis; he also appealed to majority rule and to the rights of local governments to determine the purposes for which tax dollars would be spent. Bryan argued repeatedly that the majority of citizens in a state should not be forced to pay for teaching that would undermine their children's faith. He believed that public schools were under the jurisdiction of state governments and should not be coerced to conform to national educational standards. The fundamentalism that Bryan represented suffered the defeat of public humiliation through journalistic accounts that portrayed it as a backward, rural, unlearned faith, but fundamentalists did not waver, and they remained a deeply egalitarian and democratic political constituency that could be readily marshaled under the right circumstances.

Another popular political crusade of the 1920s that revealed fundamentalism to be more than simply an otherworldly faith was Prohibition. Of course, temperance reforms had deep roots in Anglo-American Protestantism, and the criminalization of the sale and distribution of alcohol was no more exclusively a fundamentalist issue than it was a modernist one. For instance, during the 1920s, when the northern Presbyterian Church found ways to tolerate modernist theology, it also repeatedly issued official support for the Eighteenth Amendment and the Volstead Act.

Even so, the cause of Prohibition reveals that fundamentalists were not as apolitical or as otherworldly as caricatures imply. Here the case of Billy Sunday is instructive. Arguably the most popular evangelist in the twentieth century prior to Billy Graham, Sunday was a professional baseball player who got religion and left the major leagues for the sawdust trail. For the first three decades of the twentieth century Sunday took his unique pulpit antics and vivid colloquial style across the United States in hopes of converting the lost. One of his most popular sermons was entitled "Get on the Water Wagon." In it he railed against the saloon as the chief source of vice in urban America; he also identified the major breweries and distilleries as monopolies intent on profiting from human weakness. Alcohol was also a threat to the family and home. According to Sunday, "the American home is the dearest heritage of the people, for the people, by the people, and when a man can go from home in the morning with the kisses of his wife and children on his lips, and come back at night with an empty dinner bucket to a happy home, that man is a better man." Conversely, he warned, "whatever invades the sanctity of the home, is the deadliest foe to the home, to church, to state and school, and the saloon is the deadliest foe to the home, the church and the state, on top of God Almighty's dirt."[4] After 1907 Sunday delivered this sermon in each of his city crusades and frequently gave it as a stand-alone exhortation in smaller towns and communities. Historians estimate

4. Billy Sunday, "Get on the Water Wagon," quoted in Lyle W. Dorsett, *Billy Sunday and the Redemption of Urban America* (Grand Rapids: Eerdmans, 1990), 190.

that his popular and vigorous opposition to alcohol enabled nineteen states to pass dry legislation. Sunday also campaigned actively for national prohibition and was clearly responsible for rallying support from a large swath of born-again Protestants.

Sunday's crusade on behalf of prohibition tapped Anglo-American Protestant ideals of domesticity and the middle-class family. Ever since the middle decades of the nineteenth century, when Protestants established a variety of voluntary associations to check moral license and promote personal and social godliness, evangelicals looked at American society and its political order through the lens of the nuclear family. This made sense because of the family's crucial role in passing on habits and virtues to the next generation. Public education was another issue that motivated Protestant political engagement; Protestants put great stock in the capacity of schools to nurture a civil religion that grounded public virtues in a generic form of Protestantism. The saloon and its menu of beverages, as Sunday's sermon indicated, directly challenged Protestant ideals of hearth and home. As Thomas R. Pegram has observed in *Battling Demon Rum*, "Many native Protestant households felt themselves under assault from a reckless saloon trade that separated husbands from wives and parents from children." "In defense of their families," he adds, "they marshaled the weapons of democracy — political parties, the public schools, and ultimately the power of the state — to defend community standards and suppress the noxious traffic in intoxicants."[5] Billy Sunday's campaign against booze advanced this approach to American public life. Not even their beliefs about the imminent return of Christ and the need to proselytize the lost could dissuade conservative Protestants from a deep-rooted sense of being responsible for the moral health and stability of the republic.

Despite the consolidating power of the federal government that reforms such as Prohibition encouraged, fundamentalists feared big government and easily enlisted for opposition to communism in the Soviet Union and any hint of socialism in Washington. Gerald Burton Winrod (1900-1957), a religious publisher and antag-

5. Thomas R. Pegram, *Battling Demon Rum: The Struggle for Dry America, 1800-1933* (Chicago: Ivan R. Dee, 1998), 77.

onist during the church controversies of the 1920s, was one fundamentalist who eventually ran for the Senate in Republican primaries
in Kansas because of opposition to the New Deal. His understanding
of biblical prophecy and the role that European nations and the
United States would play in the events leading to the return of Christ
at times pushed Winrod toward conspiracy theories and anti-
Semitism. These peculiar ideas prevented Winrod's candidacy from
ever gaining a wide following and eventually in the 1940s prompted
federal authorities to suspect Winrod of Nazi sympathies that were
supposedly responsible for insubordination in the armed forces.
But as bizarre as Winrod's outlook may have appeared to non-
fundamentalists, his anxiety about big government tapped born-
again Protestants' fears of expanding federal programs that might
take the United States down a socialist path.

Carl McIntire also nurtured hostility to communism and Washington's bureaus through a small empire that included radio, publishing, schools and churches. For preachers like McIntire, communism
was chiefly objectionable as a form of atheism. It denied God, Christ,
and the spiritual reality of human existence and closed churches and
Christian missions wherever it was tried. But for McIntire, communism was also opposed to the West's ideals of human freedom. Consequently, in order to protect the United States, Christians needed to oppose communism in all forms. This included opposing any political or
religious institution that was soft on communism.

These examples demonstrate that fundamentalism was by no
means an apolitical religious movement completely absorbed exclusively with soul-winning. Its political ideals may not have been coherent, but they tapped longstanding American notions about freedom,
limited government, and the importance of the family. To these convictions fundamentalists added conspiracy theories and millennial
ideas about America's status as a redeemer nation that informed
both their militant opposition to theological liberalism and their engagement with the nation's politics. Despite their reliance on basic
Protestant assumptions about American public life, fundamentalist
politics gained the reputation for being extreme, divisive, and even
paranoid. It was obvious that evangelicals needed to seek an alternative identity.

Conservative but Not Combative

The new evangelicals who emerged as a distinct constituency within American Protestantism during the 1940s wanted to escape the reputation that haunted conservative Protestants like Bryan, Sunday, Winrod, and McIntire. This was true not only in the realm of politics but also in religion itself. Evangelicals believed that fundamentalists would fail to capture the hearts and minds of many Americans, let alone rally the energy and resources of conservative Protestants, because fundamentalism was only negative all the time. The strategy that evangelicals believed would win was a positive mission and outlook. It was not sufficient merely to stand *against* liberalism. Evangelicals intended to stand *for* basic Christianity.

The creation of the National Association of Evangelicals in 1942 became the institutional outlet for evangelicals' positive mission. The organization's first magazine was *United Evangelical Action,* and the title said a good deal about the positive thrust of the new evangelicals. The NAE was an effort to unite conservative Protestants for specific activities that would lead America back to Christ during a time of cultural crisis. The Second World War and the negative image of conservative Protestants prompted the creation of institutions that would rival the liberal Protestant churches in as winsome a manner as possible.

On simply practical grounds, the war posed a number of hurdles that prompted evangelicals to start a new agency. For instance, if born-again Protestants wanted to serve in the military as chaplains, they would have had to go through channels established and controlled by the Federal Council of Churches, the mainline Protestant ecumenical agency from which most evangelicals were alienated. A related difficulty, though not directly resulting from the war, was the new medium of the radio and the acquisition of time for religious broadcasting. During the 1940s some of the most popular radio preachers were ministers outside the mainline Protestant fold, such as Charles Fuller in Los Angeles, Paul Rader in Chicago, and Donald Grey Barnhouse in Philadelphia. These radio preachers used their entrepreneurial gifts and charisma to establish national audiences on the existing networks. But in the 1940s the Federal Communications

Commission began to regulate religious broadcasting and teamed up with the Federal Council of Churches to determine which Protestants would have access to the airwaves. The new evangelical organization, the NAE, was designed to represent the interests of conservative Protestants before the federal government and demonstrate that the mainline denominations had no monopoly on American Protestantism. It would be a mistake to call the NAE a lobbying endeavor, but the new evangelical organization sought to promote born-again Protestantism in a way that could readily spill over to a variety of advocacy outlets.

The Second World War and the growth of the federal bureaucracy it fed during the 1940s did more than reveal the need for an evangelical organization to counter the mainline churches' control of Protestantism's public voice. The war also proved to be an incentive for born-again Protestants to show why the world still needed the good news of the Christian faith. As Harold John Ockenga, pastor at Boston's Park Street Church and founding president of the NAE, declared to the Association's first delegates:

> Let us learn something from the Soviets and the Nazis. If the children of this world are wiser than the children of light, then it is time for the children of light to open their eyes and learn how to carry on God's work. This is the time, the day for the offensive. Personally I am just as tired of defensive tactics in ecclesiastical matters as the Americans are tired of defensive tactics on the part of the United Nations. . . . Do not be so foolish as to think that though your own personal work is thriving at the present time you will escape.[6]

The particular offensive that Ockenga had in mind was an evangelical parry to the thrusts of Roman Catholicism, liberal Protestantism, and secularism. In fact, the leaders of the NAE believed that the fortunes of Western civilization both in Europe and the United States depended on a vigorous assertion of orthodox Protestantism. Never

---

6. Harold J. Ockenga, "Unvoiced Multitudes," in *Evangelical Action! A Report of the Organization of the National Association of Evangelicals for United Action* (Boston: United Action Press, 1942), 19.

mind that Roman Catholics and mainline Protestants also believed and asserted that their version of Christianity best preserved the political ideals and cultural conventions of the West. Like most Anglo-American Protestants before them, the new evangelicals assumed that the health of a free society depended on a virtuous people, and that the true source of virtue was their own brand of Christianity. According to Ockenga, a revolution had already taken place in the United States with dire consequences for conservative Protestantism. "The crisis is greater than any of us realize," he warned. "Now, if ever, we need some organ to speak for the evangelical interests, to represent men who, like myself, are 'lone wolves' in the church."[7]

These close ties between evangelism and preserving a Christian America meant that the NAE had implications for politics, even if the organization was explicitly religious in purpose and the rise of the Religious Right was three decades away. One indication of the implicit political engagement of the new evangelicalism came from Carl F. H. Henry in a book long regarded as the manifesto for this new breed of conservative Protestants. Published in 1947, *The Uneasy Conscience of Modern Fundamentalism* tapped evangelical discontentment with the belligerency associated with fundamentalism and tried to position the new evangelicals as the harbinger of a more winsome and socially engaged faith.[8] This faith would not be narrowly religious but would strive to address the needs of postwar America.

At the time of its publication in 1947, Henry was a young Baptist theologian completing a doctorate in theology at Boston University and soon to become a member of the faculty at Fuller Seminary, a school founded to be the think tank of the new evangelicalism. *The Uneasy Conscience* actually stemmed from a more ambitious book Henry had written the year before; in that book, *Remaking the Modern Mind,* he argued that Western civilization was bankrupt because of its humanistic philosophy. This situation provided the new evangelicals with a tremendous opportunity to include cultural renewal as part of their mission.

7. Ockenga, "Unvoiced Multitudes," 19.
8. Carl F. H. Henry, *The Uneasy Conscience of Modern Fundamentalism* (Grand Rapids: Eerdmans, 1947).

The Uneasy Conscience critiqued fundamentalists for failing to tackle the West's cultural crisis. Unless born-again Protestants were willing to move beyond questions of ecclesiastical purity and personal morality, Henry warned, the gospel would be dismissed as irrelevant. He complained in one of the more memorable illustrations from the book that while fundamentalists were debating the propriety of playing cards, "the nations of the world are playing with fire."[9] Henry proposed a "progressive fundamentalism" that would tap the sort of social activism that had characterized nineteenth-century evangelicalism, such as crusades against drunkenness and slavery. In effect, the new evangelicalism would go beyond fundamentalism and add social involvement to soul-winning. Henry believed this was a viable combination because the world's problems could only be solved through Christianity.[10] Of course soul-winning was still primary, but for Henry social reform followed naturally from evangelism.

In hindsight, Henry's attempt to provide an evangelical alternative to the mainline churches' Social Gospel lacked muscle even while opening a wedge for later evangelical political involvement. As some critics have claimed, the social evils that *The Uneasy Conscience* listed were not far removed from the sort of sins that animated fundamentalists. Billy Sunday and William Jennings Bryan would have applauded Henry's denunciation of "aggressive warfare, racial hatred and intolerance, the liquor traffic, and exploitation of labor or management, whichever it may be."[11] Furthermore, his invoking of Jesus' teaching in Matthew 5:17 for bi-partisanship in Washington — "seek first, not a Republican victory, or a labor victory, but the kingdom of God and His righteousness"[12] — sounded idealistic and naive. Even so, Henry's bland social imperatives indicated that the new evangelicalism was not simply going to be a religious identity. These born-again Protestants wanted a seat at the proverbial table to counter the influence of the mainline denominations and to insure the continuation of America's Christian heritage.

9. Henry, *The Uneasy Conscience*, 20.
10. Henry, *The Uneasy Conscience*, 45.
11. Henry, *The Uneasy Conscience*, 17.
12. Henry, *The Uneasy Conscience*, 85.

Evangelicalism before the Religious Right

As much as the new evangelicals wanted to have a voice in the public sphere, especially since they regarded the United States as a Protestant country and their variety of Protestantism as the genuine article, they also believed the church's primary task was religious. The Social Gospel of liberal Protestantism had damaged the Protestant denominations' credibility while also embracing a variety of reforms that were unhealthy for a free society, such as increasing the size and role of the federal government in American life. As such, the political engagement recommended by born-again Protestants was right of center but not particularly reflective. Most evangelicals during the middle decades of the twentieth century defended and advocated liberty, democracy, and small government and viewed totalitarian forms of government such as the Soviet Union as the exact opposite of a free and just society.

A variety of political scientists and historians who have written on American evangelicalism of the 1950s and 1960s era have concluded that these Protestants were in fact conservative. According to University of Wisconsin scholar Robert Booth Fowler, evangelicals supported such "standard conservative ideas as a balanced budget and the prevention of any more erosion of America's traditional freedoms."[13] This outlook also meant that evangelicals were generally much more willing to defend America's political institutions, heritage, and Cold War foreign policy than the 1960s chorus of critics who faulted the United States for racial, class, and gender discrimination. Of course, Protestants who stood as heirs to a religious tradition that had regularly lamented the decline of Christian standards in American society were not likely to be uncritical of aspects of postwar American life. Among the most objectionable facets of the United States during the twenty-five years after World War II was materialism. As one writer in *Christianity Today* put it, Americans were increasingly "hedonistic, materialistic, . . . hungry for profit."[14] Even so, despite

13. Robert Booth Fowler, *A New Engagement: Evangelical Political Thought, 1966-1976* (Grand Rapids: Eerdmans, 1982), 25.
14. Fowler, *A New Engagement,* 30.

certain acknowledged faults of the United States, evangelicals remained patriotic. And despite their nation's blemishes, born-again Protestants held that the church's place was not to reform society or engage in political activism. Individual evangelicals might well be called to perform public service. But the religious mission of the church was a task that transcended politics, and churches that forgot this truth, like the mainline Protestant denominations, tended to substitute a social gospel for the genuine article.

Arguably, the most serious threat to the American way of life for many evangelicals was the Soviet Union. Between 1958 and 1967 the NAE issued seven different resolutions on communism, the most of any topic. The first in 1958 expressed concern over the infiltration of communism in American institutions, including the inability of men in the armed forces to "meet the inroads" of such ideology. To address the problem the Association called on public schools to do a better job of teaching "the principles of our democracy, with its Christian heritage in contrast to the atheistic materialism of Marxian Communism." Two years later, the NAE highlighted communism's atheistic assumptions and hostility to faith: "Coexistence with the devil is repugnant to any Christian and as followers of Christ we cannot pursue a policy of 'live and let live' with hell. We cannot close our eyes to the slavery, cruelty, theft and deceit with which Red Communism has enveloped more than a third of the human race and is creeping relentlessly forward to engulf the whole world." The Association called upon its members as well as all American Christians to engage in an "aggressive and unrelenting campaign against this enemy of righteousness and freedom."

These two initial resolutions captured the tenor of evangelical reflection on American society and its political ideals. For most Protestants, the United States owed its freedom and respect for the rule of law to its Christian origins. Communism was not simply a political threat, however, but first and foremost a religious one. As a 1962 resolution put it, "communism is only one of many avenues through which Satan employs his powers of spiritual wickedness." Consequently, the Association called on Americans to fight communism not by political means but by religious ones. "The church should endeavor to use this emphasis to call Christians to prayer and the rededication of their lives to God and the fulfillment of their Christian responsibilities," it read, because a spiritual awakening in the church and nation "is the most effective way to combat communism." Part of the motive for spiritualizing communism owed to missionary efforts by evangelicals to proselytize in Soviet-dominated societies. Without access, evangelicals understandably regarded communism as another religion.

When evangelicals attempted to expose the *political* deficiencies of communism, they invariably spoke in terms of tyranny versus free markets. In a 1963 resolution the NAE determined that mere opposition was insufficient in combating communism; evangelicals also needed to *affirm* the sort of political and economic system that was most compatible with Christianity. Consequently, the statement expressed gratitude for "the larger liberties we enjoy," and called upon evangelicals to "dedicate ourselves afresh to those biblical principles of duty and freedom promotive of social justice and enduring peace." These principles included the state as a means for restraining evil and "man's right of private property and responsibility for its voluntary stewardship as a divine entrustment." These were standards that just four years later prompted the NAE to express concern over a growing disregard in American churches and the federal government for "the rights of the private sector" along with an increasing acceptance of the doctrine, "'from each according to his ability, to each according to his need' not as a Christian principle but as a fixed economic law." In fact, the NAE declared in 1967 that restraints on free-market economics went hand in hand with a "total secularization as a way of life" and a "passion to eliminate distinctions or differences of any kind."

The evangelical approach to public life may have involved a fear of big government, but this concern did not outweigh the perennial Anglo-American Protestant activism that used legislation to curb vice. A favorite target was beverage alcohol. Although many evangelicals believed that personal consumption was wrong, the Association's rationale for opposing alcohol at an institutional and policy level was not individual but social. In 1957 its resolution identified several ways that alcohol was harming the body politic: it aggravated the "disintegration of the American family," it placed "spiritual, mental, and physical strain" on the health of the American people, and the liquor industry was "having a corrupting influence" upon American politics. For these reasons the NAE advocated all forms of legislation to protect "the home, the church, the state and the economic order" from advertising for liquor and favored educational and promotional campaigns to persuade Americans of the deleterious consequences of beverage alcohol. The 1957 resolution also commended Congress for its recent passage of legislation prohibiting "liquor service" on board all American commercial and military flights, and it deplored the use of alcohol by public officials, those to whom had been committed the responsibility for policies affecting the "destiny of our own country" and even the destinies of other nations.

Two years later the NAE noted the social problems posed by drunk driving and the use of alcohol in criminal activity, declared opposition to all forms of consuming liquor, and called upon its member churches to institute educational programs on alcohol's dangers. At the same time, the NAE attempted to keep pressure on Congress to pass legislation that would "eliminate the interstate advertising of alcoholic beverages as a major step in protecting the homes and highways of our nation against the devastating effects of alcohol." The Association took similar stands, for instance, against gambling (1966) — especially state lotteries — and obscene literature (1965). In each case it assumed a proprietary relationship between Protestants and the United States, while skimping on the specific implementation of policies and ignoring the relationship between federal and local government.

One last indication of evangelical political conviction in the era before Reagan was religion and education. Here the NAE's members tried to affirm the separation of church and state while also holding that the United States government possessed an obligation to support rather than suppress religion in public institutions. On the one hand, evangelicals endorsed religious liberty and conceived of the United States as the product of Protestant endeavors to find a political shelter for the freedom to worship and teach according to the dictates of conscience. This meant that evangelicals were regularly on guard against any policy or legislation that might regulate and limit religious freedom. As the Association put it in a 1957 resolution, "we view with growing concern acts of government that would control religion and

34

education, and policies of church that would dominate government." The necessary balance was to protect "our great American heritage of freedom and . . . protest against compromise of the historic principle of separation of church and state."

One point of possible compromise was state funding for church-related schools, but in 1963 the Association asserted that public funding for parochial schools was at odds with the separation of church and state. Although evangelicals affirmed the necessity of maintaining the church's independence from state control, the subtext of its argument was to restrict state funding for Roman Catholic schools. This ulterior motive was evident in the Association's disapproval of the Supreme Court decision in *Everson v. Board of Education* (1947), which upheld the constitutionality of public funding for the bus transportation of Roman Catholic students in New Jersey. In fact, in a separate resolution in 1964 the Association held that because bus transportation was a "necessary part of most modern educational systems," "any educational system motivated by religious and/or sectarian purposes should provide its own facilities and tax funds should not be appropriated to convey children to schools providing religious instruction." This would, of course, have included Lutheran, Episcopalian, and some Reformed private schools. But like most American Protestants before them, evangelicals of the time saw Catholic schools as a threat to a unified, Christian (read: Protestant) America, and they appealed to the separation of church and state to restrict Roman Catholic access to public funds.

On the other hand, evangelicals stated the separation-of-church-and-state principle differently when the subject was religion in public schools. Here the effort was to keep religion and politics distinct without succumbing to a secular public realm. In a 1963 statement, the NAE held that a firm commitment to the separation of church and state "should not imply an espousal of secularism or practical atheism through the exclusion of all reference to God in the public schools." Although public schools needed to be kept free from the specific tenets of any one sect or denomination, "they should by all means provide the students with an atmosphere of friendliness to and acceptance of the concepts of the existence of God, man's responsibility to God and to fellowmen, and the benefits of promoting godliness."

To that end, the Association endorsed six "courses of action" to maintain a religion-friendly system of public education. The first called upon Congress to amend the Constitution in a manner that would "strengthen the present provision for the free exercise of religion in our national life and allow reference to, belief in, reliance upon, or invoking the aid of God, in any governmental or public document, proceeding, activity, ceremony, school or institution." The second reminded Americans of public education's duty to expose students to the contribution that the Christian tradition had made to the development of American society. The next called for public schools to teach "the Bible as history and/or literature" as a legitimate and integral part of the curriculum. Fourth, the Association asserted the need for academic freedom for "Christian teachers to teach from a Christian standpoint and to witness by example and personal life to the effects of Christian commitment." The resolution was also directed to families; its fifth recommendation called upon parents to conduct religious devotions in the home to develop children's "moral and spiritual nature." The final point called upon evangelicals to resist "any hostility toward a religiously based view of life as it may appear in the public schools" and raised the possibility of establishing Christian day schools "to safeguard the American Christian heritage." (The Association did not mention whether the buses taking evangelicals to such schools should benefit from public funding.)

The final sentence of the NAE's statement on the separation of church and state captured the dilemma that evangelicals had inherited from their Protestant forebears. Evangelicals believed that America was "a nation under God" to which applied the scriptural admonition, "Blessed is the nation whose God is the Lord." The problem was how to reconcile the biblical norm of a state based on the true faith (i.e. Old Testament Israel) with the modern expectation that church and state be separate. The way around this dilemma was to keep religion formally out of public institutions while supporting it informally.

The problem with this approach was that evangelicals were not the dominant figures in American public life that they had been before the split between fundamentalists and mainline Protestants of the 1920s. Before it balkanized into its theological right and left wings, Anglo-American Protestantism was sufficiently established in the nation's elite institutions that a strategy of informal establishment for Protestantism worked relatively well. It allowed Protestants the ability to affirm the national ideals of religious liberty and separation of church and state while still possessing more political leverage than any other religious group in the United States. Evangelicals knew no other approach to public life. But informal establishment assumed a form of cultural hegemony that evangelicals abandoned when they left the mainline Protestant institutions to form their own.

Aside from the structural problems inherent in the new evangelical ideas about American politics, intellectual confusion also riddled the new born-again Protestant activism, as the rhetoric and proposals of the NAE indicate. Evangelicals desired to preserve a society that reflected a specific form of Protestantism; they also believed that born-again Protestants should be active in American politics in a way that was less bellicose than fundamentalists but still truer to older Protestant ideals than the mainline Protestant churches were willing to espouse. But aside from these aims, the new evangelicals gave little attention to the formal arrangements of American politics or to theoretical reflection on the nature of the good society and the forms of government that encouraged both public and private virtue. In that sense, evangelicals may have looked conservative because they desired to protect traditional American society. But they were several steps removed from the debates and institutions in which American conservatives weighed the future of their ideas.

Indicative of evangelical confusion was the indifference that *Christianity Today* displayed toward the candidacy of Barry Goldwater, the first presidential nominee to be clearly identified with the American Right. While conservative pundits offered support and counsel — William F. Buckley Jr.'s brother-in-law, Brent Bozell, even ghostwrote Goldwater's bestseller, *The Conscience of a Conservative* (1960) — evangelicals remained aloof. In fact, *Christianity Today* carried only two news stories, and the main point of both concerned the lack of objectivity about Goldwater in the secular and religious press. In these reports, the one item that stood out as the most significant religious aspect of the campaign was Oregon governor Mark O. Hatfield's speech at the 1964 Republican convention. Hatfield's call for a "spiritual renaissance" and government to set an example for "high standards of ethics and morality" was encouraging. But Goldwater's choice of a Roman Catholic, William E. Miller — the first ever on a Republican ticket — raised evangelical eyebrows.

Conventional Protestantism

Evangelicals may have considered themselves a different kind of Protestant from both the liberal mainline churches and the strident fundamentalists, but their political assumptions were actually fairly close to mainstream American Protestant thought, even if they had abandoned the historic institutions of mainstream Protestantism. For most intents and purposes, the defining moment for American Protestant politics was not the Scopes Trial but the formation in 1856 of the Republican Party. From the middle of the nineteenth century until today, most Protestants of Anglo-Saxon stock, whether religiously liberal or conservative, have identified politically with the Whig-Republican tradition. This close identification between American Protestants and Republicanism stemmed from a peculiar blend of religious devotion and political motivation.

At the risk of oversimplifying a complicated situation, the division between Republicans and Democrats on the eve of the Civil War reflected a basic difference between low-church and high-church expressions of Christianity. The newly founded Republican Party was the political outlet for Protestants who had been deeply influenced by revivalism and the Second Great Awakening. This form of devotion was characterized by individual zeal, commitment to Christ, and the self-conscious resolution by each convert to lead a disciplined and holy life. This version of Protestantism emphasized individual responsibility and self-denial, and it dovetailed well with Whig-Republican attitudes that promoted "rational order over irrational spontaneity" and "self-control over self-expression."[15] Revivalist Protestantism also fit well with the demands of an expanding market economy, which the

15. Daniel Walker Howe, "Religion and Politics in the Antebellum North," in Mark A. Noll, ed., *Religion and American Politics: From the Colonial Period to the 1980s* (New York: Oxford University Press, 1990), 124.

Whigs and Republicans favored, and provided the rationale for any number of social reforms that were designed to Christianize America (a revivalist desire) and enforce Anglo-conformity (a Whig-Republican goal).

Revivalist Protestants gave first the Whigs and then the Republican Party a Protestant character after the arrival in the 1840s of large numbers of Roman Catholic immigrants who identified with the Democratic Party. Democratic candidates did not merely appeal to Roman Catholics but also to Episcopalians, Lutherans, German and Dutch Reformed, and some Presbyterians. The Democrats' efforts on behalf of populist and limited government provided high-church Christians (who were often, though not always, part of ethno-cultural minorities) with a measure of reassurance that the state would not encroach on their churches, parochial schools, or the lives of their members. In contrast, low-church Protestants in the Republican Party trusted government to enact laws based on eternal truths which would nurture virtuous citizens and a righteous society.

The legacy of Protestant republicanism was a peculiar blend of religious and national ideals that assumed a privileged place for low-church Protestantism in maintaining and defending the United States' political order. Mark A. Noll summarizes well this mixture of religion and politics at the beginning of the twentieth century:

> Protestants in the progressive era relied instinctively on the Bible to provide their ideals of justice. They believed in the power of Christ to expand the Kingdom of God through the efforts of faithful believers. They were reformists at home and missionaries abroad who felt that cooperation among Protestants signaled the advance of civilization. They were thoroughly and uncritically patriotic. On more specific issues, they continued to suspect Catholics as being anti-American, they promoted the public schools as agents of a broad form of Christianization, and they were overwhelmingly united behind prohibition as the key step toward a renewed society.[16]

16. Mark A. Noll, "The Scandal of Evangelical Political Reflection," in Richard John Neuhaus and George Weigel, eds., *Being Christian Today: An American Conversation* (Washington, D.C.: Ethics and Public Policy, 1992), 73.

This was the outlook shared by Protestants on both sides of the 1920s fundamentalist controversy. As much as they disagreed about the nature of genuine Christianity, they thought about the United States and the place of Protestantism in American society in remarkably similar ways. One group might insist on the necessity of the virgin birth of Christ and the other might have reservations about Christ's deity, but both sides were confident that Protestantism provided the right amount of religious direction for a free people and a republican form of government.

Instead of representing a new approach to American public life, mid-twentieth-century evangelicals were simply heirs to the politics that had sustained Protestants since the middle of the nineteenth century. But the America of which they claimed moral and cultural leadership had changed, and the shifting of the religious landscape had fractured the Protestant majority beyond repair. In fact, across the theological spectrum, the Protestant outlook on the United States was generally oblivious to the sort of structural changes that had transformed America from a decentralized, largely agrarian republic into a liberal democratic superpower. And for American Protestants, whether theologically doctrinaire or tolerant, Protestant Christianity was still crucial to the well-being of the United States. Only after 1970, when a variety of Supreme Court decisions, policy initiatives, and protest movements challenged the Protestant character of the United States and threatened evangelical institutions, would evangelicals switch from silent minority to Moral Majority.

TWO

Young and Leftist

―❦―

O ver the Thanksgiving weekend of 1973, a group of fifty evangelicals, primarily young faculty and students, gathered at the YMCA in Chicago to express dissatisfaction with the political status quo. To suggest that this meeting was an instance of baby boomer evangelicals rebelling against the politics of born-again Protestants' Greatest Generation would be simplistic. Even so, the Protestants who digested their holiday meals while hammering out a call for evangelical social engagement were fed up with the direction in which the United States was heading — and not particularly pleased by their parents' support for the Republican Party or its indifference to the concerns of America's blacks, women, and impoverished.

The work of this group duly appeared as the "Chicago Declaration of Evangelical Social Concern." It mixed Christian themes of faith and repentance with American realities of poverty and war. First, these evangelicals declared that God requires justice, and then they confessed that American conservative Protestants had been woefully delinquent in pursuing a just society. "We deplore the historic involvement of the church in America with racism," the signers declared, and "we have failed to condemn the exploitation of racism at home and abroad by our economic system." The statement went on to call for an "attack" on America's materialism and the "maldistribution of the nation's wealth and services." "Before God and a billion hungry neighbors, we must rethink our values regarding our present standard of liv-

41

ing and promote a more just acquisition and distribution of the world's resources." Also, as citizens the signers acknowledged a duty to challenge "the misplaced trust of the nation in economic and military might — a proud trust that promotes a national pathology of war and violence that victimizes our neighbors at home and abroad." For good measure, the "Chicago Declaration" addressed men's and women's roles by confessing the error of teaching that led men to "prideful domination" and women to "irresponsible passivity." In turn it called men and women to "mutual submission and active discipleship." If the authors of this document felt better for having gotten these objections off their collective chest, their parents may have experienced indigestion that extended beyond holiday overeating.[1]

No matter what the older evangelicals thought of the "Chicago Declaration," the early returns were favorable. Writing for the *Washington Post,* Marjorie Hyer speculated the young evangelicals' discussions "could well change the face of both religion and politics in America."[2] Meanwhile, the *Chicago Sun-Times* religion reporter wrote that "Someday American church historians may write that the most significant church-related event of 1973 took place last week at the YMCA hotel on S. Wabash." That estimate gave historian Joel A. Carpenter room to conclude that the "Chicago Declaration" represented a "radical shift" among evangelicals from a form of political meddling that an older generation believed sold out the gospel to a pursuit of "the righteousness that exalts a nation."[3]

In point of fact, the rise of the Religious Right at the end of the 1970s would swamp the nascent radicalism expressed in the fall of 1973 among the evangelicals assembled in the Windy City. Yet for a brief period, especially in the immediate aftermath of Richard Nixon's scandals, baby boomer evangelicals believed they were forging a new initiative for faith-based activism. But their arguments also revealed a confusion that ran deep in the political soul of born-again Protestants.

1. The "Chicago Declaration of Evangelical Social Concern," reprinted in Ronald J. Sider, ed., *The Chicago Declaration* (Carol Stream, Ill.: Creation House, 1974).

2. Hyer quoted in Joel Carpenter, "Compassionate Evangelicalism," *Christianity Today* 47:12 (Dec. 2003), 41.

3. Carpenter, "Compassionate Evangelicalism," 41.

The Socially Concerned

In 1970, Philadelphia publishing house J. B. Lippincott announced a new book series, "Evangelical Perspectives" — a somewhat surprising move, since it endowed conservative Protestants with greater intellectual heft than they typically enjoyed outside the evangelical publishing houses of Grand Rapids, Michigan. The series editor, John W. Montgomery, then teaching church history at Trinity Evangelical Divinity School in suburban Chicago, explained the need for this particular collection of titles in the series foreword. Polarization between fundamentalists and liberals continued to plague the contemporary church. The former were so intent on preserving the truth that they turned a blind eye to "the live issues and compelling challenges of a world in crisis." In contrast, for liberal Protestants pursuing the kingdom of God, "the church has become indistinguishable from the ideological and societal evils she is supposed to combat."[4]

The evangelical authors that Montgomery had corralled to write for the series were supposed to triangulate this Protestant antagonism. On the one hand, they were committed to historic Christianity, as expressed in the Apostles' Creed, the Protestant Reformation, and the revivals of the eighteenth century. On the other hand, the series' authors found "little comfort in the reiteration of ancient truth for its own sake." The "staggering problems" of the age demanded more than the "repetition of formulas." "The race problem, social revolution, political change, new sexual freedom, the revival of the occult, the advent of the space age," Montgomery wrote, "these are areas of modern life that demand fresh analysis on the basis of the eternal verities set forth in the Word."[5] The *evangelical* perspective that this new series would articulate was an "all-embracing and genuinely relevant theological perspective for the emerging twenty-first century" as revolutionary as the Protestant Reformation was in the sixteenth.

If the "Evangelical Perspectives" series was indicative of fresh thinking among born-again Protestants, a noticeable lurch to the left

---

4. Montgomery, Preface to Richard V. Pierard, *The Unequal Yoke: Evangelical Christianity and Political Conservatism* (Philadelphia: Lippincott, 1970), 5.

5. Pierard, *The Unequal Yoke*, 6.

was part of the renaissance. Of the seven titles that this Lippincott series produced, two specifically addressed American politics and took issue with the predictably conservative, or at least Republican, loyalties of evangelical Protestants.

Richard Pierard, a historian at Indiana State University, started the critique of the born-again Protestant status quo with *Unequal Yoke: Evangelical Christianity and Political Conservatism* (1970). Pierard's title drew upon biblical admonitions for Christians to avoid being unequally yoked with unbelievers (2 Cor. 6). Although the Apostle Paul's instruction applied specifically to marriage, Pierard expanded the point to include evangelicals' political conservatism. "The evangelical church," he began, "has tied itself to the *status quo* of contemporary middle-class America and traded its prophetic ministry for a pottage of public acclaim and economic well-being." To underscore the point, Pierard cited Brown University historian William G. McLoughlin for one of the epigrammatic quotations to introduce the argument: "The N.A.E.'s outlook on political and economic affairs is so deeply committed to nationalistic, laissez-faire ultra-conservatism that it shocks even the most chastened Liberal Protestant." The pressing question for evangelicals, according to Pierard, was whether conservative Christianity would "exchange the worldly yoke for that of Christ."[6]

Crucial to Pierard's case was his own understanding of conservatism. Here he turned to the *National Review* and Barry Goldwater's manifesto, *The Conscience of a Conservative,* to spell out the mainstream American political convictions about freedom and limited government. Conservatives believed in balancing personal freedom and social order, and to maintain this stability they affirmed that government power had to be specifically delegated. The U.S. Constitution's ideal of a coordinated system involving federal and state government was designed to restrain the tendency of political centralization. Twentieth-century conservatives, Pierard further explained, were alarmed by the growth of the federal government and hoped to return greater authority to local governments that were better situated to address the needs of neighborhoods, towns, and re-

6. Pierard, *The Unequal Yoke,* 19, 15-16.

gions. Pierard also described conservatism as upholding the essential "right of each person to property and to enjoy the fruits of his labor." The emphasis on free markets led conservatives to suspicion of taxation and federal schemes that thwarted economic growth. Finally, conservatives were convinced of the "moral superiority of America" and opposed various international policies or agencies that weakened the United States' sovereignty — especially those promoted by a communist ideology.[7]

If not for the inclusion of extremist anti-communism, this fair-minded description of conservatism might have appealed even to Pierard. But the subject of communism prompted his most important reasons for considering conservatism a yoke of bondage. He devoted a chapter to the "Parasites of the Far Right." Here were the usual suspects: such figures as Billy James Hargis (a prominent anti-communist Church of Christ minister), Carl McIntire, and such organizations as the John Birch Society, The Christian Anti-Communist Crusade, the Christian Freedom Foundation, and the Church League of America. Characteristics of the Far Right included a tendency to view the struggle with communism in absolutist terms and a "full-blown individualism in social, economic and political relationships." For Pierard, the Far Right was a threat both to American democratic institutions and to Christianity. "The Rightists are unwittingly undermining faith in civil liberties, the two-party system, and the integrity of elected officials, and they have made a mockery of American patriotism." The Far Right also undermined Christianity by diverting attention and financial resources away from missions and evangelism to anti-communist organizations and activities. It also linked faith to conservatism in an "idolatrous manner."[8]

But if Pierard thought anti-communism overwrought, he had trouble avoiding extremism himself. The Far Right did often make an enemy of anyone who would not embrace its anti-communist cause — thus targeting both communists and those who were "soft." Yet Pierard manifested a similar outlook when he not only condemned the Far Right but also the evangelical mainstream for being "soft" on

7. Pierard, *The Unequal Yoke*, 23, 24.
8. Pierard, *The Unequal Yoke*, 44, 69, 72.

conservative extremism. The book was peppered with quotations not only from anti-communists but also from mainstream evangelicals, leaders of the NAE, popular authors, even Billy Graham himself, which showed how large the yoke was. These figures had not, in Pierard's view, satisfactorily condemned extreme anti-communism. Of course, to make this case, Pierard needed to show that the views of the Far Right were not on the fringe but readily available in ordinary evangelical outlets. But this need for evidence also betrayed a deeper conviction, namely, that militant anti-communism was an outgrowth of political conservatism.

Pierard's hostility to conservatism was evident in two aspects of the book: first, his brief treatment of the history of American evangelicalism, and second, his sympathetic rendering of communism. He understood evangelical Protestantism to be essentially a form of Christianity in which the desire for personal holiness led to social, economic, and political reforms. "Conversion had the effect of shifting the individual's controlling motivation from self-interest to Christian concern, and this marked not the end but only the beginning of life," Pierard wrote. In the evangelical revival movements of the late eighteenth and nineteenth centuries, "the Gospel" demanded that society be "reconstructed . . . and evils like slavery, poverty and greed [be] eliminated." Evangelicalism originally moved Christians to "relieve the miseries of the urban poor by the distribution of food and clothing, aiding immigrants in finding employment, and providing medical aid for the lowest classes." Such improvements in society would hasten "a millennial reign of justice and righteousness."[9]

But sadly, according to Pierard, twentieth-century evangelicals had abandoned this commitment to social justice. During the Gilded Age, as the problems of industrialization and massive immigration confronted Americans, evangelicals threw up their hands and "concluded there was little they could do about the wretched social conditions except pray." It did not help, in Pierard's narrative, that evangelical preachers poured more energy into opposing new ideas like Darwinism and Marxism than into addressing social problems. Finally, evangelicalism lost its radical edge by depending on wealthy

9. Pierard, *The Unequal Yoke*, 28-29.

businessmen. Here Pierard cited numerous revivalists, such as Dwight L. Moody and Billy Sunday, whose patrons included wealthy industrialists and entrepreneurs. The result was a doctrine of individualism that "undermined the position of the church as the Christian community, emphasized noninvolvement with the problems of the world, and played directly into the hands of political rightism." Twentieth-century evangelicals, accordingly, had betrayed their radical roots.[10]

Pierard's understanding of evangelicals' past might have informed his mild defense of communism. First, he wondered if collectivism were as bad as the Far Right hysterically insisted. Welfare systems and concern for the well-being of an entire society was simply what states do. "The very nature of government," Pierard wrote, "requires such action, as the phrase in the preamble to the Constitution 'promote the general welfare' so clearly indicates." Second, despite communism's materialistic conception of human existence, its revolutionary instincts, and its functioning as a pseudo-religion, it had obvious appeal. Anti-colonialism, anti-capitalism, and the laboring class's resentment of the rich were all parts of communism's lure. It also promoted a sense of community, and through the Soviet Union's example had made "an impression" on many in developing nations. Pierard concluded that communism "has definite positive achievements," and that "The communist vision of a better world is a clear reminder to Christians that they must redouble their efforts to achieve social justice for all men."[11]

To be sure, Pierard admitted that communism was defective. One error was atheism. Another was its "lack of concern for human beings as individuals." Finally, its denial of human depravity was "diametrically opposed to the ethical standard of Jesus Christ." But the proper response to communism was not anti-communism, but instead to be good Christians and manifest the kind of concern for social and economic conditions that made communism attractive: "Everywhere Christians should be at the forefront of the struggle against poverty, disease, starvation, ignorance, overpopulation, and racial

10. Pierard, *The Unequal Yoke,* 29, 34.
11. Pierard, *The Unequal Yoke,* 99.

discrimination." In effect, what communists did, Christians should do better.[12]

By the time Pierard reached the conclusion of his book with the chapter title "This World is My Home," readers were likely not surprised to see the author assert that "Evangelicals should stand up for the weak, the poor, and exploited in today's society, because that is what Jesus did in his day." Pierard not only appealed to the example of Jesus; he also quoted a number of prominent evangelicals who were beginning to question a stress on personal salvation that denied Christian responsibility to society. Of course, these references to evangelical leaders arguably undermined Pierard's argument that the born-again Protestant mainstream was too conservative. Even so, the book should have alerted the politically astute that, if pushed to argue on religious grounds about social order and governmental responsibilities, evangelicals were unreliable members of the Right. To their credit, evangelicals' ultimate loyalty was to the God of the Bible. But finding ways to harmonize the American pattern of limited government, free markets, and strong national defense with biblical religion was next to impossible, at least for evangelicals like Pierard, because of the born-again Protestant assumption that the Bible or the teachings of Jesus were models for everyday life, *including the ordering of society.* How Pierard had changed the stakes of political contests was another question. If anti-communists were guilty of dividing the world between the forces of capitalist light and communist darkness, could Pierard's appeal to Jesus' earthly example restrain the habit of viewing politics as a contest between good and evil?[13]

The other book in the Lippincott series that revealed what many younger evangelical academics thought about American conservatism was David O. Moberg's *The Great Reversal: Evangelism versus Social Concern* (1972). As the subtitle indicated, Moberg's concern was to address the assumed division between evangelicals as "soul winners" and mainline Protestants as Social Gospelers. The former either ignored social problems because of the world's ephemerality or believed that the conversion of individuals would fix society's difficul-

12. Pierard, *The Unequal Yoke,* 100, 101, 104.
13. Pierard, *The Unequal Yoke,* 179.

ties. In contrast, the proponents of the Social Gospel believed that the ills afflicting modern social structures required social rather than individual or personal solutions. Moberg traced this divergence to the fundamentalist-modernist controversy of the 1920s and argued that the division was unnecessary and even unbiblical. "There was a time," he argued, "when evangelicals had a balanced position that gave proper attention to both evangelism and social concern." This was the time before the "great reversal," the period of the early twentieth century when evangelicals abandoned social reform and focused exclusively on personal evangelism.[14]

Moberg echoed Pierard in several matters, but his distaste for conservatism was the most noticeable. Both authors revealed the increasing acceptance among evangelical academics of a narrative of born-again Christianity that regarded evangelicalism as originally on the forefront of social reform in the nineteenth century and then taken over by middle-class, free-market individualism in the twentieth century. In effect, both authors argued that authentic evangelicalism was not content with inequality or deprivation but sought always to establish a righteous social order. Conservatism, consequently, was unnatural for born-again Protestantism. "As a result of the Great Reversal," Moberg argued, "conservatism in theology is often equated with conservatism in economic, political, and social affairs." He borrowed Pierard's phrase of "unequal yoke" and faulted evangelicals for being conformed to the world: "We have equated Americanism with Christianity to such an extent that we are tempted to believe that people in other cultures must adopt American institutional patterns when they are converted." Instead of helping the poor, evangelicals criticized those who tried to help. Moberg quoted one anonymous evangelical leader who said in 1967, "With all the clamor about the poor and minorities in our society, it's time someone speaks up in defense of the White-Anglo-Saxon Protestant Puritans. I'm for the upper dog." Moberg thought it completely understandable that "sensitive youth" would reject the "hypocrisy of such leaders."[15]

14. David O. Moberg, *The Great Reversal: Evangelism versus Social Reform* (Philadelphia: Lippincott, 1972), 25-26.

15. Moberg, *The Great Reversal,* 38, 42-43.

Moberg's gloss on sociological data may have rendered this defense of WASP society obviously hypocritical, but his evidence did not necessarily prove that America's cultural patterns were defective, nor did it make clear why Moberg should be interested in overturning them. Moberg cited a half-dozen surveys of American clergy and church members conducted during the 1960s and 1970s that confirmed a correspondence between conservative faith and conservative politics. One particular study by Jeffrey K. Hadden showed that conservative theology, in contrast to liberal theology, corresponded to "the belief that government is providing too many services that should be left to private enterprises, agreement that most people who live in poverty could do something about their situation if they really wanted to . . . support [for] Goldwater in the 1964 presidential election . . . and an unfaltering commitment to the free enterprise system as 'the single economic system compatible with the requirements of personal freedom and constitutional government.'" On the other hand, a study of the Episcopal church indicated that those who believed the church's mission was primarily one of preparing pilgrims for the world to come were guilty of the Marxist lament that religion functions as the opiate of the people, and another survey of American attitudes toward salvation and forgiveness demonstrated that people who did not go to church "were more compassionate than churchgoers."[16]

Despite the data against conservative religion, Moberg surprisingly resisted the conclusion that evangelicals conformed to this thesis about conservatism and religion. Instead, Moberg was in the middle of conducting his own survey, which found many church members who were evangelical in their beliefs and also "very 'liberal' in their perspectives toward blacks, welfare recipients, and members of other socioeconomic minorities and ethnic subcultures." The preliminary evidence seemed to indicate that Christian orthodoxy "leads less to racial and religious prejudice than more." Moberg's unwillingness to let the majority of sociological findings color his own conclusions about the social concerns of evangelicals certainly fit with the book's argument, even if it suggested special pleading more than rigorous analysis and poignant critique.

16. Moberg, *The Great Reversal*, 50, 52-53, 55.

His concluding chapter indicated as much. His desire was to restore the older balance between personal evangelism and social reform. "Personal regeneration that brings new self-conceptions and an orientation of love for God and others," Moberg concluded, "is essential to social regeneration." For that reason, he warned, socially oriented Christians needed to be on guard against their own self-centeredness: "As long as the power elite, together with the voters who support them politically, consumers who enrich them economically, stockholders who insist that they produce high yields on investments, and others who give them authority, wealth and power, are selfishly oriented, they will resist reforms to correct the numerous structural defects of society."[17]

Curiously lacking in Moberg's warning was the recognition that self-centeredness might also afflict politicians who supported welfare and social programs in order to gain re-election. His understanding of selfishness, which showed no trace of Alexis de Tocqueville's notion of "self-interest rightly understood," only seemed to apply to the economic markets, not to the ones in which politicians pitched for votes. This thin account of the self, individual responsibilities, and the multifaceted nature of civil society may explain why Moberg could assume in an almost Manichean fashion that "the avoidance of social involvement is equivalent to blessing the growth of evil in society."[18]

Moberg's analysis of American society displayed additional weaknesses. Even if his equation of WASP culture with American business interests was plausible, to reduce the political contest between American liberals and conservatives to a referendum on cultural intolerance and prejudice was to miss a basic reality. American politics had always involved a balancing act not only among the powers within the federal government — the executive, legislative, and judicial branches — but also the relationship between federal and state governments. American republicanism and federalism were rooted in the history of British politics and the experience of the English colonists who debated the contours of America's political order. In a very real sense, then, the WASP character of American culture sharpened

17. Moberg, *The Great Reversal*, 62, 157.
18. Moberg, *The Great Reversal*, 178.

and nurtured the political structures within which activist evangelicals would need to work if they wanted either to alleviate the needs of their nation's poor or to address the needs of the world. But Pierard and Moberg said nothing about the specific structures or traditions of American government. For them, it was sufficient to talk about religious obligation in the pursuit of a compassionate evangelicalism. The limits and exigencies of the people and institutions of the United States were simply inconsequential to the born-again Protestant pursuit of equality.

Richard Mouw, a philosopher at Calvin College (later president of Fuller Theological Seminary) and signer of the "Chicago Declaration," increased the distance between evangelical political reflection and the realities of American politics with his book *Political Evangelism* (1973). Mouw's argument avoided the stridency of Pierard and Moberg; he took few if any swipes at American conservatism or evangelicals' alliance with the Right. Like a good philosopher, Mouw tried to walk systematically through the logic that would lead Christians to regard political involvement as part of religious duty — hence the phrase *political evangelism*. Like Pierard and Moberg, Mouw was endeavoring to leave behind the old dichotomy that resulted in an either/or choice between evangelism and politics. "Political evangelism," he averred, "is one aspect of the overall evangelistic task of the people of God."[19]

One piece of Mouw's argument was the insistence that the church could not avoid politics, since it was by its very nature a political institution. This took readers into some comparisons between the church and Israel, the differences between religious and secular societies, and the place of the church in the history of salvation. The church was called to be active in the world, to live as a "paradigmatic community, whose life together demonstrates the triumphs of God's grace in human communal existence." In addition, the church had its own political structures of authority and accountability. The institutional church possessed real power. The aim of this power ultimately was to oppose evil in the world, thus drawing the church into a concerted conflict with worldly powers that corrupt and distort God's

19. Richard J. Mouw, *Political Evangelism* (Grand Rapids: Eerdmans, 1973), 15.

truth. If the political aspect of human life, Mouw wrote, had to do "with those patterns of authority, accountability, collective decision-making, and corporate responsibility in some form for community life," then the church's mission would inevitably draw Christians into politics. In effect, the church was, to borrow the Apostle Peter's phrase, a "holy nation" that embodied an ideal political community. But the church's political claims were even more basic than its example. "No matter what 'earthly' allegiances we have to political powers, we are members," Mouw exhorted, "of another society that places significant obligations on us, namely, the theocratic community over which Jesus Christ is King."[20]

For Mouw this understanding of the church as *polis* implied a break with both the perceived evangelical indifference to politics and a repudiation of the middle-class status quo. He faulted evangelicals for a self-serving selectivity when it came to the church's role in society. Here Mouw echoed other young evangelicals who were clearly sympathetic to the Left's critique of American society. Christians, he wrote,

> have denounced the sex habits of Hollywood while ignoring graft and corruption in the centers of political power. They have called for legislation to control Sunday business and the sale of alcohol but have refused to "meddle in politics" on voting rights and discriminatory employment practices. They have been concerned over the failure of science textbooks used in the public schools to emphasize man's creation in God's image, but they have too seldom spoken out against public laws and practices that oppress races of men who reflect that image. In the name of "separation of church and state" they have remained silent on matters of their nation's foreign policy, while freely criticizing the domestic policies of Communist countries. Under the guise of awaiting the transformation of all things they have enthusiastically supported the status quo. They have denounced the false prophets of political radicalism, while praying at the breakfasts of faithless kings and endorsing a spiritually destructive culture dispensed by greedy secular high priests.

20. Mouw, *Political Evangelism*, 41, 49.

In a book that spoke predominantly in moderate, even soft, tones, this riff was almost as radical as Pierard's. Even so, this passage expressed Mouw's reason for writing the book. Political evangelism was finally not a political question, but a spiritual one. "The demands of discipleship," Mouw warned, "require us at least to struggle to become more obedient in the areas in which we have erred."[21] Political engagement, in other words, was fundamentally a question of sanctification.

Rather than formulating the politics of Jesus as political theologians like John Howard Yoder would, the philosopher in Mouw could not resist his own theoretical efforts. In the most original part of the book Mouw appealed to the idea of social bonds. He argued that people were not created to be autonomous individuals, but instead were designed for community both with God and with each other. This basic reality of human existence should inform the shape of government for a given society. The proper form of governance would be one that minimized individualism and maximized a community's ability "to serve the Lord who is head of the church." The Christian community would also enable the diversity of gifts given to people to flourish. Authority would involve service and self-sacrifice, not a democracy *per se* but one that valued dialogue and decision-making with the input of all members. This form of community was little more than a description of the church without specifications about church polity, liturgy, or creedal requirements. It was also idealistic because it constituted "a radical alternative to contemporary styles of living." It was unclear how applicable Mouw's community would be for American society — or any other social group for that matter — since to be part of this social bond depended on being a Christian. What Mouw did not recognize was that this vision of community depended on a form of separatism assumed in the old bogeyman: fundamentalism.[22]

Nevertheless, Mouw and the other young evangelical academics believed they were resisting the status quo and rescuing their religious compatriots from conservative naiveté. For these young evangelicals, conservatism was simply a function of middle-class inter-

---

21. Mouw, *Political Evangelism*, 33, 32.
22. Mouw, *Political Evangelism*, 67, 71.

ests, individualism and personal liberty, indifference to the poor, and opposition to the welfare state. This political outlook was worldly and far removed from Christ's ideals of compassion and self-denial.

Yet for all of the younger Protestants' disdain for fundamentalism and the stridency associated with it, the evangelical critics of conservatism revealed a remarkable continuity with their parents and grandparents. For them, politics was still basically a matter of doing God's will, and the criteria for public policy and just rule continued to be the goal of avoiding worldliness. In effect, the young evangelicals sounded as preachy, moralistic, and separatist as fundamentalists, and possibly even more idealistic than their parents because of an almost utopian belief that with the right motives and arguments they could implement a more just society and a better form of government. Rather than looking for patterns of the American order that could be employed to improve the United States, the young evangelicals preferred to invoke godly standards and believed in their own righteous ability to follow, or at least divine, those ideals for society.

What Jesus Would Do

Some scholars have tried to distinguish two groups among the young evangelical activists: the reform-minded and the radicals. The problem with the radicals was, according to Paul Henry, the son of Carl Henry and a Republican Congressman from Michigan, "an unattractive fondness for 'rhetorical overkill.'"[23] Henry found it virtually impossible to take seriously people who dismissed much of institutional Christianity, the United States, the middle class, and the military. University of Wisconsin political scientist Robert Booth Fowler explained the difference as one of tone; the radicals were negative, but the reform-minded evangelicals tried to be positive. The reformers were still critical of American society, yet they believed that the United States could be changed in healthy ways and that Christians could lead lives in America that were consistent with the imperatives of

23. Paul B. Henry quoted in Robert Booth Fowler, *A New Engagement: Evangelical Political Thought, 1966-1976* (Grand Rapids: Eerdmans, 1982), 98.

their faith. Radicals like Jim Wallis of *Sojourners* magazine, on the other hand, adopted too many extreme positions.

To observers without a program or interpreter, spotting the differences between the evangelical "reformers" and "radicals" was not as easy as this distinction suggested. In the book that accompanied the "Chicago Declaration," for instance, Paul Henry and Jim Wallis each contributed short reflective pieces that were, as it happened, positioned right next to each other. Henry went first and attacked "the social indifference of evangelicalism," or at least he welcomed the Chicago gathering for pointing out born-again Protestants' apathy. The statement was "a bill of impeachment passed upon the evangelical church itself." As such, the evangelicals who drafted and signed the statement had placed the "blame and the remedy for our social evils right where they belong — on the shoulders of the 40 million evangelicals in this country." Henry went on:

> If we can't solve the problem of racism in our own churches, what right do we have to pontificate to the rest of the world? If we can't place our loyalty to the demands of God over and above our loyalty to the nation, how can we truly call ourselves soldiers of the Cross? And if we can't divest ourselves of our captivity to suburban, materialistic American culture, how can we speak to the maldistribution of wealth in our country and around the world?[24]

In comparison to Henry's reformist and "positive" rhetorical questions, Wallis, the so-called radical, sounded moderate. To be sure, the young activist used the word *radical* more than Henry. "Many are coming to believe that the gospel of Jesus Christ," Wallis wrote, "is indeed a radical message: in its demand for personal transformation, in its spiritual and intellectual power, and in its dynamic ethic that drives toward social justice." He also stated explicitly what Henry and the reformist evangelicals only affirmed implicitly, namely, that evangelicals might be the future of a new and improved version of the Left. "With the decline of the New Left and other movements for social change," Wallis conjectured, "it is highly probable that the strongest thrusts toward prophetic witness and social justice may well spring

---

24. Paul B. Henry, "Reflections," in Sider, ed., *Chicago Declaration,* 137, 138.

from those whose faith is Christ-centered and unapologetically biblical." Even so, he employed none of the language of "the cultural captivity of evangelicals" that Henry had. Wallis would, of course, go on to engage in such critiques in *Sojourners* and in numerous books. But the differences between evangelical reformers and radicals appeared to be so subtle as to be a distinction without a difference.[25]

The politician who embodied the activism of the young evangelicals was Mark Hatfield, a Republican Senator from Oregon. An Oregon native, Hatfield served in the Navy during World War II, witnessing both the enormities of war at Iwo Jima and in Japan after the destruction caused by two atomic bombs. After his time in the service, Hatfield studied political science at Stanford University and wrote a master's thesis on Herbert Hoover, a Quaker politician whose moderate policies the student admired. Back in Oregon, Hatfield taught political science and served as dean of students at his alma mater, Willamette University. In 1950 he was elected to Oregon's state legislature, and six years later he ran successfully for governor, a position he held for two terms. Although philosophically a proponent of limited government and a critic of centralization, as governor Hatfield helped to rewrite Oregon's constitution and increased the authority of the government in the state's capital, Salem. In 1966 he ran for the Senate; he won and would remain in that post for five terms. Hatfield's political heroes included not only Hoover but also Dwight D. Eisenhower, another moderate Republican. Hatfield was in fact one of the first Republicans to argue that the GOP draft Eisenhower for the head of its 1952 national ticket.

By 1964, when Hatfield gave the keynote speech at the Republican national convention, he had gained a reputation as a political maverick. Although Republicans were on the verge of nominating Barry Goldwater, Hatfield was an outspoken critic of the alleged extremism that Goldwater represented. Just a year before the convention, Hatfield had delivered a speech in Goldwater's hometown, Phoenix, in which he said, "I have no time for extremists' or fanatics' right-wing infiltration of the Republican Party. . . . The right wing frequently comes under the guise of patriotism and [catches] up unthinking adherents." In his speech at the national convention, Hatfield also at-

---

25. Jim Wallis, "Reflections," in ibid., 141, 142.

tacked extremists, lumping the John Birch Society with the Communist Party and the Ku Klux Klan. But his sharpest criticism was for the Johnson administration and its handling of the war in Southeast Asia. "Why, why do they fear telling the American people what our foreign policy is?" he entreated. "Tragic as is the tomb for an unknown soldier, still more tragic is the fate of the unknowing soldier whose life may be lost in a battle the purpose of which he has not been told."[26]

Hatfield's outspoken criticism of the Vietnam War would play fairly well in Republican circles as long as Democrats were in power in Washington. Richard Nixon even considered Hatfield as his running mate in the 1968 presidential contest against Hubert Humphrey. Even so, Hatfield's position on the war went beyond party lines and included opposition to most forms of armed conflict. This outlook alienated Republican faithful and conservatives who viewed a militarily powerful America as a necessary check upon Soviet expansion. Still, although Nixon selected Spiro T. Agnew as his running mate, he used Hatfield on the campaign trail, assigning the Oregonian especially to college campuses to explain how as president Nixon would handle the war. Hatfield later admitted that during his campaign stops he would portray Nixon as the least objectionable of the three candidates (including George Wallace). Yet his criticism of the war eventually forced Nixon as president to distance himself from Hatfield. In 1970 Hatfield joined with George McGovern to produce the Hatfield-McGovern Amendment, which prescribed withdrawing soldiers from Cambodia within a month, Laos by the end of the year, and Vietnam by the end of 1971. The Senate defeated the measure by a 55-39 vote, but Hatfield emerged as the liberal Republican, a reputation on which he thrived. According to Hatfield, liberalism means the ability "to put oneself in the position of the other fellow, to evaluate contradictory evidence and look at the many sides of one issue."[27]

By this time, Hatfield was also well known as an evangelical Christian. He had been reared in a Protestant home and was religiously active throughout his life. But in 1953, while dean of students

26. Mark O. Hatfield quoted in Robert Eells, *Lonely Walk: The Life of Senator Mark Hatfield* (Chappaqua, N.Y.: Christian Herald Books, 1979), 49, 51.
27. Hatfield quoted in Eells, *Lonely Walk,* 31.

at Willamette, Hatfield was forced to field questions about Christianity that he could not answer. Through interactions with evangelical students, he recognized, as he would later put it, that "for thirty-one years I had lived for self and decided I wanted to live the rest of my life only for Jesus Christ." Initially, the biggest change that Hatfield's conversion had on his life was a willingness to speak to church groups about the need for spiritual renewal in the United States and abstinence from smoking and drinking. But his born-again identity was also responsible at least in part for anti-establishment instincts, which included animus toward conservatism. In speeches he was critical of the institutional church as so much posturing compared to the vitality of personal religion. Likewise, Hatfield would be outspokenly critical first of Democratic and then of Republican administrations for putting pragmatic considerations ahead of principle. His evangelical faith was especially important for Hatfield's opposition to the Vietnam War. "I do not believe," he declared in 1965, "that in the ideals of both our Judaeo-Christian faith and our great political idealism can we say that bombing of nonmilitary targets . . . can ever be condoned as an action of foreign policy."[28]

As Senator, Hatfield regularly spoke to evangelical gatherings, where he usually upset his audiences with quips about the United States. In 1967 he told a group of Southern Baptists, "God does not intend that human beings should suffer endlessly under pressures of poverty, hunger, social decay, racial persecution, disease, ignorance, unemployment, war, or violence." Whether listeners were upset with Hatfield's criticisms of American society or his refusal to cheerlead for the nation is hard to say. But when evangelicals heard Hatfield criticize the Vietnam War at the United States Congress on Evangelism in 1969, some took issue with his politics as well as his theology. He asked them, "Why should we — a nation founded by those seeking a New World blessed by God — now be bound by 'an eye for an eye, a tooth for a tooth'? Do the fruits of the Spirit — love, joy, peace, patience, kindness, generosity . . . have any relevance to the concrete realities we face?" For his remarks Hatfield received numerous objections from the evangelical rank-and-file. One correspondent wrote to

---

28. Hatfield quoted in Eells, *Lonely Walk*, 29, 56.

the Senator's office, "I and a lot of other Christian people are extremely disappointed in your performance ... for you who claim to be a Christian and have access to our Almighty God should have a better understanding of human nature and evil in the human heart."[29]

Hatfield did not react kindly to such criticism and often responded sanctimoniously. He was tapping the frustrations that the signers of the "Chicago Declaration" had expressed about political conservatism. In his 1971 book, *Conflict and Conscience,* Hatfield swiped at a "theological 'silent majority'" that wrapped "their Bibles in the American flag, who believe that conservative politics is the necessary by-product of orthodox Christianity, who equate patriotism with the belief in national self-righteousness, and who regard political dissent as a mark of infidelity to the faith." Hatfield did not seem to notice that he may have been baptizing his own political dissent with the holy water of Christian devotion.[30]

Even so, his criticism of the evangelical mainstream and its support of the social and political status quo, which included backing a highly controversial war that nevertheless fit with the dynamics of the Cold War, made Hatfield increasingly sympathetic to the social justice rhetoric of the emerging evangelical Left. According to one of his biographers, Robert Eells, he moved in the direction of a "radical Anabaptism" that faulted the institutional church for trying to alleviate only spiritual needs; as Hatfield put it, "With the serious issues of war, race, hunger, and poverty impinging on us, the Christian must follow Christ in deeds as well as words." In the same way that the "Chicago Declaration" had called for overturning the otherworldly outlook of evangelicals that separated the temporal and eternal aspects of human existence, Hatfield was equally convinced that these spheres could not be separated and even that the temporal could embody the eternal. "The notion that being evangelical means that one does not have to concern himself with social problems," Hatfield wrote, "or that ministering to social ills is different from an evangelical concern, is simply heretical."[31]

---

29. Eells, *Lonely Walk,* 72-73.
30. Hatfield quoted in Eells, *Lonely Walk,* 81.
31. Eells, *Lonely Walk,* 86, 82.

Hatfield initiated any number of pieces of legislation on domestic and foreign policy that struck many as naively idealistic. From issues of American food consumption and dependence on fossil fuels to the United States' production of a nuclear arsenal, Hatfield was often ready with proposals that reflected his own understanding of what Jesus would do if he were an American Senator. Aside from legislative proposals, the Oregonian also used his own limited bully pulpit to prick the conscience of fellow Americans. Two resolutions from the 1970s stand out. In 1974 Hatfield called for a National Day of Humiliation, Fasting, and Prayer on which Americans would humble themselves, acknowledge their dependence on their creator, and "repent of their national sins." The Senator's home newspaper referred to the proposed day as the time "we all eat humble pie." The same year, Hatfield proposed a "Thanksgiving Resolution" that called upon Americans to identify with the world's hungry and encouraged fasting on all holidays between the Thanksgiving Days of 1974 and 1975. To publicize this resolution, Hatfield hosted a luncheon in the Senate where eaters were treated to a one-course meal consisting of a hard roll.[32]

Hatfield's political sensibility made no sense to conservative leaders in the GOP, but it resonated with young evangelicals' desire for a religiously motivated politics. In several books, such as *Between a Rock and a Hard Place,* Hatfield insisted that politicians and citizens who followed Christ should be committed to four basic ideals: identifying with the poor and oppressed against exploitative institutions and social structures, opposition to all forms of violence and militancy, resisting a materialistic lifestyle, and understanding political authority as essentially a form not of rule but of service. "Our witness within the political order must hold fast," Hatfield wrote, "with uncompromised allegiance, to the vision of the New Order proclaimed by Christ."[33] As such, the role of the Christian politician was always prophetic — the Senator drew much inspiration from the Old Testament prophet Jeremiah.

For Hatfield, whose close exposition of the Bible was more sub-

---

32. Eells, *Lonely Walk,* 126, 127, 136.
33. Mark Hatfield, *Between a Rock and a Hard Place* (Waco: Word Books, 1976), 29.

stantial than most of the evangelicals who were writing about politics, a fundamental tension existed between Christianity and politics. This world's structures of governance and economic productivity were essentially corrupt. But rather than regarding the role of the civil magistrate as one of restraining such evil until the return of Christ and the establishment of a new order, Hatfield believed the Christian politician's duty was to implement those longed-for patterns of justice and righteousness in the present. As utopian as such an ideal might appear, Hatfield's reliance on the Bible forced evangelicals to take him seriously. For younger evangelicals, and especially those attracted to an alternative form of politics, Hatfield's arguments expressed exactly the themes that should characterize Christian social concern. Still, even older evangelicals, who were more comfortable with the label of conservative and who channeled their political energies into the GOP, could not dismiss Hatfield because of his standing in the Senate and his appeal to Scripture. If evangelicals had been comfortable with political theories derived from reflection on human nature and the created order instead of searching for those derived from holy writ, they might have dismissed Hatfield as just one more radical idealist who happened to know his Bible. But because he imbibed the language of Bible-based, Christ-centered social activism and political responsibility, Hatfield became another in a long line of American Protestants who believed they were doing the Lord's work.

Poised but Out of Position

A story in *Newsweek* during the 1976 presidential contest could have given the young evangelicals a vote of confidence that their politics were the future of born-again Protestants in America. The piece pronounced the nation's bicentennial to be "the year of the evangelical." Since that time journalists and academics have viewed evangelicalism as not simply a religious style or constituency, but also as a political force. The main reason for the attention to evangelicals and politics was Jimmy Carter's admission that he was a born-again Christian. This self-revelation sent reporters scurrying to their reference works and to religion scholars, whereupon they discovered that a lot of

Americans claimed to be born again. Jimmy Carter's denomination, the Southern Baptist Convention, alone counted some 13 million members. The "God vote" might be decisive in the 1976 election, the story concluded. That Carter's chief rival, Gerald Ford, a member of the Episcopal Church, also claimed to be an evangelical was not coincidental.

In addition to reporting the religious proclivities of Carter and Ford, *Newsweek* noticed the emergence of an activist strain of politics among young evangelicals. The reporters here followed the arguments of Pierard and Moberg on the alliance between born-again Protestants and American conservatism as a betrayal of evangelicalism's inherently reformist impulse. "Embarrassed by the evangelical establishment's opposition to the civil-rights, peace and anti-poverty movements of the '60s," *Newsweek* observed, "the younger believers are reexamining the social teachings of the Bible . . . in the hope of closing the gap between private and public demonstrations of faith." For evidence of this shift, the story noted the "historic" Chicago Declaration, *Sojourners* magazine, and Mark Hatfield, "whose Scriptural defense of political liberalism is new to most evangelical ears." These signs indicated that evangelicals were turning back to an older version of "public Protestantism," the one that the mainline churches had embraced and that fundamentalists had rejected. It held that "Christians can and should change society through social reform, ecumenism and moral influence on secular learning, leaders and politics."[34]

But "the year of the evangelical" was not all good news for born-again Christians or their increasing visibility. The reporters conceded that evangelicalism had been growing for a decade, "offering certainties of a fired-up faith as an alternative to secular disillusion." But just as the mainstream media was beginning to take notice, "evangelicals find their house divided." Indeed, the 1976 election was exacerbating differences on social and doctrinal matters so profound that a loss of "cohesiveness as a distinct force in American religion and culture" might be the price evangelicals would pay for putting one of their own in the White House.[35]

34. "Born Again! The Year of the Evangelical," *Newsweek*, Oct. 25, 1976, 70, 75.
35. "Born Again! The Year of the Evangelical," 76.

But within three years, after the founding of the Moral Majority, *Newsweek's* foreboding conclusion would come to look like wishful thinking for the evangelical Left. By the time that Jerry Falwell, James Dobson, and Pat Robertson became household names, barely anyone knew about *Sojourners,* the "Chicago Declaration," or that Mark Hatfield was a card-carrying evangelical. In fact, with Ronald Reagan's victory in 1980, the Religious Right so thoroughly routed the nascent evangelical Left that journalists would for more than a generation equate born-again Christianity with political conservatism.

Even so, for a brief period during the early 1970s evangelicalism looked like it was poised to leave conservatism behind and turn left. In other words, the politics of born-again Protestants were never more uncertain than just before the emergence of the Religious Right. This instability stemmed from a form of political reflection that was long on recourse to the Bible but short on the kind of considerations germane to a federal, constitutional republic inhabited by people of diverse faiths. Instead of regarding politics and civil society as matters properly belonging to the earthly city, young activist evangelicals spoke of America as if it were, or could be, the City of God. The result was not simply that the reform-minded rejected conservatism. At a time when traditionalists, libertarians, and anti-communists were conducting lively debates about the future of the American republic, politically interested evangelicals with Bibles in hand were talking primarily to themselves. To be sure, their discourse was more thoughtful than some of the pronouncements of their fathers and grandfathers. Still, the young evangelicals' ideals bore the imprint of a "what would Jesus do" approach to religion and politics that had shaped American Protestants for the better part of two centuries. They may have believed that by distancing themselves from conservatism as they understood it, they would be better positioned to engage the American political mainstream. But their overtly Christian approach would turn out to be as divisive and sectarian as the Religious Right's in the wider world of public opinion, academic reflections, and policy debate.

THREE

The Search for a Usable Past

The year 1976 was a benchmark for evangelical Protestants. Not only were the two national political parties choosing presidential candidates who wore the moniker "born again"; the nation was also celebrating two centuries of existence. The younger evangelicals who objected to political conservatism had already begun to reflect on the authentic character of born-again Protestantism by turning to the past. They pointed to nineteenth-century reformers and activists who conjured up notions of a twentieth-century recovery of evangelical leadership against social evils from war to poverty. But the bicentennial of the United States invited evangelicals across the spectrum to reflect on the meaning of America's political and religious identity — with a broad spectrum of results.

In the periodical literature, two responses were immediately evident. The editors at *Christianity Today* used the bicentennial fairly predictably to reflect on the benefits of religious liberty. American independence was "from a biblical point of view" a mixed bag. Even if the founding fathers owed a great debt to their Puritan heritage, "most of them were at best theists." And trying to baptize the birth of the republic in the zeal of the eighteenth-century's Great Awakening would not fly, because the revivals of George Whitefield and Jonathan Edwards had occurred "a full generation" before the revolution. Meanwhile, "revival fires had been considerably dampened by the fervor for independence and by the acceptance of Enlightenment skepticism about the truthfulness of biblical religion." But America's shaky relationship to evangelicalism did not invalidate the nation's achievements. A tribute to the founders' efforts was the wave of immigrants who had come to America "to take part in the experiment in self-government." The other huge benefit was the separation of church and state. In the United States the church had fared "much better" than in Europe where "official ties were considered highly desirable." The danger confronting twentieth-century evangelicals was a form of defeatism that only saw hostility to Christianity in the United States. The revolutionary era of evangelicals might have been similarly tempted to see around them only infidelity and skepticism. But within a generation another revival swept across the United States and reshaped the new nation. Thus the bicentennial was a reminder for contemporary evangelicals not to give up, to "live boldly for God," and to hope for another outpouring of true religion.[1]

The "radicals" at *Sojourners* paid little attention to the bicentennial. Instead, the editors decided to devote the issue that appeared closest to July 4, 1976, to the subject of torturing political prisoners. Most of the articles discussed the conditions of believers and missionaries who had experienced great cruelty in South America, Asia, and Eastern Europe. But the import for Christians in the United States was not hard to discern: the economic interests of America and the West favored political stability even if it came with "a little fascism and torture." The *Sojourners* editorialist observed that in the Bible a clear connection existed between violence and wealth: "Building and protecting wealth seems inevitably to involve violence in countless ways, even the torture of innocents in foreign lands." The "issue" before Congress was what to do about the "utter sin" of allowing a nation's economic and political interests to justify the use of torture or physical intimidation.[2]

Although *Sojourners* did not invoke the past for its call to oppose torture, the magazine's outlook rested upon a historical perspective that took a very specific view of evangelicalism's social significance.

1. "Knowing the Future in 1776 . . . in 1976," *Christianity Today* 20 (July 2, 1976), 24.

2. John Alexander, "Threats to Freedom," *Sojourners,* July-August, 1976, 4.

The Bible, for these evangelicals, demanded opposition to injustice and immorality without qualification. The clear mandate of evangelicalism in its recovery of biblical truth was the pursuit of a righteous social order that was not limited to the borders of the United States but extended to the entire world. This outlook drew directly on the reforming zeal of nineteenth-century American Protestants such as Charles Finney, Lyman Beecher, and Theodore Weld, who in the pursuit of winning the nation to Christ were intent on establishing a holy society. Consequently, while the mainstream evangelicals at *Christianity Today* reflected on the meaning of the United States' history for evangelicalism, the activist Protestants at *Sojourners* were considering the meaning of the gospel for the history of the world.

To say that evangelicals were in the grip of the past would be a mistake. Born-again Protestantism had always exhibited indifference to history because of prior commitments to Scripture and religious experience. But to figure out the proper form of their political involvement, evangelicals turned to history for clarity. The most obvious need, which the bicentennial nurtured, was to understand the American founding. The result was a series of debates about the role of Christianity and even divine providence in the formation of the United States. Equally important was the history of evangelical Protestantism in the United States. Wherever they came down in the past, evangelicals were unanimous in contending for a faith-based politics, a consensus that would pave the way for the emergence of the Religious Right.

Intelligent Design

Peter Marshall Jr. was the David McCullough of evangelical historiography. The son of Peter Marshall, the Scottish-born Presbyterian minister who served as chaplain to Congress during the 1940s and was memorialized in his wife Catherine's memoir, *A Man Called Peter,* the younger Marshall exceeded the fame of either of his parents as one of the most popular evangelical interpreters of American history. His first book, *The Light and the Glory,* published in 1977 by evangelical publisher Fleming H. Revell, sold close to one million copies. It also supplied evangelicals with inspiration and exhortation as it made its case for America's providential role in history.

Marshall's was providential history with a vengeance. The idea for the book came while Marshall had been speaking at a community church in East Dennis, on Cape Cod, a place rife with historical associations about Massachusetts' original English settlers, the Pilgrims. In the audience was an editor who was fascinated by the idea that God had shaped the founding of the United States and entered into a special relationship with its citizens. After their initial meeting, writer and editor set off to Cambridge, Massachusetts, to conduct research at Harvard on the religious origins of America. Unable to gain access to Widener Library, they decided to head for Boston's Public Library. On the way, as if being led by God's providential hand, Marshall and his editor, David Manuel, walked past Harvard's book store and decided to check its history titles. They happened, as if by coincidence, upon Ernest Lee Tuveson's *Redeemer Nation.* As Marshall read the dust jacket, he later recalled, "it became clear to us that here we were indeed onto something — that there had been others who had felt that God did have a specific and unique plan for America." Further browsing in Harvard's store confirmed that America's first settlers "consciously thought of themselves as a people called into a continuation of the covenant relationship with God and one another which Israel had entered into."[3]

Despite the book's New England origins, Marshall was more ambitious in his argument than to claim simply that God had providentially directed the English Protestants who founded Massachusetts Bay colony. His interpretation extended all the way back to Christopher Columbus, who represented for Marshall a reluctant prophet whom God needed to humble before he could bring the true religion to another land. In fact, the original presentation in East Dennis that led to the book included excerpts from Columbus's *Book of Providences,* which included the explorer's confession of his sinfulness, his need for divine mercy, and his acknowledgment that God had placed in his mind the idea of sailing from Europe to the Indies. "All we had ever read or been taught," Marshall lamented, "had indicated that Co-

3. Peter Marshall, *The Light and the Glory* (Old Tappan, N.J.: Revell, 1977), 19.

lumbus discovered the New World by accident." No one seemed to consider anymore that Columbus had been "guided by the Holy Spirit every league of his way — and knew it."[4]

Where God's indirect ordering of man's affairs began and his direct intervention into the lives of individual saints ended was a question that did not occur to Marshall. As he researched Columbus's life, the author became convinced that the explorer had entered into a covenant with God: "Because Christopher had dedicated his life to serving Christ, God had given him an assignment that would test him to the limit." What is odd about this account is that despite the attribution of redemptive significance to Columbus's quest, Marshall refused to sugarcoat what a despotic explorer and captain Columbus was. Marshall showed how poorly Columbus treated his crew, how greed fueled his search for gold, how delusional he was when he thought he had discovered Solomon's mines. But, in each of these episodes, "Columbus may have turned away from God, but God did not turn away from Columbus." "By sheer grace," God brought Columbus with many of his men back to Spain having fulfilled his purpose, which was in effect to lead the Europeans into the promised land of the New World. The closing scene for Columbus was Marshall's imaginary account of his last words. After having sung the *Te Deum* with King Ferdinand and Queen Isabella, Columbus retired to his deathbed and confessed to God, "Father, I'm afraid I have not done well in carrying the Light of Your Son to the West," and "I pray that others will carry the light further." God's reply was, *"They will. You are forgiven."*[5]

If Columbus was for Marshall the Moses of American Christianity, John Winthrop was Joshua. The parallels were not exact. In some ways, Columbus's discovery of the New World was more like the scene in Genesis 1 after God had created the world and chaos prevailed before God established order over the course of the creation week. Soon after Columbus's death, settlements in the New World descended into a "debacle of rape, murder, and plunder." The situation prompted Marshall to wonder how a place that the Puritans could regard as the New Israel could "go to seed so badly for a whole century."

4. Marshall, *The Light and the Glory*, 17.
5. Marshall, *The Light and the Glory*, 52, 65.

One way out of the dilemma would have been to abandon the idea of America's divinely appointed place in the history of redemption. But short of that, Marshall needed to connect the unlikely — the Spanish exploration of Central America to the English colonies in North America; the Roman Catholic missions of the Spaniards to the Puritan ideals that motivated the settlers of Massachusetts Bay. This was a real challenge to Marshall's ability to weave a coherent narrative. But a man who could turn Columbus into a born-again Christian was up to the task.[6]

In point of fact, Marshall did acknowledge the need to connect the dots between Columbus and Massachusetts Bay. He did so by highlighting the sacrifice and piety of French and Spanish missionaries to North America and by contrasting their labors with the sordid efforts of the English at Jamestown. The missionaries represented the "first pinpricks of Christ's light," "thrusting deeper and deeper into the heart of a dark and murderous continent." Marshall did not shy away from the brutal treatment of the Native Americans. But his maxim for historical interpretation ran as follows: "God does not take the measure of men's lives by the sum of their accomplishments," but rather by "the quality and depth of commitment." Their lives functioned as the soil into which God would plant "the seeds of the nation which was to become the New Promised Land." The first harvest in Virginia was a disappointment; the English at Jamestown talked a devout game and promised to be on a mission from God, but their rhetoric turned out to be "Fools Gold." "Damn your souls! Make tobacco," was the response of General Edward Seymour to the request for the founding of a college in the colony of Virginia. This outlook stood in marked contrast to the Roman Catholic missionaries — and accounted for the early failures at Jamestown. While the colony's leaders may have "acknowledged God's existence," hardly anyone was actually living a life of sacrifice and devotion. The first English settlement, "undertaken without Christ," would await a better group of Christians.[7]

Marshall did not mention the Puritans until a third of the way

6. Marshall, *The Light and the Glory,* 67.
7. Marshall, *The Light and the Glory,* 78-79, 104-5.

into his book. This was remarkable, if only because many scholars were accustomed to looking to the Puritans for the basis of American identity. Marshall could have easily started his account of America as the Christian promised land by going straight to Massachusetts Bay. Indeed, by the time he reached the Puritans he acknowledged what many readers had long suspected, that these English Protestants "made possible America's founding as a Christian nation." At the base of the project was one word: *covenant.* This term summed up the Puritans' commitment both to God and to each other, for in fact the task of building the kingdom of God "requires total commitment." Even so, that Marshall put Columbus, French, Spanish and Anglicans ahead of the Puritans was significant. It underscored his larger point about the providential design behind the flourishing of Christianity in the United States.[8]

The Puritans were different from the other Europeans who came to the New World, because "they really believed it" — that is, they believed, according to Marshall, that "the Kingdom of God really *could* be built on earth, in their lifetimes." In sum, they were committed to living under the Lordship of Christ. Their reason for coming to America was that England had made Christian living impossible: "London was not the sort of place you would want to take your child for a walk, even in the morning." Meanwhile, church conditions were not much better. Church of England officials resisted efforts to reform the church and even considered the Puritans to be sanctimonious. But in the new setting, Puritanism flourished. Contrary to the perception that New Englanders were killjoys or theocrats, Marshall regarded them as serious Christians who lived quiet, decent, humble lives in pursuit of serving God. "Those who had eyes to see it recognized [New England] as a miracle of God, of a magnitude which had seldom been equaled in the previous sixteen hundred years of the Church's history." This conclusion did not prevent Marshall from documenting the Puritans' treatment of Roger Williams and Anne Hutchinson, whom they banished for deviant views, or their punishment of witches. Nor did Marshall overlook the failure of second- and third-generation Puritans to follow in the ways of the original settlers. But

---

8. Marshall, *The Light and the Glory,* 146.

the Puritans had planted good seed, so good that it could not help but bear equally good fruit.[9]

The next challenge for Marshall's narrative was that he had to cover almost eight decades, from the decline of Puritanism to the founding of the United States, and he needed to link the history of Puritan godliness with the later declaration of national independence. The only way to accomplish this feat was by way of the First Great Awakening. The revivals conducted by the likes of Jonathan Edwards, George Whitefield, and John Wesley became literally the "re-awakening of a deep national desire for the Covenant Way of life." The religious vitality of the Puritans may have gone dormant, but it eventually produced a "generation of clergymen who would help to prepare America to fight for her life." The non-political aspects of these revivals, or the reality that they transcended national boundaries and flourished on both sides of the Atlantic under the leadership of English and colonists, did not bother Marshall. The important feature was that revival had aroused a small group of Christians and transformed a would-be nation into a people "spiritually tough enough to face its supreme test."[10]

In case readers had missed it, Marshall's principal claim was that the United States had been established by providential control and had entered into a national covenant in which the country would enjoy God's blessing if faithful and suffer curses if disobedient. In some ways, the assertion of independence in 1776, the subsequent war, and the achievement of constitutional order were simply outworkings of divine purpose and religious devotion. Yet beneath the surface of this narrative was a flattening of political theory. Marshall endorsed political freedom, democracy, and the U.S. Constitution with little consideration of the debates that informed these outcomes or whether the American ideals he backed were actually compatible with his covenant theology. For instance, democracy for Marshall was both a divine blessing and a threat that needed divine protection from its excesses:

9. Marshall, *The Light and the Glory,* 145, 147, 191.
10. Marshall, *The Light and the Glory,* 240, 252.

It is difficult for us, with ten generations of democracy behind us, to appreciate just how radical were the words of the Declaration of Independence that "all men are created equal." Never before in history had the world actually *believed* in the equality of man. That is why, beginning with the Mayflower Compact, a century and a half earlier, the American system of government under God had been so unique. *Under God* — that was the key. Democracy would be subsequently tried in many places through the next two centuries, but only in nations where the one true God was worshiped would it succeed. For the study of man's history shows that equality, without the unifying hand of Almighty God, inevitably breeds chaos and anarchy.[11]

When it came to the problems posed by American acts of rebellion against a ruler established by divine providence, Marshall demonstrated greater urgency in ironing out wrinkles. For example, he did wonder at one point "how could the American revolution be justified" if Jesus and the apostle Paul taught the importance of submission to civil authority. The answer: political resistance was justifiable not for personal liberty but to serve God. God had given the Puritans "a land where there was no immediate civil authority, where, by the guidance of the Holy Spirit, they were to establish their own civil authority." To have submitted to the king of England would have been to abdicate the God-given authority of the colonists to govern themselves. They would have been like the Israelites: "After all that God had done for them to bring them out of Egypt — turning around and inviting Pharaoh to bring his troops to Canaan and put them back under servitude." The revolution, notwithstanding the leadership of Deists and Anglicans in Virginia, or Presbyterians in New Jersey, was a recovery of the rights that Massachusetts Bay originally had and that Charles II had revoked in 1683 when he demanded the return of the Puritans' charter. As early as the 1680s, it was clear to "even the most undiscerning Puritan that passive, docile submission to English rule would mean the reimposition of the oppressive authority of the Church of England from which God had delivered their forefathers."[12]

11. Marshall, *The Light and the Glory,* 255.
12. Marshall, *The Light and the Glory,* 257-58, 260.

But the United States was still not out of the woods. Even after the defeat of the British, Americans were not united, and the point of the new nation was hardly obvious. In stepped George Washington, giving all credit to God, to lead the Constitutional Convention. Ben Franklin also made a cameo appearance, according to Marshall, during a particularly significant deadlock in the proceedings to invoke divine providence on the Constitution's behalf: "We have been assured, Sir, in the Sacred Writings that except the Lord build the house, they labor in vain that build it. I firmly believe this." And finally the Constitution, the embodiment of the Puritans' original covenant, prevailed. No matter what difficulties the United States would face, even as early as the campaign of heterodox Thomas Jefferson, the Constitution was nothing less than the guardian of "the Covenant Way of Life for the nation as a whole!" As such, the Constitution guaranteed that American Christians could still restore the nation's covenant and return the United States to her original divinely blessed status. If these Christians would humble themselves and pray, God would heal the land and America would become again "the citadel of light which God intended her to be from the beginning."[13]

Marshall may not have single-handedly etched in the evangelical Protestant mind the point about America's Christian origins. As James Davison Hunter remarked, the evangelical account of America's divinely blessed status was a story told by Protestants beginning with John Witherspoon and Timothy Dwight and continuing in the popular imagination through such Protestant political figures as Woodrow Wilson or popular evangelists such as Billy Sunday. In other words, the United States had always signified for Anglo-American Protestantism the triumph of "Providential wisdom."[14] Or, as Michael Lienesch summarized the evangelical perspective on American history, "America is God's country."[15] Although many Protestants assumed this outlook as basic to their patriotism and sense of national purpose, Marshall's bestselling book functioned

13. Marshall, *The Light and the Glory*, 343, 348, 359.
14. James Davison Hunter, *Culture Wars: The Struggle to Define America* (New York: Basic Books, 1991), 109.
15. Michael Lienesch, *Redeeming America: Piety and Politics in the New Christian Right* (Chapel Hill, NC: University of North Carolina Press, 1993), 141.

as the forerunner of a bevy of books, partly inspired by the bicentennial, that provided the rationale for evangelicals moving confidently and aggressively into the public square. Within the next decade evangelicals attempted to stake their rightful claim to a place in the nation's history through books such as Jerry Falwell's *Listen, America!* (1980); Charles Stanley's *Stand Up, America!* (1980); Pat Robertson's *America's Dates with Destiny* (1986); Tim LaHaye's *Faith of Our Founding Faithers* (1987); and Rus Walton's *One Nation Under God* (1987).[16]

America and the Crisis of the West

If Marshall fleshed out the deep-seated American Protestant belief about the city-on-a-hill-like purpose of the United States, Francis Schaeffer provided a theoretical platform — a worldview — for the Religious Right. Born in 1912 in Philadelphia, Schaeffer was closely linked to the controversies that played out in his hometown during the first four decades of the twentieth century. After graduating from the Virginia Presbyterian liberal arts college Hampden-Sydney, where he majored in philosophy, Schaeffer returned to Philadelphia to study at Westminster Seminary, a school founded in 1929 by J. Gresham Machen, a distinguished New Testament scholar and Presbyterian controversialist who eventually led a small remnant of conservatives out of the mainline Presbyterian Church to form the Orthodox Presbyterian Church. When the new denomination itself split, Schaeffer switched teams and joined Carl McIntire, a fundamentalist Presbyterian who would become legendary for his anti-communism. Schaeffer's bond with McIntire in the Bible Presbyterian Church eventually led him to Europe in 1948, where he promoted McIntire's plans for a world alliance of fundamentalist churches and worked as a missionary for the Bible Presbyterian Church.

16. Walton's book was originally published in 1975 by Revell, the same publisher of *The Light and the Glory*. For whatever reason, Walton's book did not receive the popular attention that Marshall's book did. It is not the most responsible way to demonstrate this claim, but at Amazon.com sixty other books scholarly and popular cite Marshall, while only thirteen do so for Walton.

Schaeffer did not emerge as an influential evangelical thinker until the 1960s, a full decade before he would become, in the estimate of Garry Wills, the intellectual father of the Religious Right. In his book *Under God: Religion and American Politics* (1990), Wills wrote that although non-evangelicals "would consider Schaeffer's art criticism philistine," the apologist "deserves more credit than anyone else" for galvanizing evangelicals to recover America's Christian roots.[17] The turning point for Schaeffer's influence came during a series of speaking engagements he conducted at evangelical colleges during the 1960s. By then he had broken with McIntire and established L'Abri in Switzerland — then almost a decade old — as a study center and Christian community for doubting and troubled young men and women who questioned the truth of Christianity. His first book, *The God Who Is There,* did not appear until 1968 and was based on lectures given in 1965 at Wheaton and Gordon Colleges. In rapid succession came a flurry of short books in which Schaeffer theorized about modern theology and philosophy and the decline of the West. All told, Schaeffer produced twelve books in the course of a decade. Then in the year of the bicentennial, the future leaders of the Religious Right discovered Schaeffer. In the weeks running up to the presidential election, he made his first appearance on Pat Robertson's television show, *The 700 Club.*

What many evangelicals found intriguing about Schaeffer — aside from his appearance, complete with knickers and goatee — was the way he looked beneath the political surface to diagnose the metaphysical reality. In a sense, he was following Russell Kirk's insight that political problems were essentially religious and moral problems. Throughout his early career, Schaeffer was devoted to showing how developments in the arenas of philosophy, painting, music, film, and politics stemmed directly from first-order considerations about man's relationship to God and his place in the universe. This understanding of the spiritual foundation of human existence was everywhere present in Schaeffer's first three books, where he diagnosed the decay of the West through its philosophy and artistic expressions.

17. Garry Wills, *Under God: Religion and American Politics* (New York: Simon and Schuster, 1990), 321.

He did not elaborate fully the connection between religion and culture, but the direction was unmistakable:

> People have presuppositions, and they will live more consistently on the basis of these presuppositions than even they themselves may realize. By *presuppositions* we mean the basic way an individual looks at life, his basic world view, the grid through which he sees the world. Presuppositions rest upon that which a person considers to be the truth of what exists. People's presuppositions lay a grid for all they bring forth into the external world. Their presuppositions also provide the basis for their values and therefore the basis for their decisions.[18]

From these basic convictions flowed all of history and culture. Schaeffer may have had a peculiar understanding of the logical structure of cultural development, such as the priority of philosophy and its trickle-down effects upon science and art. Even so, he was doing for evangelicals what Kirk had done twenty years earlier, showing that political and cultural disorder is nothing less than a manifestation of spiritual malaise.

Schaeffer applied this point to the history of the United States in his widely read book *How Should We Then Live?* (popular in part because accompanied by a film of the same title). Coming out as it did just before the emergence of the Religious Right, Schaeffer's diagnosis of the decline of the West and America's part in that fall became a staple in evangelical arguments about the nation's founding, its need to recover its Christian basis, and the dangers of secular humanism. The basic narrative in Schaeffer's approach to the West was typically Protestant. One of the points stressed throughout his writings was the unhealthy separation of nature and grace in Thomas Aquinas's thought. Although many evangelical academics would later dissent from Schaeffer's understanding of Thomism, he argued that Aquinas was responsible for the rise of human autonomy in the West and its destructive consequences for philosophy, art, and social order. Thomas's teaching on nature and grace rendered the particulars of

18. Francis A. Schaeffer, *The God Who Is There* (Downers Grove, Ill.: InterVarsity Press, 1968), 19.

nature autonomous, without reference to God, and so lacking a religious or spiritual meaning. Of course, Schaeffer believed that Renaissance humanism and the Enlightenment did far more to sever the connections between human flourishing and divine significance than Thomism did. Even so, from his perspective the Protestant Reformation stood out as providing a proper grounding for the relationship between nature and grace, while also placing human freedom in its proper context:

> [A]s the Reformation returned to biblical teaching, it gained two riches at once: It had no particulars-versus-universals (or meaning) problem, and yet at the same time science and art were set free to operate upon the basis of that which God had set forth in Scripture. The Christianity of the Reformation, therefore, stood in rich contrast to the basic weakness and final poverty of the humanism which existed in that day and the humanism which has existed since.[19]

The founding of the United States was the embodiment of Reformation politics. The Reformation's "return to biblical teaching gave society . . . the opportunity for tremendous freedom, but without chaos." The mediator of Protestant politics to North America was Samuel Rutherford, a Scottish minister and member of the Westminster Assembly. His book *Lex Rex* (1644), according to Schaeffer, established the importance of political rule by law rather than the arbitrary decisions of men — "because the Bible [was] the final authority." This was an advance upon the institution of church councils or medieval parliaments because the Bible gave an objective authority that transcended "inconsistent church pronouncements" or "the changing winds of political events." In Schaeffer's genealogy of the American founding, Rutherford's views came to the United States by way of John Witherspoon and John Locke. Schaeffer conceded that Locke secularized Christian teaching; still, Locke drew heavily on the Presbyterian political tradition. The reason was axiomatic. "To whatever degree a society allows the teaching of the Bible to bring forth its natural con-

---

19. Francis A. Schaeffer, *How Should We Then Live?: The Rise and Decline of Western Thought and Culture* (Old Tappan, N.J.: Revell, 1976), 86.

clusions," Schaeffer deduced, "it is able to have form and freedom in society and government."[20]

In his 1981 book, *A Christian Manifesto,* Schaeffer applied the lessons of America's founding to the contemporary situation in the United States. American Christians knew that their nation had gone seriously wrong. They were rightly disturbed by pornography, the conditions of public schools, the dissolution of the family, and abortion. But they only regarded these problems as individual challenges rather than as symptoms of a larger problem. That more basic difficulty was a secular worldview that regarded "the final reality [as] impersonal matter or energy shaped into its present form by impersonal chance." Secular humanism stood in marked contrast to the worldview that had dominated America from its eighteenth-century origins down to World War I. The framers of the Constitution understood that man's inalienable rights came from God, and that these liberties were closely linked to divine law. This is why the first Congress opened with prayer. America's statesmen knew that without God or his law, "the Declaration of Independence and all that followed would be sheer nonsense." But the United States had lost this worldview thanks to the rise of materialistic philosophy and its effects on law and jurisprudence. Abortion was the logical consequence, the "natural," "inevitable" result of the "humanistic concept of the final basic reality."[21]

Schaeffer and Marshall provided a powerful right jab and left hook for a group of Americans excited by the commemorations of America's founding and despondent about its recent past and immediate future. If Marshall offered the inspirational account of God's intelligent design in establishing a beacon for Christianity in the modern world, Schaeffer added pessimistic caution by describing the ideological fault lines that confronted American Christians if they were to try to restore their nation's spiritual greatness. Even so, the recovery of America's Christian past was not free from mixed messages for evangelicals. In fact, professional evangelical historians were an-

---

20. Schaeffer, *How Should We Then Live,* 105, 109, 110.
21. Francis A. Schaeffer, *A Christian Manifesto* (Westchester, Ill.: Crossway, 1981), 18, 33, 48.

noyed with some of the glibness of accounts like Marshall's and Schaeffer's and offered a significant correction.

The Search for a Christian America, written by Mark Noll, Nathan Hatch, and George Marsden, evangelical scholars who would emerge as the historical guild's most significant interpreters of American Protestantism, was a response to the efforts of Marshall and Schaeffer to recover America's Christian roots. In fact, the book stemmed specifically from correspondence between the authors and Francis Schaeffer regarding his interpretation of America. On the one hand, the purpose of the book was to set the historical record straight. Was it theoretically possible to identify any state or society as Christian? The authors took their stand with Roger Williams, who taught that "no nation since the coming of Christ has been uniquely God's chosen people." In fact, the biblical record of nations that desired or possessed a chosen status, such as Israel, needed to meet incredibly high standards of piety. As such, a nation that claimed a Christian identity needed to acknowledge that God "hates religion that is not truly Christian more than the absence of religion." A consequence of God's exacting standards was that claims on behalf of America's Christian identity and past needed to take into account "not merely the religious professions that people make," but also the extent to which "Christian principles concerning personal morality and justice for the oppressed are realized in society." This perspective led to the conclusion that "no lost golden age" of a Christian America existed. Even worse, a careful examination of the past showed that evangelicals were "partly" to blame for the rise of secularization in America.[22]

On the other hand, the book was designed to add greater caution to contemporary efforts by the Religious Right to use the past to combat specific ills in American society, especially the bogey of "secular humanism." The authors acknowledged the problems in American policy that made abortion-on-demand possible, that minimized religion in public education, and that undermined families. Yet the authors also believed that many evangelicals engaged in the culture wars "have too often been indifferent to the oppressed and the unrepre-

22. Mark A. Noll, George M. Marsden, and Nathan O. Hatch, The Search for Christian America (Westchester, Ill.: Crossway Books, 1983), 25, 24, 17.

sented, the very ones to whom the Old Testament prophets, Jesus himself, and the inspired apostles directed our specific attention." In fact, the policies often advocated by the Religious Right too often looked to military strength rather than God's sovereignty to protect personal property and civil rights. "We have serious questions," they added, "about the morality of a defense posture that rests primarily on the threatened use of strategic nuclear arms." Consequently, the ability to evaluate the past wisely and accurately was necessarily bound up with an aptitude to assess a Christian's duty in the present.[23]

These questions of historical judgment were no more jarring than in the chapter on Puritanism. In contrast to Marshall's inspiring account of the original covenant between the founders of Massachusetts Bay and their God or the providential beginnings of New England, Noll, Marsden, and Hatch found the Puritans to be defective in efforts to establish a godly commonwealth. The standard for evaluating a Christian society ran as follows:

> Justice and charity would normally be shown toward minorities and toward the poor and other unfortunate people. The society would be predominantly peaceful and law abiding. Proper moral standards would generally prevail. Cultural activities such as learning, business, or the subduing of nature would be pursued basically in accord with God's will. In short, such a society would be a proper model for us to imitate.

By these criteria the Puritans failed. The many jeremiads that preachers pronounced in pulpits indicated that New Englanders were hardly following God's will. The right to vote was limited to church members, just one indication of how the Puritans confused church and state. These Protestants also engaged in abusive treatment of Native Americans. Aside from these obviously negative features of New England society, the long-term effects of Puritanism also left Christians with little room for encouragement. The moral influence of the Puritans was indeed great and could be seen in such important figures as Benjamin Franklin. Even so, the unintended consequence was secularization. By removing moral duty from its proper framework in

23. Noll et al., *Search for Christian America* (1983), 22.

Christian teaching about sin and grace, Puritans sowed the seeds of a failed legacy. The authors conceded that Puritanism did help to foster a Protestant work ethic and public notions of virtue and social reform, but "in their secularized versions the offspring of the Puritan ethic turn out to be at best the works-righteousness of Pelagianism, of self-salvation, or even secular modernism."[24]

If the Puritans failed to achieve Christian standards, the American founding fathers had no chance of measuring up. First, they were of questionable theological pedigree, since many of the most prominent held to Deism. Second, although the framers esteemed the Bible and knew its contents, their own political convictions, a combination of Whig and republican ideals, hardly emerged from a close reading of Scripture. According to Noll, Hatch, and Marsden, "the founding fathers may have read the Bible, but explicit references to Scripture or Christian principles are conspicuously absent in the political discussions of the nation's early history." Indeed, a close inspection of the ideals of liberty and virtue in the American founding showed a meaning that departed substantially from historic Christianity. Rather than deriving their politics from Scripture — as all Christians should, according to the authors — the American founders drank deeply from the well of Enlightenment philosophy. This generated an extraordinary but misguided confidence in the framers' ability to discern the first principles of politics: "they sacrificed an essential Christian confidence in the sovereignty of God over the structures of the world for a belief in the sovereignty of their own ability to discern the secret workings of the political world in which they found themselves." Even the most orthodox of the founders, John Witherspoon, was guilty of such hubris. Although Aquinas, John Calvin, John Knox, and Abraham Kuyper all represented efforts to ground political reflection in Christian truth, Witherspoon did not. To think that "the way in which Witherspoon reasoned about politics should ever serve as a model for Christian political thought" was even "foolish."[25]

In their 1989 afterword to the expanded edition of *The Search for a Christian America,* Noll, Hatch, and Marsden used their historical ar-

24. Noll et al., *Search for Christian America* (1983), 31, 41.
25. Noll et al., *Search for Christian America* (1983), 81, 85, 92-93.

guments to reflect on the ascendancy of the Religious Right. The result was a curious use of Augustianism to argue that Christians had no real interest in the City of Man's politics. The authors observed that Christians could legitimately claim the mantle of two traditions in American politics. The one of the Religious Right offered divine sanction to its form of government and economy, while the other challenged Americans "to use their wealth and their resources in the service of all peoples" and questioned programs "that seem to be only defending American interests." Which was more Christian, they asked, to illustrate this division in Christian ranks? Was it "a proper example" of applying Christian principles to politics "when a TV evangelist . . . argued that preserving the South African regime as a bastion against communism was more important than getting rid of apartheid?" Or was Jimmy Carter's work building homes for the poor with Habitat for Humanity "the finest model" of a politician "applying Christian principles to the problems of the world"? The authors answered by appealing to Augustine, who suggested that political regimes "are all ultimately founded by terrorist organizations" — that is, they invariably use "brutal" force to overthrow the previous regime.[26]

For this reason, Christians should not have any illusions about politics. Ultimately, politics belonged to Augustine's city of the world, where "self-interest rules." The lesson yielded from the search for a Christian America was that the church should never "play chaplain to the political order." The church's goals "are never going to be nearly coextensive with the goals of the civilization of the world."[27]

The problem with this genuinely Christian insight was that the book left the impression that Habitat for Humanity was a better form of Christian political involvement than opposition to communism. In the process, the authors lost sight of the proximate or provisional goods that come from the City of Man and consequently rejected the capacity to distinguish between different forms of tyranny and diverse kinds of social welfare. The appeal to Augustine was an effective counter to the Religious Right's providentialist impulse. But it left little

26. Noll et al., *The Search for Christian America* (1983; Colorado Springs: Helmers & Howard, 1989), 158.
27. Noll et al., *Search for Christian America* (1989), 159, 160.

counsel about American policy. For these evangelical historians, Republicans may not have been worse than Democrats, but they were certainly no better. In sum, the search for America's Christian roots left evangelicals either with a divine mandate for free markets and national defense, or without any real guidance beyond Jimmy Carter's hammer and nails.

A Usable Past Found

While evangelicals were debating the religious merits of the American founding, another historical expedition was underway that said much more about born-again Protestant political convictions than the search for either the providential origins of the United States or the religious identity of the framers. In the same year as the bicentennial, Donald W. Dayton, then librarian at North Park Seminary in Chicago, came out with *Discovering an Evangelical Heritage,* a book that dispensed with the ambiguities surrounding America's founding. Dayton shrewdly decided that determining either the religious sincerity of Adams and Franklin or the relationship between Christian theology and Enlightenment theories of man and society was beside the point. The really decisive approach to evangelical politics was to explore the political instincts and activities of born-again Protestants themselves. Here, Dayton found, was material sure to confound twentieth-century evangelical leaders' sympathy with the Republican Party and identification with the political status quo. Like King Josiah, who recovered the law for the well-being of Judah, Dayton had discovered an evangelical past that restored, for him at least, the proper role for Christians in the life of the nation.

In the prologue Dayton gave what amounted to the religious version of his political conversion. The testimony is an accepted form among evangelicals, in which they recount their turn from spiritual darkness to light. Dayton's wayward past involved a period at one of America's evangelical colleges, where rules prohibited drinking, smoking, dancing, card-playing, and going to movies. These were apolitical days generally. Support for Barry Goldwater or Richard Nixon was acceptable, but the protests surrounding the civil rights movement or Vietnam were off-limits. Dayton believed that the evangelicalism of the 1960s had a failure of conscience. What born-again Protestant leaders considered appropriate and prudential responses to America's domestic and foreign affairs Dayton believed to be the result of deifying "cultural patterns not only relative but in some cases even pernicious and demonic." Forced to choose between evangelicalism and civil rights, Dayton chose the latter: he worked for the Democrats in 1964 and lived with blacks in Harlem. Soon, however, Dayton saw that this had been a false dichotomy. During studies at Yale he discovered that evangelicalism had not always been so conservative. It had actually been "socially responsible" and even politically radical. Suddenly, Dayton knew he did not have to choose between evangelicalism and the Left; born-again Protestants had not only exhibited a faith "amenable to the development of social responsibility" but even a "biblically grounded 'Christian radicalism.'"[28]

Most of Dayton's brief historical studies of nineteenth-century figures drew almost exclusively on the examples of support for abolition and feminism. The most stunning case was that of Jonathan Blanchard, the founding president of Wheaton College, which Dayton called "the symbol of modern evangelicalism." This was the school that had attracted many of evangelicalism's post–World War II institutions to the city of Wheaton, Illinois, and that had produced such notable leaders as Billy Graham; it was also in Dayton's mind an institution in political captivity. Graham himself was guilty of political convictions that nurtured social irresponsibility. In 1973, Dayton remarked, when peace negotiations between the United States and North Vietnam had broken down and American forces resumed bombing, Graham refused to use his friendship with Richard Nixon to advise a less aggressive course. Graham's response was that God had called him to be an evangelist, not a prophet. Dayton's retort was that the Bible did not insist upon a choice between social activism and religious witness. Wheaton's first president, in fact, demonstrated that Graham's either-or mentality was misguided.

As it turned out, Dayton's brief for Wheaton College's radical ori-

28. Donald W. Dayton, *Discovering an Evangelical Heritage* (New York: Harper & Row, 1976), 3-4.

gins was sketchy. He had little trouble convincing readers that Blanchard drew upon nineteenth-century Protestant ideals about the kingdom of God and its approaching fulfillment in the United States. According to Dayton, Blanchard believed that this kingdom was a "perfect state of society" and that it was not simply a future reality. Blanchard was also an opponent of slavery, though again the evidence of a radical abolitionist position was slight. Before founding Wheaton, Blanchard had affirmed the "one-bloodism" of whites and blacks and declared that slavery was a sin. He also argued that a defense of slavery by Christians would turn their faith into one of the "privileged class." Beyond these examples of social reform in Blanchard's life Dayton did not go. But it was the hook he believed he needed to get the attention of Republican evangelicals.[29]

The rest of the historical examples in Dayton's book ranged from the notorious to the obscure. In the former category fell the revivalist-turned-moral-philosopher Charles G. Finney. His significance for Dayton stemmed from an egalitarian impulse that flouted the established mechanisms of status in antebellum America, especially the hierarchical system of slavery. Equally important for Dayton's purposes was Finney's belief that revivalism and political activism reinforced each other. Another figure in Dayton's gallery of evangelical reformers was Theodore Weld, a convert under Finney who devoted his entire life to abolishing slavery. That by the end of his life Weld became a Unitarian did not deter Dayton, since the author chalked up the rejection of orthodox Protestantism to the intransigence of the evangelical churches in opposing social reform. In addition to Finney and Weld, Dayton devoted a chapter to Arthur and Lewis Tappan, wealthy businessmen in New York City who financed most of Finney's revivalist crusades and various abolitionist organizations.

The obscure parts of Dayton's book explored various episodes in the history of abolitionism and movements that showed evangelicalism's progressive if not radical side. In the former cases Dayton highlighted the civil disobedience of students and faculty at Lane Seminary in Cincinnati and at Oberlin College against slavery. He had no reservations in suggesting that these examples of evangelical activism

---

29. Dayton, *Discovering an Evangelical Heritage,* 10, 13.

could legitimately be called "revolutionary." So pleased was Dayton with the iconoclasm of the evangelical abolitionists that he pointed out how the radicals at Oberlin were sympathetic to John Brown's raid on Harper's Ferry. In fact, two Oberlin students died in the incident, an outcome that prompted one college trustee to say of Brown that "we esteem him as one of the Wise Men of our times."[30]

In the other parts of the book Dayton looked at the evangelical roots of feminism and programs for the poor. Evangelical feminism sprouted among the Methodists, Holiness groups, and Quakers (especially the Grimké sisters). It relied on interpretations of such biblical texts as Galatians 3:28: "There is neither Jew nor Greek, there is neither slave nor free, there is neither male nor female; for you are all one in Christ Jesus." It was, in effect, an extension of the anti-hierarchical impulse that informed abolitionism. Dayton's examples of evangelicals who stressed meeting the needs of the poor came from the Christian and Missionary Alliance and the Salvation Army. Each of these groups emerged out of efforts to alleviate the poverty produced by urbanization and immigration after the Civil War. Again, Dayton relished the affinities between the Salvation Army's founders and "the emergence of socialism and related utopian visions." Even though they backed away from overt radicalism, Dayton was sufficiently impressed by these examples of "Evangelical protest against the bourgeois church" to hold them up as a model for born-again Protestants of his own generation.[31]

The point of Dayton's exercise in historical archaeology was to recover the original genius of evangelicalism, one that combined personal evangelism with social reform. Such an exercise also required him to account for the loss of this dynamism in twentieth-century evangelicalism. Dayton's explanations were mainly theological, though he did suggest in sociological terms that any reform movement, once institutionalized, loses its edge. The theological factors involved a change in beliefs about Christ's return among late nineteenth-century evangelicals that engendered a degree of pessimism and directed them to legislative initiatives, such as Blue Laws, as

---

30. Dayton, *Discovering an Evangelical Heritage,* 63, 62.
31. Dayton, *Discovering an Evangelical Heritage,* 118.

a way to preserve personal morality and purity. Dayton attributed the most blame to the influence of the Princeton Theology on evangelicalism. A system of doctrine taught at Princeton Seminary primarily to students studying for ministry in the Presbyterian Church, this theology became dominant in twentieth-century evangelicalism partly because no other system of instruction existed and partly because the Princeton Theologians had been forceful defenders of biblical infallibility. In turn, the Princeton arguments showed up among fundamentalists who insisted on the inerrancy of the Bible. Dayton himself was a critic of the doctrine of biblical inerrancy, and his disparagement of Princeton in a book devoted to evangelical activism was another way to discredit views he believed to be harming evangelical theology.

In his critique of Princeton Dayton contrasted Charles Hodge, Princeton's highly regarded theologian, with Charles Finney. Where Finney opposed slavery, Hodge argued that the Bible nowhere condemned it as a sin. Where Finney nurtured feminism by recognizing the gifts of women, Hodge was an opponent of egalitarianism. And where Finney was a libertarian on human nature and sinfulness, Hodge was a "determinist." These contrasts led Dayton to invoke again, without any hint of embarrassment, the word *utopian*. Finney's emphasis on redemption provided the utopian edge necessary for a theology that would support major social change. The importance of his theologically grounded utopianism had again become clear in recent discussions between the South American liberation theologians and the school of Christian realism that has dominated much recent American theology. Christian Realists found the liberation theologians' use of utopianism to be visionary and unrealistic. The Latin American theologians replied that without this theme, the positions of Christian Realists become in effect "ideologies of the establishment." To Dayton, Hodge's Calvinism served the ideology of establishment while Finney "found in the doctrine of redemption the utopian vision that enabled them to press toward a society free of slavery and the subordination of women."[32]

Few seemed to notice at the time, but Dayton's radicalism was radical in another sense. As much as evangelicals might debate the re-

---

32. Dayton, *Discovering an Evangelical Heritage*, 131, 132.

ligious character of the American founding, the origins of the United States did not amount to a hill of beans compared to Dayton's breathtaking view of Christian salvation. If his redemptive utopianism was at the heart of the evangelical faith, then debates about republicanism, Locke, Hume, or the Puritans were child's play next to the staggering view of human potential and civil society involved in Dayton's affirmation of Finney's perfectionist faith. Dayton had trumped the evangelical search for a Christian America by laying on the table a Christian-utopia full house.

Past Imperfect

The bicentennial in 1976 and the election of the first openly born-again president, Jimmy Carter, were catalysts for evangelicals to enter the political field self-consciously as an identifiable part of the electorate. The attention to the American founding, no matter how much its Christian character was up for debate, was also partly responsible for evangelicals enlisting with conservatives. A sense of pride in the political order established by the framers combined with the appeal of limited government naturally led many born-again Protestants to support politicians who defended the goodness of the United States and stood up to liberals and leftists who advocated an even bigger government through various schemes of social engineering. Instead of looking to the past for a way to square evangelical devotion and political allegiance as Dayton had, the majority of born-again Protestants proved eager to listen to the likes of Peter Marshall or Francis Schaeffer and enter the ranks of the Religious Right. In other words, the search for America's Christian origins found an outlet more readily in Ronald Reagan's patriotic optimism and regular invocation of the nation's civil religion than it did in even resolutely born-again Democrats who were suspicious of American greatness, the nation's redemptive purpose, or its laissez-faire ethos.

Even so, deep within the soul of the members of the emerging Religious Right beat the heart not of a Burkean conservative but of a Finneyite activist. Evangelicals may have sung "The Star-Spangled Banner" with relish, but their interest in political formalities, the

89

sorts of questions that yielded the constitutionalism, federalism, and republicanism of the framers, was of secondary importance. Before polity came morality and righteousness, whether personal or social. If the founding was a story of the triumph of true religion, the men who accomplished it were not exactly choirboys. Nor was the political order they established a complete victory for the simple principles of justice and equality. Consequently, as admirable and praiseworthy as the American founding was, most evangelicals regarded it as flawed. America's greatness still needed to find a nobler outlet than either the Articles of Confederation or the Constitution.

The need for a sequel to the narrative of American independence led evangelicals in their historical understanding of the United States invariably to regard the democratic activism and reforms of antebellum Protestantism as the culmination of the best aspects of the founding. In their sequel to *The Light and the Glory,* for instance, Peter Marshall and David Manuel took the history of the United States down to 1837. The revivals of Finney and the reforms they inspired were by no means the centerpiece of the story in *From Sea to Shining Sea,* but the authors had no trouble regarding the radical egalitarianism of the Second Great Awakening as the default setting for Christians involved in political life. They quoted one religious newspaper approvingly that declared "The grand result to which revivals are here tending, is the complete moral renovation of the world." So too they observed that Finney's efforts to abolish slavery and the consumption of alcohol and the more general effort to make every aspect of human existence — from business to diet — conform to God's will were simply the fruit of Christian duty to love one's neighbor as oneself. The revivalists' efforts to establish the kingdom of God in America were, then, simply American Christians' endeavor to avoid the fate of the world's other great civilizations — Chaldea, Egypt, Greece, and Rome. "Let the Christianity at the heart of America wither and die, and in a very short time marble monuments on the Potomac would join the ruins on the hills of Rome and the banks of the Nile."[33]

Evangelical academic historians knew better than to grant ei-

33. Peter Marshall and David Manuel, *From Sea to Shining Sea* (Old Tappan, N.J.: Revell, 1986), 315, 316.

ther the American founding or the Second Great Awakening such a providential benediction. Noll, Marsden, and Hatch, in their book on America's Christian origins, conceded that Finney and his revivalist peers possessed an awareness that "their bountiful heritage as Americans required much of them," including a fervent struggle "to remake every part of their society according to Christian standards." But they also knew enough to recognize the downside of evangelical crusades. "On the verge of inaugurating a kingdom that was essentially Protestant, democratic, and Caucasian, many evangelicals looked askance at anyone who threatened the solidarity of this image: Catholic immigrants, religious dissenters such as the Mormons, and most blacks and native Americans." These authors seconded Tocqueville's observation that, thanks to the influence of religious zeal, "Americans were more tolerant than Europeans within certain limits and less tolerant outside those boundaries."[34]

Yet even these evangelical historians had real affinity for revivalism's egalitarian ideals when it came to describing the features of a Christian society abstractly conceived. "Certainly Christianity brings many broad, obviously good influences," Noll, Marsden, and Hatch wrote, "as when families' lives are improved, charity is displayed, the poor are cared for, high moral standards are pursued, just laws are enacted, personal worth is properly valued, minorities and outsiders are regarded as persons in God's image." To be sure, these social virtues could not be realized in this life: "We should be reminded that we ourselves do not have the final blueprints for establishing the Kingdom of heaven on earth." The Augustinian outlook of Noll, Marsden, and Hatch would prevent them from following Dayton all the way down Finney's path of the kingdom of God in America. But in its broad outlines, the form of society that they believed most conformed to Christian ideals was not far from the one that Finney envisioned. The historians knew Finney was deluded to think such a society could take root in America through revivalism's conversions and reforms. Less clear was whether they fundamentally disagreed with Finney's agenda for pursuing equality and righteousness.[35]

34. Noll et al., *Search for Christian America* (1983), 116.
35. Noll et al., *Search for Christian America* (1983), 45, 46.

The evangelical search for a usable past started from a place generally different from that of other students of American polity. Evangelicals' historical judgments invariably involved moral and religious interpretations, rather than legal or political ones, because they used what they believed were Christian categories to evaluate the relative goodness of America's governmental structures. Whether they regarded America specifically as a divinely ordained nation with a commission to establish righteousness on earth or simply as one nation among the nations, their judgments did not significantly differ, because politics was a subset of Christian truth. No matter that these standards looked remarkably similar to those of political radicals intent on eliminating all forms of inequality, injustice, and oppression. The lessons that evangelicals drew from America's past were generally ethical and redemptive. The standards for the United States derived primarily from its standing before God, not from its conformity to its constitutional and cultural traditions. George Santayana once remarked that those who fail to learn from the past are condemned to repeat it. The addendum to that quip that applies to evangelicals is that sometimes those who do learn from the past learn only one lesson — the wrong one.

FOUR

Party Crashers

———

In 1985, just a year after his book *The Naked Public Square* was published, Richard John Neuhaus responded to social analysis and journalistic accounts of the Religious Right that went something like this: "The Falwells are coming! The Falwells are coming!" Neuhaus likened it to the country cousins showing up "in force at the family picnic." "They want a few rules changed right away," he explained. "Other than that they promise to behave, provided we do not again try to exclude them from family deliberations." Neuhaus did not have much to lose by defending fundamentalists in the pages of *Commentary,* a right-of-center Jewish publication; an op-ed in the *New York Times* would have been more provocative. Still, the public intellectuals that Neuhaus was trying to coax back from the brink of hysteria would likely also have scorned a piece in the *Times* as easily as they would have ignored an essay in *Commentary*. And that was the point. America's opinion class, the "'northeasternliberalestablishment' (one word)," was comparing the Religious Right to the Third Reich. This reaction was surprising if not discouraging because Falwell and others, Neuhaus pointed out, tried to calm fears by "expressing devotion to the rules of liberal democracy (yes, *liberal* democracy) and by distancing themselves from the anti-democratic theocrats who are attracted to their cause." Equally surprising was that the people who wrote for, edited, and read the *Times* "could be so easily intimidated."[1]

---

1. Neuhaus, "What the Fundamentalists Want," originally published in *Com-*

Having just written a book about the danger of secularization, Neuhaus was in a better position to score points off the carom of the Religious Right than most commentators. To do so he would have to explain away fundamentalism's less attractive features. The "fundamental" doctrines concerning Christ and the Bible were not necessarily a problem because for most Christians, Roman Catholic and Protestant, these were articles of faith. Neuhaus observed that beliefs about the return of Christ had been responsible for a pessimistic view of history that undermined political engagement by fundamentalists. In fact, one of the common complaints was that these Protestants were otherworldly, too removed from the affairs of the world. Now that the Religious Right had turned around fundamentalism's disdain for politics, to complain that they were too politically engaged was to apply an arbitrary standard that was not very liberal or democratic. Neuhaus also conceded that fundamentalist beliefs about the "end times" were especially unsettling for Jews because support for Israel seemed to be simply part of a broader Christian system in which Judaism played a partial function. But he pointed out that all Christian traditions had trouble finding a positive presence for contemporary Judaism within the ongoing Christian witness, so again, critics were holding fundamentalists to an arbitrary standard. Even so, he insisted that fundamentalists were fully capable of distinguishing between membership "in the company of the truly saved" and belonging to the Moral Majority, a distinction readily apparent to anyone who observed that both Roman Catholics and Jews belonged to Falwell's activist organization but would see no advantage to joining the pastor's Thomas Road Baptist Church in Lynchburg, Virginia.[2]

What then accounted for the hostility of mainstream journalists, academics, and political leaders to fundamentalists becoming politically active? Neuhaus believed that the problem stemmed from an overly high estimate of secularization theory. Most sociologists had presumed that the more advanced a society became, the less in-

---

mentary (1985) and reprinted in Richard John Neuhaus and Michael Cromartie, eds., *Piety and Politics: Evangelicals and Fundamentalists Confront the World* (Washington, D.C.: Ethics and Public Policy Center, 1987), 5, 17-18.

2. Neuhaus, "What the Fundamentalists Want," 15.

fluential religion would be. But scholars were discovering in fact that Americans had become more religious, not less, over the course of the twentieth century. The problem for fundamentalists was that even though they and their kin had retained older forms of faith, many elites in America had lobbied for and secured policy and legislation on the basis of the older presumption — that secularization was the rule. This was the reason for fundamentalist political engagement; "fundamentalist leaders did not just get together one day and decide to go political" but instead were "responding to an assault on their religious freedom." The most alarming aspects of that assault were the removal of prayer and Bible reading from public schools, the heavy hand of the Internal Revenue Service in restricting religious institutions' tax-exempt status for failing to comply with federal policies, and increasing openness in American public life not to faith but to drugs, pornography, gay activism, divorce, and abortion. Neuhaus argued that by any reasonable measure, these were "legitimate issues for debate in a democratic society" — unless, of course, fundamentalists were not considered legitimate members of America.[3]

Electoral politics aside, Neuhaus had a point. From the vantage of a mid-1970s consensus that regarded the United States as having entered a post-Protestant era, the rise of a Religious Right dominated not only by Protestants but by fundamentalists was not the way the story was supposed to go. People like Jerry Falwell looked like party crashers who, rather than slinking from bar to buffet in hopes of going unnoticed, demanded that the vegetarian, alcohol-imbibing hosts serve meat and tell the bartender to go home. For conservatives already present at the party before their arrival, the inclusion of fundamentalists was generally welcome, since the presence of religious conservatives altered social dynamics and swelled the Right's numbers. But welcoming the Religious Right also came with liabilities that Neuhaus's depiction of fundamentalists may have conveniently glossed. The metaphor of closing down the bar at a party may involve a caricature of fundamentalist taboos, but is also apt in the sense that including the moral, if not moralistic, seriousness of the Religious Right in American conservatism had the potential to diminish con-

---

3. Neuhaus, "What the Fundamentalists Want," 15, 17.

servative merriment at the soirée. To see secular liberal discomfort over religious conservatives was satisfying in its own way, but it also required hiding the cocktails traditionalist conservatives were holding when fundamentalists entered the conversation. As long as religious conservatives provided a demographic challenge to the secular trajectory of American society, their value to the American Right remained high. Once the Religious Right tried to assume leadership or generate policy, the burden of dry parties, metaphorically even more than literally, became apparent.

From Silent to Moral Majority

The bicentennial year of 1976 proved to be decisive for the emergence of a conservative Protestant political movement not simply because celebrations of the United States' founding provoked attention to the place of Christianity in the outlook of the nation's framers. It was also the year when a self-consciously born-again Protestant, Jimmy Carter, became not only the Democratic Party's nominee for president but also the president of the nation with allegedly Protestant roots. Of course, Carter turned out to be a different kind of evangelical than the one that would dominate the public's attention for the last quarter of the twentieth century. A Southern Baptist moderate who took his cues more from Reinhold Niebuhr than from Billy Graham, Carter proved to be a disappointment and a problem that the Religious Right would try to solve. The thirty-ninth president of the United States may have taught Sunday school in his Georgia congregation and talked of a personal relationship with Jesus Christ, but Carter had no capacity to support the policies or commandeer the constituency of evangelical Protestants for his administration or the Democratic Party. Had evangelical leaders and journalists known more about the Southern Baptist Convention than simply the reputation that followed from its being southern or trusting in Jesus, they would have seen that Carter, despite the southern accent, had more affinities to the tolerant and do-good orientation of mainline Protestants than the restrain-evil-and-promote-righteousness resolve of fundamentalists and evangelicals. In 1976 and the first few years of the Carter administration, however, the president's conversion experience placed him on the conservative side of the political spectrum.

The bloom came all the way off the Carter rose in 1980 when he held a breakfast for a group of prominent evangelical preachers, many of whom were popular through television or radio, including Falwell, Oral Roberts, Rex Humbard, Jim Bakker, D. James Kennedy, Charles Stanley, and Tim LaHaye. This was part of Carter's effort to build better bridges with evangelicals, the follow-up to his appearing before the National Religious Broadcasters the previous day. But the meal did not produce the results for which both sides had hoped. When the ministers asked Carter about his support for the pro-life position, the president's response was, in their estimation, vague. Then they asked Carter about the poor representation of born-again Protestants in his administration, and he seemed to waffle again. Tim LaHaye recalled that he asked Carter point-blank why as an evangelical and a "pro-family man" he still supported the Equal Rights Amendment. When Carter, according to LaHaye, "gave some off-the-wall answer that the Equal Rights Amendment was good for the family," LaHaye concluded that Carter was "out to lunch": "We had a man in the White House who professed to be a Christian, but didn't understand how un-Christian his administration was." In the limousine ride from the White House, LaHaye and the others "made a commitment to God that day that, for the first time in our lives, we were going to get involved in the political process and do everything we could to wake up the Christians to be participating citizens instead of sitting back and letting other people decide who will be our government leaders." Evangelicals needed a president who would be committed to moral values, "because if he's going to represent us, he's going to have to represent our moral values" — not just those of evangelical Protestants, but "the same traditional values our country was founded on."[4]

The person who needed the most persuasion to enter the political fray was Falwell. He would later admit that he had preached at many pastors' conventions and argued for his listeners not to lead

---

4. LaHaye quoted in William Martin, *With God on Our Side: The Rise of the Religious Right in America* (New York: Broadway Books, 1996), 189-90.

marches, and to focus on pulpit ministry instead of becoming bogged down in contemporary issues. He conceded that he had misled his evangelical colleagues. "I never thought the government would go so far afield," he confessed. "I never thought the politicians would become so untrustworthy, I never thought the courts would go so nuts to the left, and I misjudged the quality of government we have." Falwell even deduced that evangelicals' lack of political involvement was "one of the reasons why the country's in the mess it is in."[5]

An important explanation for Falwell's about-face was the work of Francis Schaeffer. Schaeffer's 1976 book, *How Should We Then Live?*, co-written with his son, Frank, became the evangelical equivalent of Richard Weaver's *Ideas Have Consequences,* the classic brief against contemporary culture by traditionalist conservatism. The particular ideas that Schaeffer believed were having pernicious consequences were those stemming from secular humanism. The West's rejection of Christianity, everywhere on display in philosophy, art, and politics, was responsible for the moral relativism that informed the youth culture's embrace of sex, drugs, and rock and roll. Even worse, secular humanism had provided the justification for abortion. Schaeffer's book, and the companion film of the same title, capitalized on his growing popularity as an evangelical intellectual and became a ready weapon in the emerging culture wars. Falwell himself invited Schaeffer to the Virginia pastor's school, Liberty University, and required freshmen to see and discuss the film version of *How Should We Then Live?* For his part, Schaeffer tried to convince Falwell to turn Liberty University into the evangelical Harvard.

As it turned out, Falwell's instincts ran more toward activism than academics. In 1979, with the help of Republican strategists Paul Weyrich, Howard Phillips, and Ed McAteer, Falwell opened the offices of the Moral Majority in Washington, D.C. The organization's aim was to "exert a significant influence on the spiritual and moral direction" of the United States. To accomplish this, the Moral Majority would try to mobilize Americans at the grass roots, inform them about the aims and scope of legislation in the federal and state legislatures, lobby Congress to "defeat left-wing, social-welfare bills that will further

5. Falwell quoted in Martin, *With God on Our Side,* 202.

erode our precious freedom, work for the establishment of the Family Protections Agency, and help communities to block pornography, homosexuality, and immoral teaching in public schools." Some of Falwell's associates on the staff at Thomas Road Baptist Church actually believed that their senior colleague was wrong to take on the work of political advocacy. But members of the congregation were generally supportive. According to one charter member, "Somebody had to take a stand. I think Dr. Falwell was the one to do it because he gets his wisdom and knowledge from God. That's why we're for him a hundred percent."[6]

For all of Schaeffer's influence on Falwell, the latter's 1980 book, *Listen, America!,* read more like speeches of Ronald Reagan than a gloss on Schaeffer's argument. Designed to publicize and advance the Moral Majority's program, the book began with the themes that had propelled the ascendancy of Reagan. According to Falwell, the United States faced three great crises: a weakening national defense, tax policy that enlarged government and hurt free enterprise, and a paucity of strong and virtuous statesmen. The context for this assessment was clearly the Cold War and the struggle between free societies and communism. In fact, Falwell began the book by recalling his thoughts during a return flight from a speaking engagement in Tulsa, Oklahoma. While cruising above the American heartland, he thought back to a trip the previous week to Thailand and the refugees he had seen there fleeing the brutal Communist government of Cambodia. "I thought of the little girl I had taken in my arms, being careful not to hurt her thin, fragile body and her brittle, reedlike arms and legs," Falwell recalled. "I had looked down at her swollen belly and was overwhelmed with the fact that thousands like her were dying. No one could visit the camps I visited and see the things I had seen without having his heart moved." The lasting impression he took away was that millions around the world were running from communism. "They long for freedom and they long for life. One hundred forty-seven million people have been murdered by the Communists since the Bolshevik Revolution in 1917." This global contest between tyranny and liberty had brought America to a crossroads. The United

6. Charter member quoted in Martin, *With God on Our Side*, 202-3.

States was "facing a fateful 'Decade of Destiny.'" Falwell was afraid that Americans had taken the "blessings of God for granted." "I knew that I lived in the greatest country in the world," but "I knew that I had to face the grim truth that America, our beloved country, is indeed sick."[7]

Of the basic themes that united conservatives around Reagan, free enterprise was the one that received shortest shrift in *Listen, America!* Falwell assured readers that a market economy was clearly outlined in the Book of Proverbs. Christ himself taught the work ethic. What is more, "Ownership of property is biblical. Competition in business is biblical. Ambitious and successful business management is clearly outlined as part of God's plan for His people." Yet, as valuable as free enterprise was, Falwell couched it in terms of the productivity necessary for a strong national defense. One part of the problem confronting America, then, was that the federal government was spending on the wrong programs — namely welfare — and hurting the economy. With annual deficits of over fifty billion dollars, it was time for Americans to realize that the nation could not "indefinitely carry on the burden of governmental spending." Falwell failed to acknowledge that government spending was also responsible for a strong national defense. He apparently assumed that some forms of spending, even if taking money out of the hands of entrepreneurs, was the price of freedom.[8]

That assumption prevailed again when Falwell turned to the nature of American government. "When America was founded," he wrote, "the legitimate purpose of government was to protect the lives, the liberties, and the property of the citizens." The purpose was not economic redistribution or social engineering; "Simply stated, government was to protect the God-given rights of the people." Securing and protecting the freedoms of the American people, of course, involved respecting their economic freedoms and personal property. For this reason, Falwell's discussion of American politics was an extended critique of the welfare state. By expanding dramatically the services and agencies of the federal government, the national admin-

7. Jerry Falwell, *Listen, America!* (New York: Bantam Books, 1981), 3-4, 5, 7.
8. Falwell, *Listen, America!*, 13, 14.

istration had fundamentally altered the American system of governance. Here Falwell relied heavily on the arguments of economist Milton Friedman. The University of Chicago libertarian had documented the growth of the federal government — from roughly three percent of the national income in 1933 to twenty-five percent by the late 1970s.[9]

Falwell also relied on Friedman to connect the dots between free markets and political liberty. Of course, Falwell did not care for paying what he considered to be high taxes. And he certainly objected to paying taxes for services never rendered. Yet even his critique of welfare and foreign aid stemmed as much from a concern for the health of the nation and its citizens as it did from resentment over high taxes. Government assistance invariably created a culture of dependence and consequently was at odds with the ideal of independence that had informed America's founding. As Falwell put it, "free enterprise was the best economic organization to maintain [a] free society." For support he quoted Friedman's *Capitalism and Freedom:* capitalism promotes political freedom "because it separates economic power from political power." It was in effect another check upon the balance of power so delicately established by the framers. To threaten or control a person's economic resources, through tax policies aimed either at redistribution or social uplift, was a direct assault upon the liberties protected by the United States Constitution.[10]

The protection of freedom also informed Falwell's opposition to communism. His was a free-wheeling animosity that evoked the anti-communism of the 1950s and understood the contest between God-fearing liberty in the West and God-denying tyranny in the Soviet Union as the chief catalyst of twentieth-century history. Falwell supplied quotations from Lenin and Marx that demonstrated how communism was inherently opposed to capitalism, faith, and morality. He also attempted to document, at least through the writings of Alexander Solzhenitsyn, how ruthless a regime communism had created in the Soviet Union, imprisoning and managing the deaths of millions. The point of revealing communism's brutality and aggression was to rekindle among American citizens at least but also government

9. Falwell, *Listen, America!,* 69.
10. Falwell, *Listen, America!,* 73.

officials an older hostility that had been compromised by detente and nuclear treaties. "Americans have been fooled by the Communists long enough," Falwell wrote. "It is time that key figures in our government awaken to the fact that communism is a vicious attack upon what was once the free world." Falwell even believed, as the most ardent anti-communists did, that the Soviet Union's willingness to sign agreements with the United States and NATO was simply a trick. Here he quoted a Leonid Brezhnev speech given in 1973 that explained to his comrades in Prague, "We are achieving with detente what our predecessors have been unable to achieve with the mailed fist."[11]

As much as Falwell believed that communism threatened the West's political institutions and economic system, his greatest fear was communism's atheistic foundation. At this point Falwell showed the influence of Schaeffer in his calculation of the West's success. Political and economic freedom, according to Schaefferian logic, were the direct result of Christian beliefs about God, humanity, and the purpose and patterns of social relations. To deny Christianity, and to do so blatantly, as Communists did, could not help but result in tyranny of the worst sort. In fact, Falwell argued, the "first thing that happens" when communism takes over a nation "is that the churches are shut down, preachers are killed or imprisoned, and Bibles are taken away from the people." Just as bad, communism also intentionally destroyed the family. According to Falwell, the three most common reasons that Soviet officials removed children from parents were the insanity of the parents, alcohol or drug addiction, and the practice and teaching of Christianity in the home. Contempt for churches and family was simply the outworking of the original rules of the 1919 revolution: "Corrupt the young; get them away from religion. Get them interested in sex. Make them superficial. Destroy their ruggedness."[12]

As grave a threat as communism was to international affairs and the prospects of political liberty, it was even more revealing for Falwell of America's faltering character. He repeated the lament, "Why are we as Americans so apathetic to the threat of communism?"

11. Falwell, *Listen, America!*, 86.
12. Falwell, *Listen, America!*, 87, 90.

That question was key to distinguishing true patriots from poseurs. Obvious to America's founders was the tie between religion and freedom. That truth enabled Falwell, the conservative Baptist, to quote John Adams, the Unitarian, with nary a qualification: "Statesmen may plan and speculate for liberty, but it is religion and morality alone upon which freedom can securely stand. A patriot must be a religious man." Unfortunately, by the 1970s the American people had lost the convictions of the framers. For Falwell this explained why Americans were losing their resolve against communism — they were also losing their faith. "When God is taken out of a society," he maintained, "all freedom is lost." For that reason, the people responsible for secularizing the United States were also the greatest threats to the nation's political ideals and institutions:

> It is communistic to destroy the concept of God. We have already taken prayer and Bible reading out of our public schools. Madelyn Murray O'Hair is now proposing that God's name be removed from the Pledge of Allegiance and "In God We Trust!" be removed from our currency. With the removal of God from a society, there is a removal of liberty.

The close tie between Christian faith and political liberty helps to account for the way *Listen, America!* so easily moved between questions of domestic policy or international affairs and religious convictions. To be sure, skeptical readers might have accused Falwell of using politics to advance his own version of Protestant Christianity. But because of the connection between spiritual and political realities, Falwell saw no impropriety in mingling faith and politics. This was particularly evident when he took up a subject — namely, humanism — already weighed in on by Francis Schaeffer.[13]

Of the five national sins from which America needed to repent, according to Falwell, humanism was number four, behind abortion, homosexuality, and pornography, just ahead of "the fractured family." He defined it as a "contemporary philosophy that glorifies man as man, apart from God," the "outgrowth of evolutionary science and secular education." Its most popular expressions were "do your own

---

13. Falwell, *Listen, America!*, 93, 95, 90.

thing" and "if it feels good, do it." Although it ranked only fourth in his list of national sins, in Falwell's diagnosis humanism, along with naturalism, was the chief cause of the nation's crisis of morality. "We can talk about inflation, about big government, about crime in the streets, about America's lack of defense, and about a host of other critical subjects," but the root of America's problems was "the decay of our individual and national morals." The "decadent state and instability of everything else" followed directly from the country's moral bankruptcy, which in turned stemmed from the rise and influence of unbelief.

> Men and women cannot ignore God, live as they please, and expect to be happy and blessed. This is, however, precisely what has happened. Men and women have placed their priorities on acquiring tangible possessions and achieving tangible goals. Man, rather than God, has been placed at the center of all things. Humanism in some form has taken the place of the Bible. Secular humanism has become the religion of America. Through education and the media, man is constantly being told that he is nothing more than a machine.

How man was the center of all things and merely a machine was a conundrum Falwell did not pause to solve.[14]

The relationship between Christianity and the United States ultimately was as clear as it was neat. America prospered as a free society and the defender of liberty in world affairs when its citizens were God-fearing and its government acknowledged the nation's dependence on divine blessing; in contrast, tyranny within the United States and America's unwillingness to combat tyranny internationally characterized a nation that had turned its back on God. The history of the British colonies in North America as well as the debates of the founding fathers provided the evidence for this unambiguous relationship between faith and American liberty. According to Falwell, the framers of the Constitution were "deeply religious men" and scriptural teaching guided their thinking, decisions, and writings. The early history of the United States proved that "God is the Author of our liberty, and we

14. Falwell, *Listen, America!*, 254, 56, 65.

will remain free only as long as we remember this and seek to live by God's laws."[15]

The expectation, both for rhetorical purposes and in keeping with American Protestant (and especially Baptist) reflection, was for Falwell to affirm the separation of church and state along with his acknowledgment of America's religious founding. But for whatever reason — his inexperience in public debate, strategic considerations, or perhaps genuine alarm about the nation's declining standards of public decency — Falwell did not produce reassuring bromides on the danger of religious establishment. He did feel compelled to address the question of church and state; in less than two pages he gave his support to the First Amendment, coupled with a quotation from James Madison about the Ten Commandments providing the ethical platform for the republic. In fact, according to Jesse Helms, whom Falwell invoked on this point, on the same day that Congress passed the First Amendment it also called for a national day of prayer. Clearly, the point of disestablishment was to prevent one denomination from becoming the state church, not the "separation of God and government," or a "government devoid of God or the guidance found in Scripture."[16]

If Falwell was restrained in discussing the separation of church and state, he was downright garrulous on the question of separating the authority of families from the control of government. The second part of *Listen, America!* was devoted to morality, but the heading could just have easily been the family. It contained chapters on the importance of the family, the rights of children, feminism, abortion, homosexuality, pornography, and education. Falwell considered the family to be under siege, from the sanctity of unborn life to the ability of parents to rear their children according to their own convictions. For many who decided to join the Moral Majority, the media, public school officials, the Internal Revenue Service, and state and federal legislators were cultivating an environment that undermined the norms and assumptions of middle-class families about the best way to conceive, rear children, and pass on their way of life.

15. Falwell, *Listen, America!*, 47.
16. Falwell, *Listen, America!*, 54.

In a section on the threat of the government to the family, Falwell itemized three federal initiatives that demonstrated the state's abuse of its powers in undermining the legitimate authority of parents. The first was a domestic violence bill that was designed to eliminate physical aggression in the home, especially the conduct of men against wives and children. Falwell objected not simply because in the specifics this legislation identified corporal punishment as an improper mode of disciplining children, but also because it set up a federal agency to regulate family life. Another bill before the Senate would have restricted the government's ability to restrain pornography. Falwell's conception of federal power revealed a measure of inconsistency here, because he did not object in this case to federal law as long as it abetted the efforts of a family "to protect itself from the onslaught" of pornography. Even so, the Baptist pastor prided himself on a keen sense of discerning when the state was trespassing on civic space it had no business invading. Finally, Falwell pointed out a series of initiatives by federal agencies, such as Health, Education and Welfare and the Internal Revenue Service, that were undermining parental control of education in private schooling. Here federal policies were either aimed directly at the curriculum or using the leverage of tax-exempt status to regulate admissions and hiring policies of Christian schools. Falwell was obviously going overboard when he also griped that the federal government was hostile to families by allowing the Soviet Union to achieve nuclear superiority to the United States, thus "providing its families far less protection from nuclear attack than is the Soviet Union providing its families." Still, that he raised this objection in relation to families, as opposed to churches, was an indication of the institution the Religious Right was most concerned to protect from a secularizing state.[17]

At the same time, Falwell's pro-family case against the United States government did not presume that parents were faultless. If the government was going to respect the sphere of parental responsibility, parents needed to be responsible in rearing their children. Not surprisingly, Falwell invoked biblical teaching to specify the positive duties of parents to rear children in the faith along with the negative

17. Falwell, *Listen, America!*, 130, 131, 132.

tasks of punishing kids when they strayed. This provided cover for him to take shots at programs from the United Nations and policies of Scandinavian countries that sanctioned the breakdown of traditional parental responsibilities, whether state-sponsored daycare or legislation that forbade corporal punishment. It also produced a fulsome endorsement of The Eagle Forum's enumeration of a child's basic needs. These essentials ranged from familial ("to have the care of a mother who makes mothering her No. 1 career, at least in the all-important preschool period"), to educational ("To have sex education taught by parents, churches, or others who believe in the Ten Commandments"), to the political ("To know that the United States of America, in the words of our Declaration of Independence, is founded on the 'self-evident' truth that each child is 'created' by God and 'endowed' by his 'Creator' with 'certain inalienable rights'").[18]

As much as anti-communism and a defense of American greatness functioned as the pretext for Falwell's emergence as a political spokesman for born-again Protestants, the subtext was the family. Of course, the two were related. The original political order of the United States assumed a large degree of decentralization both for states and mediating structures, such as churches, neighborhoods, schools, voluntary associations, and families. The growth of power in the hands of federal legislators, judges, and bureaucrats for the sake of efficiency and organizational unity would necessarily threaten lesser authorities. Because evangelicals continued to rely on families (with churches and schools often functioning as natural extensions of families) for propagating the born-again faith, Falwell's defense of the family was his most plausible point. And the fact that language of the family rather than the church might be seen as more appealing to a broader base didn't hurt, either. Still, for family values to gain a hearing on the domestic agenda, leaders of the Religious Right needed to sound convincing in their opposition to communism and their defense of American freedoms. The unresolved tension was whether a nation that encouraged decentralization for the sake of families could organize sufficiently to fight an international war against communism.

18. Falwell, *Listen, America!*, 148-49.

In but Not *of* the Party

When Republican strategists courted born-again Protestants, they likely thought that the Religious Right represented more benefits than costs. A relatively new demographic that caught pollsters off guard, evangelicals could claim to constitute as much as forty percent of the American people. The electoral advantage of cultivating such a constituency without clear ties to the Republican Party was obvious, and the establishment of an organization like the Moral Majority seemed like a plausible mechanism for luring evangelical voters and donations. At the same time, conservative organizers needed to consider the public relations problems that the Religious Right could pose.

The possible damages were twofold. First, the United States was still under the influence of a theory of secularization that expected faith to decline in importance the more a society modernized. For almost two decades before the election of Ronald Reagan, the country had appeared to be progressing according to plan. Even if conservative leaders disbelieved the theory or held that faith should still matter in public life, putting the spotlight on the most religious Protestants could make the Republican Party look extreme. Indeed, the extremeness of the Religious Right highlights the second problem inherent in sidling up to born-again Protestants: evangelicals like Jerry Falwell were not shy about identifying themselves as fundamentalists. Unlike the evangelical leaders of the National Association of Evangelicals or Billy Graham, or unlike mainline Protestants who had figured out how to modify their religious convictions for public consumption, many of the Religious Right's leaders took pride in speaking directly and without equivocation on controversial matters of faith. Shining the spotlight on these newly invigorated Protestants had the potential of introducing into public debates speech and arguments that sounded familiar to evangelicals but strange to everyone else.

One of the born-again Protestants who played to the fundamentalist stereotype was Tim LaHaye, a California Baptist pastor, popular author, and activist who would eventually become best known for the enormously popular Christian pop fiction *Left Behind* series. While a minister in San Diego during the 1960s, LaHaye began to engage in political activism in response to the introduction of sex education in the state's public school system. LaHaye's wife, Beverly, rallied born-again women against feminism through Concerned Women for America, an association designed to rival the National Organization of Women. Together the LaHayes co-chaired Family America, an organization founded in 1979 to be a clearinghouse for conservatives on "pro-moral, family-oriented" issues. Although he always had an eye on the political landscape, LaHaye was most comfortable and popular as a speaker and author dispensing advice on marriage, spiritual psychology, and assorted biblical topics. His first venture as a political commentator came with the 1980 book *The Battle for the Mind,* dedicated to Francis Schaeffer, "the renowned philosopher-prophet of the twentieth century." America was on "a collision course with Sodom and Gomorrah" because of the increasing dominance of humanism. The only way to avoid the fate of those ancient cities was for another great revival on the order of what LaHaye called "Great Awakening II." Clearly, if Family America overlapped with the Moral Majority or *The Battle for the Mind* echoed Schaeffer's *How Should We Then Live?,* the repetition didn't bother LaHaye. The circumstances demanded as many institutions and voices as possible to alert believers to the nation's dire situation.[19]

Aside from a fairly simplistic and almost materialistic account of the human mind designed to justify the Weaver-like notion that ideas have consequences, LaHaye's basic argument was to contrast the wisdom of man with the wisdom of God. He rendered the distinction starkly: "Only two lines of reasoning permeate all of literature: biblical revelation (the wisdom of God) and the wisdom of man. All books are based either on man's thoughts or God's thoughts." LaHaye borrowed freely here from Schaeffer, especially in his account of the rise of secular humanism. Greek philosophers were the first to elevate human wisdom over God's, and medieval theologians, such as Thomas Aquinas, committed a similar error when they tried to engraft the branch of the ancients on the root of Christian truth. From

19. Tim LaHaye, *The Battle for the Mind* (Old Tappan, N.J.: Revell, 1980), 205, 5, 10.

there the descent to secular humanism was inevitable. It took shape in the Enlightenment and especially the French Revolution. The United States might have continued on the same path were it not for the nation's "Bible-based form of government." LaHaye did not want this to be construed in a way that excluded Jews, so he emphasized the biblical as opposed to the Christian foundation of the United States. The Bible-based government of America was so inclusive that it did not "exclude any but the most anti-God, antimoral humanist thinkers of our day" — about four percent of the American population, according to LaHaye.[20]

The battle between human and divine wisdom for LaHaye was as basic as the lines between secularism and faith were clear. A Bible-based philosophy yielded truth about God, creation, and morality, while secular humanism produced atheism, evolution, and amorality. The evidence of secular humanism that LaHaye marshaled came from the two *Humanist Manifestos,* the first produced by John Dewey and Unitarian clergy in 1933 and the second, an updated version of the first, written in 1973. Secular humanism, as such, was not "the weird ideas of a few obscure imbeciles" but the beliefs of "some of the most influential people in America," especially those engaged in the education of the nation's young people. If allowed to destroy and disarm the United States, a Communist takeover would necessarily follow. For this reason, the 1980s was a "decade of destiny." "As long as biblical thought prevailed in the public-school system, there was no real need for pro-moral people to put on a drive to get moralists elected to government office." But since the end of World War II secular humanists had "surreptitiously commandeered our once-great school system" and were effectively taking the reins of political power "where they continually pass laws that favor the advancement of humanism and chaos, at the expense of the biblical base for a moral society."[21]

But despite some basic resonances with conservative thought, LaHaye appealed to ideas likely to embarrass the traditional political Right. Toward the end of *The Battle for the Mind* the author made a cu-

20. LaHaye, *The Battle for the Mind,* 27, 37, 38.
21. LaHaye, *The Battle for the Mind,* 95, 46.

rious reference to the "humanist tribulation." If readers to this point had thought LaHaye a tad rough on secular humanism, the reason for such harsh treatment was now apparent: LaHaye believed that secular humanism was part of the unfolding of biblical prophecy regarding the end times before Christ's second coming. For the Protestants for whom the book was written, LaHaye's point was important. Conservative Protestant teaching about Christ's return, known as premillennial dispensationalism, could conceivably breed a form of political passivism because of its pessimistic view of the direction of human history. Unlike the postmillennial views that had dominated American Protestantism throughout most of the nineteenth and early twentieth centuries, which had inspired any number of progressive reforms in hopes of establishing the kingdom of God on earth, premillennial dispensationalism taught that history was in decline and would continue to spiral downward until Christ's return. In fact, the worse human affairs became, the closer the return of Christ must be. If the degeneracy of human culture were inevitable — even more, if it were desirable because it hastened the return of Christ — then why would Christians want to enter the political fray for the purpose of restoring Christian morality? LaHaye conceded that this was a valid question when he acknowledged that a possible reading of Bible prophecies was that "a takeover of our culture by the forces of evil is inevitable, so [we] do nothing to resist it."[22]

But LaHaye didn't accept that interpretation of prophecy; he responded instead by appealing to biblical imperatives for Christians to "resist the devil" and "put on the whole armor of God." But he went further and tried to explain how the pre-tribulation conditions of cultural depravity need not exist on a global scale. Instead they could be quarantined in certain sectors of world civilization, and Christians in America could occupy a safe sector outside divine judgment on a global scale. Russia was already past the point of no return, thanks to its anti-Israel foreign policy. Meanwhile, countries like Sweden were on the brink of a humanist tribulation because "godly Christians and pro-moral citizens did nothing to stop the socialist, humanist takeover of their government." The Swedes had turned "that delightful land

22. LaHaye, *The Battle for the Mind*, 217.

into Sodom and Gomorrah." Leaving aside his dubious and selective reading of salvation history that managed to exempt the United States from divine judgment, LaHaye's attribution of eschatological dimensions to the conflict between Christian morality and secular humanism was not the best strategy for persuading those outside the fundamentalist fold, whether liberal or conservative, to take the Religious Right seriously. Granted, the book was publicized among those believers for whom such prophetic speculation was routine. Even so, the book revealed that just below the surface of legitimate concerns about the health of families and declining cultural standards was a cauldron of theology that would perplex or even horrify outsiders.[23]

To be sure, evangelicals did not lack more respectable outlets than the Moral Majority or Family America for expressing their concerns about moral degeneracy in the United States. The National Association of Evangelicals was in the habit of adopting resolutions that echoed LaHaye's and Schaeffer's observations about America's cultural decadence. The NAE's policy proposals were much less colorful and quotable than the vituperation of fundamentalist preachers. But worries about the family and serious misgivings about the health of the culture demonstrated the degree to which evangelicals and fundamentalists, despite rhetorical differences, shared assumptions that had provoked direct political engagement.

In 1981 the NAE issued a statement that defined secular humanism — synonymous with atheistic humanism — as a denial of "any need for God," and a campaign for the right of individuals to "modify or abandon the customs, traditions and standards of behavior in the Judeo-Christian tradition, thus making good and evil relative to a particular time and place." The result was a way of life in which "men and women answer only to themselves . . . having personal desire and emotional satisfaction as their major goals." The authors of the declaration blamed secular humanism for "unrestrained materialism," ecological carelessness, pornography, and all forms of sexual deviation, whether hetero- or homosexual.[24]

Secular humanism may have been the mantra of the Moral Ma-

---

23. LaHaye, *The Battle for the Mind*, 217, 218.
24. http://www.nae.net/resolutions/302-secular-humanism-1981.

jority's leadership, but it could also carry a lot of water for the way the broader evangelical community diagnosed America. In fact, the NAE's declaration on secular humanism posited a trickle-down theory of cultural decline that attributed to humanism the downfall of public education and even the family. The public schools, according to the NAE's 1981 statement, were "increasingly controlled by the secular humanist viewpoint." The courts had not helped by removing "Bible reading, prayer and the teaching of creationism." As a result, children were "systematically exposed to an atheistic humanism that leads to hedonistic and unbridled lifestyles," and parents were bewildered over what was happening to their children. Even so, the NAE stopped short of repudiating public schools. Seven years after its statement on secular humanism, the Association issued what seemed like a compromise declaration on education that neither condemned public schools as unfit nor recommended private Christian schools as appropriate for believing families. Clearly at work was the American Protestant view of the public schools as an extension of the United States' Protestant ethos. For that reason, the Association provided advice to parents on such factors as a school's worldview, educational practices, cost of tuition, and the Christian duty to be salt and light in choosing between public and private schools. At the same time, the NAE reminded parents and churches of the justified trend of criticizing public schools for their "secular, 'morally neutral' character."[25]

While secular humanism may have been the root of America's disorder, the family was the institution that the NAE considered to be most threatened. During the early 1980s, the very years that witnessed the formation of the Moral Majority and the rise of Falwell and LaHaye as spokesmen for evangelicals, the Association joined them in highlighting the theme of family values. In 1984 it issued a resolution against the Equal Rights Amendment that rejected the argument that equality for women was simply an economic consideration. The language of the amendment was instead so far reaching that it could be used by the courts to disrupt the family and related mediating institutions. So while affirming its support for "legislation specifically designed to remedy economic injustices to women," the NAE refused

---

25. http://www.nae.net/resolutions/302-secular-humanism-1981.

to endorse the Equal Rights Amendment without qualifications regarding abortion, women serving in the military, or the rights of schools and churches to teach biblical roles for men and women.[26]

In addition to its affirmation of traditional roles for men and women, the NAE also underscored the importance of the family for the health of both the nation and the church. In its 1982 resolution "Save the Family," the Association primarily catalogued the consequences of the "enlightened rebellion" against the family begun during the 1960s. Instances of divorce had increased, esteem for marriage had declined, couples living together had become more common, and more and more young adults regarded parenting children as an obstacle to self-fulfillment. The resolution had no policy implications; its function seemed to be a collective lament for the family. But in the same year the Association came out with another resolution, this one aimed not at the state but at families themselves. "Parental Responsibilities" called upon husbands and wives to recommit themselves to the Lordship of Christ in the home, to each other irrespective of implications for career or self-fulfillment, and to rearing their children in the ways of faith and obedience. "The National Association of Evangelicals calls upon both parents and churches," the resolution concluded, "to join hands in a concerted effort to strengthen family life and restore biblical family values to the home. We believe this is not only desirable, but essential if our nation is to survive." In words that echoed Falwell and LaHaye, the evangelicals at the NAE deduced, "As goes the home, so goes the nation."[27]

Although the NAE resisted the apocalyptic tones of LaHaye and Falwell, the worries of its members matched those of the Moral Majority and Family America. This meant that trying to tell the difference between fundamentalists and evangelicals within the Religious Right was like spotting differences between Norwegian Americans and Swedish Americans. All sides rallied under the banner of organizations that endeavored to protect the traditional nature, function, and purpose of the family. The sexual revolution, the women's movement, legalized abortion, changes in public schools, and the use of tax pol-

26. http://www.nae.net/resolutions/140-equal-rights-amendment-1984.
27. http://www.nae.net/resolutions/147-save-the-family-1982.

icy to engineer private schools all assaulted the ordinary way of life of many American Protestants. Those believers possessed varying abilities to articulate their primarily personal and religious concerns in the idiom of mainstream American politics. But conservatism, not liberalism, had become the most congenial outlet for family-values Protestants. The question remained whether the political structure representing conservative values — namely, the Republican Party — could in post-Protestant America accommodate the Religious Right's defense of white Anglo-Saxon Protestantism.

Morals without Manners

The initial excitement created by the Moral Majority and similar organizations was short-lived. By 1985, LaHaye had formed another activist association, the American Coalition for Traditional Values. In preparation for the midterm elections, ACTV sponsored a conference on "How to Win an Election." But skeptical journalists discovered that LaHaye had solicited support for the organization from Sun Myung Moon's Unification Church, an embarrassing source of funding for any conservative hoping to achieve mainstream status. By 1986 the American Coalition had closed its doors. The same year saw Jerry Falwell decide to shut down the Moral Majority. At first it survived as part of an umbrella organization, the Liberty Federation. But the Federation did more to consolidate Falwell's other efforts, such as Liberty University and his television broadcasts, than it did to mobilize voters or influence policy. In fact, by 1986 opinion polls revealed widely held negative views of Falwell, the Moral Majority, and the Religious Right. It turned out not only that running things was difficult, but also that trying to influence the running of things was almost as burdensome.

With the exit of fundamentalist spokesmen from the naked public square, the mantle of leadership passed to another television personality, Pat Robertson. But the transition was by no means smooth. LaHaye and Falwell surely had quirks, and fundamentalist beliefs about the return of Christ were not an easy sell to the general public. But they were not charismatics or Pentecostals like Robertson — that is, Christians who spoke in tongues as evidence of spiritual flourishing. A tension between Falwell-style Baptists and charismatics like Robertson had always existed and was evident, for example, when Falwell did not include Robertson within the leadership of the Moral Majority. Falwell joked once that speaking in tongues was the equivalent of eating bad pizza. But Robertson did not need Falwell or the Moral Majority, because he had his own political outlets, such as the Freedom Council, founded in 1981 to educate like-minded evangelicals, Roman Catholics, and Jews in how to be effective in American politics. With Falwell and lesser Religious Right leaders more and more out of commission, by the end of Ronald Reagan's second term Robertson was the identifiable figurehead of born-again Protestant political activity and the search for family values.[28]

The exact timing of Robertson's decision to run for the presidency and succeed Ronald Reagan is obscure. Throughout the 1980s he had received encouragement from fans and supporters. His television broadcast, *The 700 Club,* gave Robertson name recognition and celebrity. Furthermore, the Freedom Council was fairly effective in combining Robertson's media popularity with grassroots political activism. Not to be discounted was Robertson's family background; his father, Absalom Willis Robertson, served in Congress for fourteen years before being elected to the Senate in 1946, first to complete the term of a vacant seat, and then two terms in his own right. But when Senator Robertson ran for re-election in 1966, Pat determined that he could not campaign for his father. In his 1972 autobiography, Pat Robertson wrote, "you cannot tie eternal purposes to the success of any political candidate . . . not even your own father." By 1984 Robertson began to have second thoughts about the difficulties of serving Christ and Caesar. He courted campaign advisors while conservative strategists like Paul Weyrich provided counsel.[29]

As farfetched as the idea of a television evangelist campaigning meaningfully for president of the United States sounds — it reads more like the plot of a bad Upton Sinclair novel than actual history — from 1985 through the early 1988 primaries Robertson repeatedly re-

28. Falwell joke retold in Martin, *With God on Our Side,* 259.

29. Robertson quoted in David Marley, *Pat Robertson: An American Life* (Lanham, Md.: Rowman & Littlefield, 2007), 30.

versed expectations. Robertson was particularly deft in those electoral environments not controlled by party machines, especially in the caucus states. He maneuvered supporters from the ranks of the Freedom Council as early as the spring of 1986 to nominate precinct captains for the midterm elections. Then in an Iowa straw poll in September 1987, Robertson beat Senator Bob Dole and Vice-President George Bush handily, a victory that Robertson likened to the early stages of Jimmy Carter's 1976 campaign. During the 1988 primary season, Robertson scared the Bush campaign when he scored impressive victories in numerous rump conventions. But in a disorderly process in which the party establishment and Bush's staff had a say in determining how the caucuses were counted, Robertson ran a distant second to Bush in the final tally of delegates, fifty percent to twenty-two. In Iowa, the next month, another caucus state, Robertson did not win but ran well, finishing second behind Dole and beating both Bush and Jack Kemp. He also continued to look strong in Hawaii, Nevada, Alaska, Minnesota, and South Dakota, finishing either first or second. But the limits of the Robertson campaign were obvious by the New Hampshire primary; there Bush recovered his command of the party's faithful and Robertson came in fifth, well below enthusiastic expectations. After New Hampshire, the only hope for the Robertson campaign was Super Tuesday with its collection of southern states. Yet in South Carolina Robertson received only nineteen percent of the vote, and in his home state, Virginia, Robertson finished a weak third. After Super Tuesday, Bush looked unbeatable.

In turn, Robertson began to look more like a televangelist than a viable presidential candidate — at the worst possible time. As early as the spring of 1987, the first of two major scandals rocked religious broadcasting and nurtured suspicions of Robertson. The first involved former associates of Robertson, Jim and Tammy Faye Bakker, whose Heritage USA amusement park and retirement complex came under an IRS investigation that revealed significant financial improprieties and confirmed the popular impression of televangelists as Elmer Gantry figures. Then in 1988, just before the primaries on Super Tuesday, came revelations of Jimmy Swaggart's liaisons with a prostitute in New Orleans. Robertson believed that the Bush campaign was the source of this leak, but it turned out that Jim Bakker was responsible. Robertson's advisors had actually tried to portray the candidate's television show, *The 700 Club,* as a news and information broadcast. They also tried to persuade reporters to refer to Robertson as "Mr." rather than "Reverend." That interpretation had helped with the Bakker scandal, but after the news of Swaggart's misconduct, and in the heat of the primary season, turning Robertson into a figure more like Dan Rather than Oral Roberts was a hard sell.

Chances are that Robertson would have had trouble succeeding in the primaries even without the scandals. The reasons had much to do with Robertson's own particular brand of religiosity and with the devotion of evangelicals more generally. Polling data from the primaries revealed that Robertson, a charismatic Protestant, was appealing mainly to charismatics or Pentecostals within the evangelical constituency. For evangelicals who were dubious about speaking in tongues or other "Spirit-filled" practices, Robertson seemed suspicious. But even more basic than the tension between charismatic and noncharismatic evangelicals was a deeper problem of harnessing religious zeal for the good of the republic. One Republican official and Bush campaign figure observed that the Religious Right constituted many "decent, God-fearing people who had a lot of the same dreams and desires that Republicans had" but pursued those aims in a very different way. "These people felt they were working for God, and if I was on the other side, who was I really working for? . . . It was pretty hard to tell them they were wrong, because they were 'working for the Lord' and we were working for someone who wasn't on that level."[30]

The problem facing Robertson, then, was the difficulty that afflicted born-again Protestantism more generally. Evangelicals may have lacked the experience in politics and the connections in the Republican Party to avoid looking like wedding crashers during the Reagan revolution. But the awkwardness of born-again Protestants in American politics went deeper. On the surface, these Protestants stood for family values and against declining standards of decency. As Robertson himself explained in his campaign, he was committed to restoring "the greatness of America through moral strength." The nation was experiencing moral decline, "a break-up of the American

---

30. Bush official quoted in Martin, *With God on Our Side,* 273.

family, the rise of crime and drug addiction and abortion." To give poignancy to that apparently moralistic stance, the leaders of the Religious Right added themes from the Cold War, arguing implicitly that America's might depended not simply on military stockpiles but on the character of her people and the institutions that shaped them. But that argument faced serious internal tension for anyone who wondered how the nation could have both a centralized, efficient government of superpower proportions and a decentralized society that gave freedom to families, schools, and communities to rear children according to local custom.[31]

Still, the tougher argument was convincing the average American that family values was not a moral imposition by the Religious Right on the rest of the nation. According to one aide to Senator Jesse Helms, electing a religious leader as president was an "insupportable burden" because it was at odds with "this type of pluralistic society."[32] To be sure, the political order of the United States has always had mechanisms for sorting out the diversity of its citizens, from federalism to voluntary associations. And a long line of religious groups in American history have entered the public square, not to make the United States Amish, Roman Catholic, Mormon, or Seventh-Day Adventist, but to seek protection for the community's religious practices and convictions. The Religious Right did not consider cultural diversity an option for nurturing family values or even as a politically conservative conviction. Instead, the prize was putting a man of faith in the White House, and the goal was a restoration of America's presumably uniformly Christian past. For the Religious Right's leaders, the stress on religion and morality was obviously a conservative impulse. According to Robertson, his campaign was "the wave of the future . . . which is toppling historic liberalism and will bring about a conservative era in the United States." Ironically, instead of fueling American conservatism, by failing to avail themselves of American political traditions, evangelicals' faith-based politics actually generated confusion about the meaning and identity of political conservatism.[33]

---

31. Robertson quoted in Martin, *With God on Our Side,* 298.
32. Helms aide quoted in Martin, *With God on Our Side,* 279.
33. Robertson quoted in Martin, *With God on Our Side,* 298.

FIVE

The Faith-Based Right

———⊸๛⊷———

J udging influence by appearances on the cover of *Time* magazine is not a method approved in the American Historical Association's guidelines on research. Even so, appearing on the cover of one of the nation's premiere newsweeklies says something about a person's relative worth among America's so-called newsmakers. And for some reason, in all of his days in the spotlight as a born-again Protestant with senior status in the United States Senate, Mark Hatfield never generated enough buzz to qualify for *Time's* esteemed cover. In contrast, Jerry Falwell, known primarily within a certain demographic of religious broadcasting, appeared on *Time's* cover only six years after founding the Moral Majority. On September 2, 1985, the pastor who described himself as a "big-F" fundamentalist was splashed across the cover for a story on "the growth of fundamentalism." This was publicity that Hatfield was probably glad to avoid. Journalists had not had to use the f-word since the 1920s, when William Jennings Bryan was leading the charge against evolution. Fundamentalism's re-emergence in the 1980s as part of a conservative coalition cobbled together within the Reagan revolution was a threat sufficiently alarming to merit front-cover coverage. For some journalists and editors, political conservatives were scary by themselves. Did they need the additional goblins of the Virgin Mary, inerrant Bibles, and prayer breakfasts?

Despite the fears that Falwell encouraged, his appearance on the cover of *Time* was also revealing of significant changes in the relationship between religion and politics between the 1970s and 1980s. In the earlier era, Hatfield's religiously motivated politics were not particularly alarming. Nor were they significantly novel. Mainline Protestants had already made the turn toward opposing America's military policies, ill-treatment of the poor and minorities, and degradation of the environment. Hatfield might be a curiosity because of his ties to evangelicalism. But because most journalists knew little about born-again Protestantism or its social and political attitudes, Hatfield's faith was merely idiosyncratic.

Falwell, however, stood for something completely different. The Lynchburg Baptist pastor was three things that Hatfield was not. First, Falwell was a fundamentalist. He believed the Bible was inerrant, that Christ was born of a virgin, that he died and rose from the dead, and that the Christian's duty was to evangelize. This meant — first point, subpoint "a" — that Falwell was also a separatist. He believed that Christians should separate from the world and from worldly practices, and that true Christians should separate from liberal churches. Second, Falwell was a conservative, at least as he understood the term. "The federal government was encroaching upon the sovereignty of both the church and the family," he explained. Abortion on demand, feminism and equal rights, and gay rights were the policies that fused Falwell's adherence to small government and his social conservatism. Finally, he was the leader of a political organization that had a constituency much larger than Hatfield's electoral support in Oregon. In 1981 Falwell estimated that the Moral Majority stood for millions of Americans, including 72,000 pastors, priests, and rabbis, "Catholics, Jews, Protestants, Mormons, Fundamentalists . . . Americans from all walks of life united by one central concern: to serve as a special-interest group providing a voice for a return to moral sanity in these United States of America."[1]

Falwell's organization was not the most felicitous vehicle for the kind of conservatism that he promoted. As the editors of *Time* sensed, the Moral Majority functioned better as a target, with Falwell as the

---

1. Jerry Falwell, "An Agenda for the 1980s," in Richard John Neuhaus and Michael Cromartie, eds., *Piety and Politics: Evangelicals and Fundamentalists Confront the World* (Washington, D.C.: Ethics and Public Policy Center), 119-20, 112, 113.

bull's-eye, than as a movement for real restraint on the federal government, especially the judiciary, or for defending the traditional duties of husbands, wives, fathers, and mothers.

Nevertheless, Falwell's national popularity, and hence the political constituency that he represented — born-again Protestants who believed the United States was losing its virtue — opened up the public square for voices that had not been audible since the 1950s, when the mainline Protestant churches could be counted on to articulate and defend from a Protestant perspective the American way of life. These faith-based conservative voices sang in the same choir with traditionalists, neo-conservatives, and libertarians on some pieces. But the intellectual leaders of the evangelical activists were not always on the same page of the hymnbook.

Politics with Only a Little Illusion

Whether Chuck Colson was up to the challenge of adding political depth to the populist zeal of the Religious Right depended on how evangelicals would view his credentials. His service in the Nixon administration gave him more experience with how Washington worked than any spokesman for evangelicalism could boast. At the same time, Colson's specific involvement in the imbroglio known as Watergate raised questions that might prompt born-again Protestants to keep the "evil genius" of the Nixon administration at arm's length from the constituency that would be a majority of moral Americans. Colson himself admitted that he was valuable to Nixon because he was willing to be ruthless.

The Watergate scandal revealed the depths of that ruthlessness. As an administration figure involved with the Committee to Re-Elect the President (CREEP), Colson was implicated in this group's decision to thwart the Democrats' campaign by breaking into psychiatrist Daniel Ellsberg's office and obtaining names and information that would discredit the opponents of the Vietnam War. Colson would later admit to leaking details secured in the break-in to the press, but denied responsibility for approving the burglary. In 1974 he pleaded guilty to conspiring to cover up the Watergate incident.

Meanwhile, Colson underwent a conversion experience, mainly through the counsel of a friend and by reading C. S. Lewis. This religious transformation became the basis for *Born Again,* Colson's book-length testimony of his conversion, and for the 1978 movie of the same title. Colson's spiritual rags-to-riches story gave him instant credibility among evangelicals. Evangelicals did not mind that he had firsthand knowledge of the United States presidency's power. He became a regular columnist for *Christianity Today* and the voice of commentaries for Christian radio networks.

Because of Colson's own experience with the dark side of the American political soul, he was less tempted by electoral success than other Religious Right leaders. The primary outlet for Colson's day-to-day activity was Prison Fellowship, a parachurch agency that aimed to rehabilitate prisoners and care for their families. From organizing and sustaining Bible studies in prisons to furnishing convicts' children with Christmas gifts, Colson's organization was a highly visible example of the sort of faith-based initiative that would attract the attention of both the efforts of the Clinton and Bush administrations. In fact, Colson's first book with an overtly political theme cautioned evangelicals about the illusions that so often afflicted the machinations of politicians.

Kingdoms in Conflict, published in 1987, was a typical Colson effort (it was co-written for starters) that combined thoughtful encouragement with a measure of wisdom about the ways of politics and delivered within a stream of anecdotes either historically momentous or personally endearing. The part of a longish book that would have obvious appeal to evangelicals was the section where he exposed the consequences of political systems that ignored or opposed faith. National Socialism (three chapters) and Marxism (one chapter) were easy targets. But they set up the broader point about the West's dependence on Christianity for avoiding ideological and utopian schemes that inevitably followed from atheism. The United States had firmly resisted the tyrannies of the Right and the Left, but it was now rapidly succumbing to the forces of secularism. Here Colson served up a plate of red meat that evangelicals ravenously devoured.

Thanks to Francis Schaeffer and others, many evangelicals by this point firmly believed that ideas had consequences. And the reasons for the string of Supreme Court decisions that removed Bible-reading and prayer from public schools had to do with faulty ideas. In the 1950s and 1960s "the long fuse lit by the ideas of Nietzsche, Freud, and Darwin finally set off an explosion of relativism." Morality was relative, and the courts could hold that "great moral issues can be decided without reference to transcendent values." Worse, however, was the increasing hostility that Christians faced in public life, either in the way the media portrayed believers, a secular bias in high school and college textbooks, or specific government policies that favored practices and convictions that religious taxpayers could not support in good conscience. Colson praised Jerry Falwell for leading "a fundamentalist stampede back to center stage" in the late 1970s. He also faulted liberal Christians for hypocritically responding to Falwell by claiming that faith was a private matter, best kept out of public life, even while belonging to communions that had abandoned the spiritual mission of the church for "weekly policy papers on social issues." The examples of this position that Colson cited were Geraldine Ferraro, the Roman Catholic vice-presidential Democratic candidate who assured journalists that faith had "no place in campaigns or in dictating public policy," and New York Governor Mario Cuomo, who tried to hold that as a Roman Catholic he opposed abortion but as an officer of the state could not impose his religious convictions on the rest of society.[2]

Colson was building his case against the *naked public square,* a phrase popularized at least among academics and pundits by his friend Richard John Neuhaus. *Kingdoms in Conflict* named a chapter after the phrase Neuhaus had popularized (though without attribution). A public sphere stripped of the protection and dignity provided by religion was the logical outcome of privatizing faith. At the same time, the United States was living with the inevitable results of a secular society. Although a "value-free society" might sound progressive and enlightened, a society free from moral norms was proving to be nightmarish. Crime, sexual promiscuity, and even the financial scandals surrounding television preachers should not have surprised

2. Charles W. Colson, *Kingdoms in Conflict* (New York: W. Morrow, 1987), 221, 211, 212.

Americans who had been taught that morality or faith was essentially a personal value.

But this was not the place from which the United States started, according to Colson. "The notion of law rooted in transcendent truth, in God Himself, is not the invention of Christian fundamentalists . . . [but is] as much in the works of Cicero and Plato as in the Bible." In fact, the argument that the Jerry Falwells of the world were distorting the American founding could be used just as effectively against secularists who were guilty of perverting "the whole history of Western civilization." From Plato, Cicero, and Augustine down to Edmund Burke, Alexis de Tocqueville, and John Adams, the West had shared the conviction that "transcendent norms were the true foundations for civil law." Colson's reading of Western civilization passed smoothly over the religious discrepancies among his litany of great thinkers. He approvingly quoted John Adams, a Unitarian, to make the point that the United States needed a moral order that could only be supplied by biblical religion: "If I were an atheist . . . I should believe that chance had ordered the Jews to preserve and propagate to all mankind the doctrine of a supreme, intelligent, wise, almighty sovereign of the universe, which I believe to be the great essential principle of all morality, and consequently of all civilization."[3] Unfortunately, the validity and utility of Adams' point prevented Colson from seeing the affinity between his own argument and the vapid one made by Dwight Eisenhower in the 1950s: "our form of government has no sense unless it is founded in a deeply felt religious faith, and I don't care what it is." Did Colson really want to put himself in the position of being zealous for faith while also showing indifference to the content of religion itself?

This hiccup in the evangelical case against secular humanism would not have troubled born-again Protestant readers of Colson compared to the Augustinian themes that seemed to undercut his argument for a vestment-clothed public square. Early in *Kingdoms in Conflict* Colson established that the kingdom of God was not a political rule, and that to look for the reign of Christ in the affairs of state was to miss the significance of New Testament teaching in ways comparable to those who assumed Jesus was going to restore the throne of

3. Colson, *Kingdoms in Conflict*, 227, 228.

King David. The kingdom that Christ inaugurated, according to Colson, was not a realm but a rule. It started with his life, death, and resurrection but was primarily an assertion of God's sovereignty that would not be realized until Christ's second coming. The rule that Christ established was not political but personal. It yielded knowing the true God, salvation from sin, ascertaining the meaning of human existence, and recognizing divine authority over all aspects of life. As Colson summarized, when Christ told his disciples to "seek first the kingdom of God," he was exhorting them "to seek to be ruled by God and gratefully acknowledge His power and authority over them." In other words, "the Christian's goal is not to strive to rule, but to be *ruled.*"[4]

Although he stressed the spiritual character of this kingdom, Colson was unwilling to limit it simply to matters of personal devotion. Yet when he turned to the outworking of the politics of the kingdom, Colson continued to refrain from political or statist applications. Instead, he advised looking for the manifestation of this kingdom in what might be called mediating structures, or the institutions that function as buffers between the state and the individual person. In one chapter, Colson gave a rendition of the Dutch Calvinist notion of sphere sovereignty that bestowed divinely ordained power among the family, the state, and the church. The family was "the most basic unit of government," "the first authority under which a person learns to live," establishing "society's most basic values." The state, in contrast, was instituted by God "to restrain sin and promote a just social order." It was rooted in the rule of law, not the whims of the ruler. And even if the state's aims included establishing social harmony, it was different from a human community; the state established an order in which humans could flourish by establishing their own communities. Along with C. S. Lewis, Colson believed that one of the primary benefits of the state was to protect and preserve simple freedoms that allowed the person "to enjoy a cup of tea by the fire with one's family."[5]

The last institution in Colson's social order was the church —

---

4. Colson, *Kingdoms in Conflict*, 88.
5. Colson, *Kingdoms in Conflict*, 90, 91, 92.

not the same as God's kingdom, but arguably the institution most responsible for encouraging it. The church's responsibilities were primarily spiritual, liturgical, and evangelistic — "to proclaim in word
and deed the same gospel that Christ announced." Even so, the
church was not the kingdom of God proper, because as a human institution it was imperfect and failed in the execution of its mission. But
the church was a constant reminder that the kingdom would not
come through the state or political means. Colson appealed to Pope
John Paul II for support. "The purpose of [Jesus'] mission embraces
far more than political order," the pope wrote. "It embraces the salvation of the entire person through transforming and peace-giving
love."[6]

Colson's personalist and even individualistic rendering of the
kingdom — it exists in the person who submits to divine rule —
sounded as if Christians could be indifferent to politics. But this was
not the case he intended to make. He appealed to William Wilberforce and his successful efforts to abolish the English slave trade as
one example of the positive influence that Christians have had on society and as a demonstration of the social transformation that radi-
ated out from the lives of believers. At the same time, Colson recognized a historic tension between church and state because of their
different responsibilities. He drew the implication that Christians
should be wary of trying to make laws and policies conform to their
own religious convictions and that rulers should respect the con-
sciences of their subjects. In fact, the balance of power between
church and state, worked out in the separation of these two institutions, was one of the great mysteries of providence by which God
achieved a "certain equilibrium" in social order.[7]

Readers used to hearing the likes of Falwell or Schaeffer on their
duties as citizens may have sensed ambivalence in the way Colson
hedged Christian efforts to cover the public square. He was, after all,
trying to do justice to the Augustinian distinction between the City of
Man and the City of God. Yet, when Colson turned to the theme of the
kingdom of God's presence in real time, he returned to arguments

6. Colson, *Kingdoms in Conflict*, 92, 93.
7. Colson, *Kingdoms in Conflict*, 121.

that reassured card-carrying members of the Religious Right. For one thing, he clarified that he was no religion-for-religion's sake advocate. He held that Christianity was the only true religion and as such it was the only religion "that provides for *both* individual concerns and the ordering of a society with liberty and justice for all." But the means by which Christianity shaped the social order was not through the state or "preferential treatment" from government. Instead it was through Christians recognizing their civic responsibilities as members of the kingdom of God. Colson believed that collectively Christians were like Edmund Burke's "little platoons," "mediating structures between the individual and government that carry out works of justice, mercy, and charity." Examples of such pockets were the 1985 marathon rock concert, Live-Aid, John Perkins's Voice of Calvary community development work in Mississippi, and Mothers Against Drunk Driving. These were the sorts of compassionate endeavors that reflected the politics of God's kingdom.[8]

Yet as much as Colson supported non-statist approaches to maintaining social order and helping the less fortunate, he was not averse to politics or what the state was ordained to do. Having served in the Nixon administration, however, Colson was deeply aware of power's corrupting aspects. And the insidious influence of politics was not simply a temptation for Washington officials. Ministers and televangelists of recent memory, such as Jim and Tammy Bakker, had exhibited the dangers of power even for those who were supposed to know better. Consequently, Colson stressed the Christian ideal of power as exemplified in Christ's own work as a suffering servant. "Servant leadership is the heart of Christ's teaching," he wrote. "'Whoever wants to be first must be slave of all.'" According to Colson, this view of power informed both the English Parliament's insistence upon autonomy from the crown and the American framers' adoption of the separation of powers. Of course, some radical Christians such as John Howard Yoder would have found Colson's perpetuation of the state to be incompatible with Christ's own example. Colson was trying to walk a fine line: to do justice to Christian ethics while also recognizing the need for the state. The problem was that in holding up Christ as a

8. Colson, *Kingdoms in Conflict*, 235, 238.

model, Colson invited the radical critique of the state and weakened his own argument.[9]

That vulnerability was particularly evident when Colson finally turned to the role of the Christian politician. As important as the mediating structures and "little platoons" might be, Colson still knew that Christian statesmen like Wilberforce were capable of exerting considerable influence. The problem was that politics was inherently at odds with moral integrity. Obviously, Colson knew this from experience, and it explained his affirmation of non-political means for establishing the kingdom of God. Still, he believed that as citizens Christians had a duty not to withdraw from politics or serving in government, and that they needed to bring moral standards into public debate. The idea of not legislating morality was a myth: "The question is not whether we will legislate morality, but whose morality we will legislate." But what about Christians holding public office? Could they do so in good conscience, given the need to be pragmatic rather than principled? Colson answered affirmatively, but his response lacked the urgency that had energized the Religious Right. Although completely opposed to the notion that faith was a private matter, Colson insisted that a believing official could not use political office to accomplish the tasks of the church, and that he or she needed to "respect the rights of all religious groups and insure that government protects every citizen's freedom of conscience."[10]

Caution about politics was Colson's overriding theme, and it was the one on which he ended the book. In a chapter on "The Perils of Politics" he reminded religious activists that the "idea that human systems, reformed by Christian influence, pave the road to the Kingdom . . . has the same utopian ring that one finds in Marxist literature." In addition, he warned against an involvement in politics that turned the church into just one more special-interest group, or that tempted Christian leaders to calculate their words and actions in relation to their access to power. In the penultimate chapter, "The Political Illusion," Colson reiterated the theme of the futility of government to fix the human condition: "Wars proliferate; political solutions fail; frus-

9. Colson, *Kingdoms in Conflict,* 272.
10. Colson, *Kingdoms in Conflict,* 279, 286.

trations rise. Yet we continue to look to governments to resolve problems beyond their capability. The illusion persists." The final chapter echoed the Augustinian theme of looking for the persistence of the permanent things in the ordinary affairs of human interaction where the City of God was most visible.[11]

Adding Moderation to Zeal

Colson's detachment from politics was easier to pull off from the offices of a parachurch agency like Prison Fellowship than it was from inside a presidential candidate's campaign headquarters, as Ralph Reed was called to do. Reed was an unlikely choice to run Pat Robertson's institutional contribution to the Religious Right, the Christian Coalition. The Coalition started formally in 1989 but functioned as the political agency for Robertson's bid for the Republican nomination in the 1988 presidential contest. It was also the de facto successor to the Moral Majority once Falwell decided to shut down his operation. Reed came to Robertson's organization a young man, only twenty-eight years old. His major accomplishment by then was a Ph.D. in American history from Emory University. His chief qualification for running the Christian Coalition came from his days as an undergraduate when he was active in Republican student organizations and enlisted members by highlighting obvious targets in the culture wars. He used a similar strategy with the Coalition. By sending direct mail pieces about controversial works of art funded by the National Endowment for the Arts, such as works by Andres Serrano and Robert Mapplethorpe, Reed hoped to enlarge Robertson's constituency. After only a couple of years at the helm, Reed could take credit for 82,000 members, financial stability, and even a measure of success in 1991 efforts to re-elect Senator Jesse Helms. But success quickly turned to failure with George Bush's defeat in 1992, the worst of any incumbent since 1912.

The question that the Religious Right and other faith-based advocates needed to answer was whether a religiously informed moral platform could actually yield the basis for a national coalition to gov-

11. Colson, *Kingdoms in Conflict,* 304, 341.

ern the nation. Reed tried to answer with his 1996 book, *Active Faith: How Christians Are Changing the Soul of American Politics.* His purpose was to provide justification not simply for the Christian Coalition but also for evangelical activism more broadly. Along the way he revealed a strain of American politics several steps removed from William F. Buckley Jr., Barry Goldwater, or even Ronald Reagan.

Reed hoped to portray "religious conservatives," as he called them, as moderate, unobjectionable, and completely within the mainstream of American politics. On the one hand, these Americans were "reluctant political actors." They had returned to the political process from a period of self-imposed retreat only because the nation faced a moral crisis of exponential proportions — "explicit sex and violence on television, rampant divorce, skyrocketing illegitimacy, epidemics of crime and drugs, and a million teen pregnancies every year." Religious conservatives' way of life was under assault. Their bumper-sticker response to the Clinton war room slogan was, "it's the culture, stupid." "Families are disintegrating, fathers are abandoning their children, abortion is the most common medical procedure in the nation, and young people attend schools that are not safe and in which they do not learn." Economic policy could not solve these problems. Only morality could. For Reed this meant that the Left and Right had reversed roles since the 1950s, when Whittaker Chambers had remarked that by joining conservatism he felt like he had left the winning side to become one of the losers. What was happening in the United States was that liberalism had lost its moral compass by rejecting faith. In contrast, conservatives sensed that "history was on their side."[12]

Reed considered himself and the Christian Coalition to be conservative. For him this meant less government, lower taxes, "tougher laws against crime and drugs, and policies to strengthen the family." He was also candid about his own "faith commitment," which taught him to be skeptical about the state's capacity to legislate morality or engage in soulcraft. His spiritual transformation was responsible for his replacing political hardball tactics with bridge-building. In fact,

12. Ralph Reed, *Active Faith: How Christians Are Changing the Soul of American Politics* (New York: Free Press, 1996), 5, 9, 11.

the kinder and gentler aspect of evangelicalism was Reed's implicit theme. The faith of religious conservatives was not fundamentalism as journalists and pundits understood the term. "Unlike fundamentalist political movements in the Middle East, religious conservatives in the United States are properly understood as an interest group within a democratic order." Their purpose was not to overturn the Constitution or to impose their faith on nonbelievers. In fact, religious conservatives were firmly in the mainstream of American politics.[13]

According to Reed, the American mainstream was flooded with faith-based politics. "Religious-based political activism is neither un-American nor undemocratic," he asserted; "there is no religion that is more thoroughly democratic than the Christian faith." Reed started his narrative of evangelical political history naturally enough with the colonial revivals of the Great Awakening. George Whitefield's preaching introduced the colonists to "new ideas about liberty and government." But those new ideas showed little respect for accepted patterns or tradition. According to Reed, "Religious revivalism smashed social conventions, eliminated distinctions between the landed gentry and the common folk, and called into question the hierarchical social relationships of the day." The Religious Right could claim to be the rightful heirs of revivalist politics in their opposition to central government and "one-world agencies like the United Nations" that become too powerful and "threaten liberty."[14]

The Second Great Awakening was equally catalytic in challenging the political order. Here the object of reform was not only slavery but alcohol. Reed drew an analogy between single-issue voters in the nineteenth and twentieth centuries who "were driven into politics by their religious commitment." In the nineteenth century, the greatest support for abolitionist political candidates came from districts where revivalism had spawned the largest number of churches. The flip side of revivalism's liberationist spirit was prohibition, a reflection of evangelicals' desire for "a more ordered and just society that reflected Biblical beliefs and primitive faith." Reed acknowledged that prohibition was easily ridiculed, but social pathologies such as

13. Reed, *Active Faith*, 23, 25.
14. Reed, *Active Faith*, 29, 31, 32.

crime, poverty, gambling, and family abandonment "all flowed from a river of booze." And although prohibition began as a reform effort of northern elites to curb the rabblerousing of the lower classes, it eventually gained support from the rank and file. One of the most popular prohibitionist organizations in Reed's account was the Women's Christian Temperance Union — which allowed him to claim that evangelicalism was the genuine source of feminism. But prohibition was responsible for more than the equal participation of women in politics. It also spawned a local, gradual, and grassroots legislative initiative that provided the Christian Coalition with a model for its advocacy of a ban on partial-birth abortion.[15]

Reed also took encouragement from the Social Gospel, which he described as "a crusade for social justice within American Protestantism that merged traditional faith with radical political reform." He approved one Social Gospeler who described the movement as the application of Christian salvation to "society, the economic life, and social institutions." With that understanding of progressive Protestantism, Reed had little trouble giving high marks to Walter Rauschenbusch, the father of the Social Gospel who produced Christian justifications for organizing labor unions, the passage of antitrust laws, temperance and prohibition, and minimum-wage legislation. Another proponent of the Social Gospel whom Reed admired was William Jennings Bryan, who advocated a more populist version of political and economic reform. "Bryan sought to change the whole political and social order" and as a result supported women's suffrage, prohibition, a federal income tax, government regulation of railroads, creation of an Interstate Commission and a Department of Labor, the demonetization of the currency, the direct election of senators, and the abandonment of the gold standard.[16]

What made Rauschenbusch and Bryan conservative in Reed's eyes was their Christian faith. As long as the individual reformer was trying to make his faith relevant to the times, then whatever he advocated, from federal regulations to direct democracy, qualified as conservative. As confusing as this political logic was, even more implausi-

15. Reed, *Active Faith*, 33, 35.
16. Reed, *Active Faith*, 41, 45.

ble was Reed's grasp of conservative Protestantism. As sons and daughters of fundamentalism, evangelicals had been inclined to dismiss the likes of a Rauschenbusch as a liberal because he put social reform at least on a par with, if not above, evangelism as the task of the church. In other words, evangelicals in their fundamentalist phase had staked their identity on opposing theologians like Rauschenbusch. To be sure, Bryan's advocacy for farmers coupled with his opposition to evolution complicated his status within fundamentalism and its religious progeny, evangelicalism. But Reed made no attempt to point out that for evangelicals, most of the Protestants in the mainstream of political progressivism were the bad guys in the history of American Protestantism.

The last episode in Reed's chronicle of faith-based politics was the Civil Rights movement and the extraordinary leadership of Martin Luther King Jr. According to Reed, King's religious credentials were unmatched — "it was the word of God preached in King's eloquent and distinctive cadence that moved not only blacks but the entire nation, for as much as the races were divided on political matters, they worshiped the same God and read the same Bible." Only someone either ignorant of or indifferent to the differences between theological conservatives and liberals — and King's theological education and mentors were all on the liberal side of the evangelical-mainline divide — could uphold the Civil Rights leader as just one more born-again Protestant pastor doing the Lord's work. But Reed consoled himself, and perhaps his readers, by reassuring them that the model for King's initial voter registration drive was Billy Graham's organization. Reed also noted parallels between the Southern Christian Leadership Conference's organization and that of the Women's Christian Temperance Union.[17]

Reed had little to say about the constitutional and legal matters surrounding King's effort to secure equal rights for African Americans. The power of the Supreme Court, the relationship between state and federal governments, and the expanded role of the federal government through the policies and programs of the Great Society — none of these topics caught Reed's eye. Instead, he was intent on baptizing the

17. Reed, *Active Faith*, 57.

Christian Coalition with the water of faith-based politics made holy by the likes of King and other Protestant progressives. "Just as [King] spoke as a black man to a largely white society," Reed explained, "we have tried as Christians to speak in a language that could be heard by a secular society." He admitted that no "crisp moral equivalence" existed between the Civil Rights movement and the "pro-life, pro-family movement of today." But the Religious Right needed to realize that King was "fired by faith and tempered by humility." If evangelicals were to succeed in politics, he speculated, it would be because "we have followed King's example always to love those who hate us, doing battle 'with Christian weapons and with Christian love.'"[18]

By the time Reed finished his survey of evangelical activism, his case for being a conservative looked incredible. The from-sea-to-shining-sea peroration of America's political tradition — "a slumbering faithful awakening from the pews and flowing into school board meetings, courtrooms, slums, and state capitols" — contained bipartisan lessons that raised doubts about not just evangelicals' but American Protestants' ability to discern the political as opposed to the religious meaning of the United States. The lesson for liberals, according to Reed, was that many of the progressive reforms they held dear actually stemmed from faith. This fact should have prevented the Left from dismissing the Religious Right as novel, bizarre, or un-American. Conservatives, Reed added, had more lessons to learn from faith-based politics than liberals. First, conservatives needed to "emulate the passion, the long-suffering, and the nonviolence of our liberal counterparts." Liberals might be morally blind about abortion, but conservatives were at least myopic on issues "ranging from anti-Semitism and anti-Catholicism to racial injustice." Conservatives also needed to learn that "liberals have been correct throughout history on issues of social justice while [conservatives] have been neglectful or derelict in applying the principles of our faith to establishing justice in a fallen world." "We quote Martin Luther King [Jr.] to great effect," Reed asserted, "but how many of us marched with him, and how many of us bear the scars of Bull Connor's billy clubs and police dogs?"[19]

18. Reed, *Active Faith*, 63, 64, 65.
19. Reed, *Active Faith*, 67, 68.

Reed's argument, however genuine, was part of a four-color-glossy effort to repackage the Christian Coalition as a moderate voting bloc that would sit squarely within the political mainstream (and, coincidentally, make the author a kingmaker). His discomfort with anything bordering on extremism was evident at the close of his book, where he contrasted the Religious Right's conservatism with Pat Buchanan's. As much as the former Reagan speechwriter stood squarely with social conservatives in the 1996 presidential contest, Buchanan's campaign "recalled the pro-family movement's previous status as the red-headed stepchild of American politics." In Reed's estimate, evangelicals were "no longer greenhorns throwing rocks at the castle" but were actually "inside the castle." To position themselves as the "permanent insurgency within the Republican Party" was akin to assigning evangelicals to the same fate as either the McGovern or Jesse Jackson wings of the Democratic Party. If evangelicals were to be taken seriously, they needed to "do more than rock the boat and panic the establishment." Buchanan's conservatism threatened more than Reed's efforts to position the Religious Right at the center of the Republican Party. For instance, Buchanan's economic nationalism had no obvious connection to the protection of the unborn or the support of religious liberty. His opposition to aid for Israel obviously stood at odds with evangelicals' historic support for Israel. To identify Buchanan as the voice of religious conservatives was, in Reed's view, a mistake, because pro-family issues were irrelevant to specific economic policies or the United States' role in world affairs.[20]

In contrast to Buchanan's populism and nationalism, Reed outlined a political theology that explained why believers were important to the political process. It began with a fundamental principle of the Social Gospel, namely, to "establish justice in a fallen world." As much as the state held responsibility in "executing the will of God," religious conservatives needed to temper this view with a commitment to keeping government small, "limited in its functions, and diffuse in its operations." The second article of Reed's political theology was the spiritual obligation of citizenship. Contrary to the old fundamentalist view of politics as worldly or evil, Christians living in a de-

---

20. Reed, *Active Faith,* 244, 245.

mocracy had an obligation to vote and be involved in politics. Reed's third point was that followers of Christ need not be persecuted for their faith, as some radical Christians argued. In fact, the Bible was filled with "accounts of heroes of the faith who served God and His people through government service." Finally, Reed exhorted religious conservatives to show grace and humility. This meant loving sinners like Bill Clinton while hating the sin.[21]

For some, Reed's moderation may have revealed the Religious Right's maturity. But just as plausible was the criticism that Reed's effort to smooth the rough edges of evangelical politics was little more than the compromise of principle for the sake of power. Reed's eventual defeat in 2006 as a candidate for Lieutenant Governor in Georgia could easily be read as the consequence of Reed's abandonment of conviction. Revelations of his ties to Jack Abramoff turned a commanding lead in the polls into a landslide defeat at the ballot box. Reed's downfall was precisely the sort of morality tale that evangelicals regularly told to make sense of the world. But that Reed himself experienced the sort of fall from grace that Colson had in the quest for a politically relevant faith was one lesson that many evangelicals ignored. Too much political capital had been invested; too many social problems needed to be fixed.

Compassionate Conservatism

Evangelical discomfort with extremism — the kind that Reed showed in wanting to distance the Christian Coalition from Pat Buchanan — is an important aspect of born-again Protestant identity. Since the 1940s, when neo-evangelicals tried to prove they were not as conservative as fundamentalists, evangelical Protestants presented themselves as a third way somewhere in between liberal Protestantism and fundamentalism. Carl Henry, the founding editor of *Christianity Today,* had expressed this outlook succinctly in a book that functioned as a watershed for conservative Protestants. His *Uneasy Conscience of Modern Fundamentalism* implored fundamentalists to reject political

21. Reed, *Active Faith,* 256, 257.

passivism and social isolation. He believed it possible to combine both soul-winning and social reform just as nineteenth-century evangelicals had. Ralph Reed may not have read Henry while growing up in a Methodist church, but his fondness for the Social Gospel evoked Henry's positive thinking about resurrecting the old Protestant hybrid of evangelism and activism. Reed concluded his book with brief reflections on the future of the Religious Right, and the issues he identified for evangelical attention were poverty and race. This was a vision for a "compassionate society" which involved "a new partnership between government and the faith community." His role model was Martin Luther King Jr., who faced "this difficult dilemma of balancing a movement's passionate faith with the requirements of political sophistication."[22]

Reed foreshadowed the arguments of Marvin Olasky. One of the original proponents of the policy program known as "compassionate conservatism" and an advisor to George W. Bush during his tenure as governor of Texas, Olasky was arguably the one most responsible for persuading conservative evangelicals to reconsider Cold War attitudes toward the welfare state. A professor of journalism at the University of Texas and since 1992 the editor of the conservative evangelical newsweekly *World,* Olasky made a splash with *The Tragedy of American Compassion* (1992). This book popularized among some of the most Republican of evangelicals the notion that Christians needed to be more concerned for the poor than their rhetoric of small government and free markets implied. The genius of Olasky's argument was his effort to cut through the partisan debates over welfare by showing that the free-market-versus-state-sponsored-welfare debate was tired and predictable. Like evangelicals on the left who had signed the Chicago Declaration, Olasky believed that Christians needed to care for the poor more than worry about a greater return on investments. But unlike evangelical critics of conservatives, Olasky rejected government welfare programs as the best way to address poverty. In fact he argued, as many critics of federal welfare had, that such programs cultivated a culture of dependence that was almost as pernicious as poverty itself. But unlike the typical conservative critique of

22. Reed, *Active Faith,* 274, 275, 280.

welfare that began and ended with an insistence on small govern-ment, Olasky was trying to add a warning about suburban compla-cency to the standard conservative fault-finding with big government.

Part of what made Olasky's book compelling was his ability to think outside the slogans that generally drove presidential contests. One example of this creativity was Olasky's several-day experiment as a homeless man in Washington, D.C. "I put on three used T-shirts and two dirty sweaters, . . . got lots of dirt on my hands, and walked with the slow shuffle that characterizes the forty-year-old white homeless male of the streets." He found that plenty of people were ready to help. Olasky received "lots of food, lots of pills of various kinds, and lots of offers of clothing and shelter." At the same time, he reported that he was never asked to do anything in return for assistance. Still, one thing he requested he never received — a Bible. At Zacheus' Kitchen, a service of First Congregational Church in Washington, Olasky asked after one meal if he could have a Bible. Because he had mumbled his request, the volunteer on duty asked, "Do you want a ba-gel? A bag?" When she finally figured out what Olasky wanted, she said, "I'm sorry, we don't have any Bibles."[23]

The method to Olasky's brief homeless madness was to reveal the limits of modern conceptions of welfare. Indeed, much of the book recounted the history of welfare in the United States. Olasky's point throughout was that earlier periods of American history had ex-hibited fruitful forms of charity, and that those examples were in-structive of basic human realities concerning those in need. In-stances of charity, from the colonial era down to the second third of the nineteenth century, were grounded in religious convictions about providence, human sinfulness, and the inherent sociability of per-sons. These beliefs taught the differences between the worthy poor and those for whom assistance would simply create unwholesome de-pendence. The Christian character of older American charity also pre-supposed a need for improvement on the part of those who received aid. Olasky conceded that this sounded cold from the perspective of modern welfare, but he believed it also demonstrated remarkable

23. Marvin Olasky, *The Tragedy of American Compassion* (Westchester, Ill.: Crossway Books, 1992), 209.

kindness. He cited Tocqueville's contrast between the European state's activities as "the sole reliever of all kinds of misery" with America's unplanned cultivation of small communities in which citizens felt "compassion for the sufferings of one another" because of close contact with those in need. The point of Olasky's historical excursus was to show that the quality of older charity was not entirely distant from that of the modern welfare state. In fact it was often superior, because it was localized and because it treated the poor with dignity. This respect led to the older compassion's holding those in need responsible. Its emphasis was always on "individual responsibility and the need to change."[24]

From this historical survey Olasky isolated several criteria by which to measure the value of charity. His list included affiliation, bonding, categorization, discernment, employment, and freedom. The actual differences among these marks were not always easy to see. But the cumulative point was that the aim of older forms of charity "was not to press for governmental programs, but to show poor people how to move up while resisting enslavement" either to state-sponsored welfare or private philanthropy. In effect, true compassion involved the dignity of the person by restoring the poor to a position of independence and responsibility.[25]

Olasky's brief for an older style of charity was one that resonated with many conservative critiques of the welfare state and explained Charles Murray's preface to the book. A libertarian public policy analyst, Murray admired Olasky's account if only because it buttressed his own complaints about the "poverty industry" — the bureaucrats, social workers, and vendors who obtained a piece of the close to $200 billion spent on welfare by 1992. The other aspect of Olasky's book that appealed to Murray was the truth that "human needs were answered by other human beings, not by bureaucracies, and the response to those needs was not compartmentalized." Murray explained that previous generations of Americans "didn't used to be so foolish as to think that providing food would cure anything except hunger, nor so shallow as to think that physical hunger was more im-

---

24. Olasky, *The Tragedy of American Compassion,* 185, 95.
25. Olasky, *The Tragedy of American Compassion,* 113.

portant than the other human hungers. " He conceded that the older form of charity might be dismissed as "moral uplift" (a phrase "overdue for resurrection"), but creating communities in which people "routinely understand and act on the responsibilities of adulthood" did in fact "work."[26]

What Murray called "moral uplift" did not adequately cover the last and arguably most unusual of Olasky's seven marks of compassion. Older forms of charity were not vaguely religiously based; they assumed the reality of God's grace. Olasky quoted one nineteenth-century editor: "True philanthropy must take into account spiritual as well as physical needs." An evangelical would interpret that sentiment as a call for spiritual renewal to be added to acts of charity, including spiritual counsel with physical forms of assistance. Olasky did not call directly for converting the poor, even if he did provide illustrations of the change that came over those in need once they were born again. He even suggested that Christians and Jews shared similar motivations for compassion and the way charity should be conducted. But deep down, Olasky, a convert from Judaism to evangelical Protestantism, knew that the sort of freedom and responsibility he advocated as the goal of charity stood a better chance when grounded in the work of the Holy Spirit. The reason for opposing government welfare programs was not simply because they were too expensive, but because "they are inevitably too stingy in what is really important, treating people as people and not animals." Ultimately, then, the crisis of the welfare state was not one of politics or conservatism. It was a religious problem, whether or not modern ideas of compassion and charity, whether public or private, were "points of light" or "shades of darkness."[27]

Eight years intervened between Olasky's *Tragedy of American Compassion* and *Compassionate Conservatism* (2000), the book that took up at least ten of Olasky's fifteen minutes of fame. In those intervening years, the editor of *World* had managed to upgrade his publisher and the person writing the foreword. From Crossway Books, a

26. Charles Murray, Preface to Olasky, *The Tragedy of American Compassion*, viii, xv.

27. Olasky, *The Tragedy of American Compassion*, 112, 233.

mid-sized evangelical publisher in Wheaton, Olasky moved to the Free Press. And instead of Charles Murray contributing the preface, for *Compassionate Conservatism* Olasky secured the services of George W. Bush, then the governor of Texas and the leading candidate for the Republican presidential nomination. The link to Bush was through Texas, where the governor, in consultation with Olasky, had begun to put the older style of compassion into place with faith-based initiatives. Compassionate conservatism became one of Bush's major policy themes once elected, and it stemmed directly from Olasky's belief that care for the poor and needy should include material and spiritual support and that it should not make those receiving aid permanent wards of the state.

Aside from Bush's foreword (and an appendix from the Texas governor explaining compassionate conservatism through one of his campaign speeches), Olasky's more popular book was filled mainly with anecdotes about churches and religious groups that implemented the older style of charity. It presumed most of the theory from his earlier book and used examples to inspire and provide instruction. Part of the program Olasky called for in his conclusion was a better understanding of charitable choice, the welfare reform legislation undertaken by Bill Clinton's administration. Olasky argued that these reforms were a good start but were still biased and prevented religious organizations from receiving government support through an overly narrow reading of the Establishment Clause in the First Amendment. Olasky also called for more advocates of compassionate conservatism, including the occupant of the White House. With Bush's election, his exhortation proved prophetic.

Lost in the details of Olasky's brief for compassion was political conservatism. Bush's credentials as a conservative were always shaky, and his definition of conservatism in the foreword to Olasky's book was much closer to Norman Vincent Peale than to William F. Buckley Jr. "Conservatism must be the creed of hope," Bush asserted. "The creed that promotes social progress through individual change." The problem for conservatives, according to Bush, was the partisan standoff between markets and big government. Free markets had produced great wealth and yet had not eliminated poverty. Welfare allocated by the state was well intentioned but ended up hurting the very people it was designed to help. For this reason the United States needed to "get beyond two narrow mindsets." The first held that only the government was capable of showing true compassion. This outlook heaps disdain upon charity that is conducted by churches and private organizations. The second mindset to be avoided was one that said the problems of poverty would be solved "if government would only get out of our way."[28]

Bush's 2000 domestic agenda, heavily inspired by Olasky, was to put compassion into conservatism. The Texan's plan was to increase charitable giving, encourage private and religious charities to become more active in a variety of social services, and coordinate better the cooperation between business and government. Compassionate conservatism was then an effort to streamline government without regarding it as the enemy of the people, markets, or freedom. "We must apply our conservative and free-market ideas to the job of helping real human beings," Bush wrote, "because any ideology, no matter how right in theory, is sterile and empty without that goal." What Olasky's recovery of compassion made possible for conservatism was supplementing justice with kindness, judgment with mercy, and zeal with love. It tells every American "this dream is for you" while doing so after the example of St. Francis — "where there is despair, bringing hope."[29]

Aside from echoing his father's rhetoric of a kinder, gentler conservatism, Bush's Olasky-inspired compassion would prove to be as difficult to execute as it would be to square with conservative ideas about the American polity. Bush's faith-based initiative stumbled most significantly over constitutional questions related to the First Amendment and whether federal support for religious charities constituted an establishment of religion. Even more difficult was harmonizing conservatism with an expansion of the federal regulations in the conduct of religious and private organizations. Did Bush and Olasky really believe that in the era of OSHA and the EPA the federal government would simply let a thousand points of light shine without

28. George W. Bush, in Marvin N. Olasky, *Compassionate Conservatism: What It Is, What It Does, and How It Can Transform America* (New York: Free Press, 2000), xi, 224.
29. Bush in Olasky, *Compassionate Conservatism*, 225, 226.

also specifying the wattage, color, and times for shining? Compassionate conservatism may have been a significant contribution by the Religious Right to American conservatism. But by redirecting the energy of conservatism away from decentralization and the integrity of local authorities (both state and voluntary) toward poverty and compassion, evangelical Protestants may have actually revealed how at odds their sentimental and humanitarian instincts were with conservatism in the first place.

One Lord, One Baptism, One Sentiment

An implicit assumption of faith-based politics is that people who hold the same religious convictions will, or at least should, look at the political order in similar ways. Some invoke the idea of worldview. Faith creates an outlook that prompts believers to see the world in a specific way, one that calls for similar forms of political engagement or similar kinds of policy and legislation. This assumption has been crucial to Republicans' cultivation of evangelicals. Born-again values voters share a perspective that will rally around certain proposals or ideals.

A moment's reflection reveals the folly of such an assumption. Evangelical Protestants are one of the least unified groups of American believers at the level of ecclesiastical affiliation and religious organization. Enough differences exist between Wesleyans and Calvinists, Baptists and Pentecostals, megachurches and small congregations to prompt a veritable cornucopia of fellowships and associations. (One could make a similar point about Roman Catholics and Jews; neither of these groups in the United States has yielded predictable uniformity.) Why then would pundits and scholars treat evangelicals as if their faith, which on Sundays divides them along a host of theological and institutional lines, would unite them when they line up on the first Tuesday in November to cast their ballots in presidential contests?

As early as 1990, James Skillen, the director of the Center for Public Justice, noticed the diversity among Christians on public matters and tried to categorize if not make sense of it. His book, *The Scattered Voice,* took stock of faith-based politics and the particular contributions of evangelical Protestants. Skillen's scope was larger than born-again Protestants; it included Roman Catholic neo-conservatives, religiously informed liberals, evangelical Civil Rights activists, "pro-justice" evangelicals, and theonomists. His classifications demonstrated that Christians, who were thought in the public media to speak with one voice, were much more cacophonous. The problem that Skillen found in most of the Christian positions was an inability to construct a comprehensive political theory of what the state ought to be. As such, many faith-based pundits started either from a conservative or liberal outlook and then looked to Christianity for justification.

Skillen's understanding of liberalism and conservatism was astute and free from much of the sloganeering that afflicted the more popular figures of the Religious Right. Liberalism, he wrote, typically "looks to government approved initiatives . . . to help people or to achieve some public good." Liberalism also connoted a progressive hope for change "away from the existing situation (status quo)" in order to improve society and the lives of citizens. In contrast, conservatism involved "holding on to what presently exists," an instinct that "seeks less government or that remains skeptical about new government initiatives designed to solve society's problems." Skillen, himself one of the more thoughtful and theoretically trained evangelicals engaged in public policy discussions, appeared to be reluctant to side with either the conservatives or liberals. The reason was his higher pursuit of "answering the questions about the nature and identity of the state."[30]

Skillen's position of non-partisanship allowed him critical distance to point out the flaws of most Christian positions on the American political spectrum, and his remarks about conservatives were telling. Finding the faults of pro-American evangelicals was arguably the easiest of Skillen's tasks. These believers too closely identified America itself with Christianity and adopted a primarily moralistic perspective on contemporary politics. "It is one thing to sense that certain kinds of immorality are expanding and that the country is in trouble because of it," Skillen declared; "it is quite another thing to

---

30. James W. Skillen, *The Scattered Voice: Christians at Odds in the Public Square* (Grand Rapids: Zondervan, 1990), 15, 17.

identify precisely and convincingly the responsibility that government should bear for addressing the situation." Many of the United States' difficulties stemmed from defects in public education, family life, and personal immorality. To try to fix these woes by lobbying efforts or winning presidential contests "is a grave error." "A political movement," he warned, "requires more than nostalgia, moral passion, and hatred of secular humanism."[31]

Skillen's critique of the red-meat evangelicals sounded responsible, but his chapter on the critical conservatives, the ones less rabidly nationalist, revealed his own ambivalence about the Right. What critical conservatives did well from Skillen's perspective was to look for biblical teaching that transcends American experience "even at its best." "They manifest a heightened sense of a unique identity above or apart from America rather than within or of America." Yet these conservatives stopped short of a "principled vision or a normative approach to politics." To recognize the pervasiveness of sin was one thing. But they ran the risk of ignoring the "deeper reality" of the created order and the implications of redemption for political authority and a just society. In the end, the evangelical conservatives who commendably avoided the search for America's Christian origins produced "an essentially negative criterion for measuring government's actions."[32]

Skillen's critique of the different wings of evangelical conservatives stemmed from his own effort to conceive of a "complete and constructive view of the political order" based on the divine command to seek public justice. Indeed, biblical notions of justice and righteousness were at the heart of Skillen's own vision. On the one hand, he conceded that Christ's kingdom was not of this world, and consequently justice and righteousness were realities that defined Christians personally or collectively as the church. But Skillen also argued that biblical accounts of justice and righteousness involved a social and political dimension. Because Christians bear the righteousness of Christ, they "should fulfill their responsibilities even in the political arena in ways that reflect their new life in Christ." "If Christ is

31. Skillen, *The Scattered Voice,* 52.
32. Skillen, *The Scattered Voice,* 57, 62, 74.

the Lord over all of life," Skillen deduced, "then Christian obedience calls for civic responsibility that promotes justice."[33]

As sensible as Skillen's analysis was, his own search for a comprehensively Christian political theory revealed the inherent fragility of the alliance between conservatives and evangelicals. The basis of that instability was precisely the effort to do political philosophy in a distinctly Christian mode. Aside from the theological tensions in Skillen's own attempt to harmonize Protestant teaching on creation and redemption, the effort to construct a comprehensively Christian political theory wound up transcending the polarities of Left and Right, liberal and conservative — and for that matter, Federalist and Anti-federalist, Whig and Democrat, Republican and Democrat. When he wrote that Christians "ought not to subsist as moralistic parasites on conservative and liberal bandwagons," Skillen made a worthwhile point. Evangelicals did appear to be pawns in a chess match between Democrats and Republicans. But Skillen had more in mind. "A Christian public philosophy will go beyond the liberal and conservative variations of Liberalism," he wrote. "It will demand more than an updating of Aristotelian Thomism or a return to Puritan theology. It will require more than an appeal to American constitutionalism."[34]

In a sense, Skillen was right. Christian teaching does in fact transcend race, class, and gender, or electoral politics and public policy white papers. But an affirmation of transcendence, as if Christians are above the tawdry issues of politics, is clearly a sticking point for evangelicals who would be politically conservative. Born-again Protestants, as Skillen's argument suggests, view conservatism as insufficiently Christian, and so identifying with the Right is tantamount to renouncing religious identity. Skillen was clearly insisting that evangelicals go beyond the slogan "What Would Jesus Do?" Even so, his own desire for a Christian political philosophy that rose above the Left and the Right revealed a political perfectionism that resonated with the older fundamentalist tendency to regard politics as "worldly" and beneath truly devoted believers.

---

33. Skillen, *The Scattered Voice,* 25-26.
34. Skillen, *The Scattered Voice,* 185, 209.

The reluctance of a smart and savvy advocate such as Skillen to side with any non-Christian political tradition helps to explain why evangelicals, who might otherwise seem to be a natural constituency for political conservatism, would turn out to be mere co-belligerents rather than members of the American Right. Because Jesus said, "you must serve God rather than mammon," evangelicals have felt uncomfortable taking cues from Friedrich Hayek, Russell Kirk, or William F. Buckley Jr. Even the most conservatively disposed of born-again Protestant thinkers have been reluctant to use conservative arguments. Instead, the evangelical habit is to rely upon explicitly Christian reasoning. By following Jesus instead of the Right, evangelicals would abandon conservatism for some positions closer to the Left. But because that shift could be justified by appealing to Jesus' ethical teaching, evangelicals like George W. Bush and Ralph Reed would try to pass off even progressive policies as conservative.

SIX

Left Turn

—⊂∾∽⊃—

A t the beginning of the new millennium the Religious Right appeared to be a permanent feature in American electoral politics. Evangelical and fundamentalist Protestants, the narrative went, had been content with religious activities on the margins of political life from 1925 until 1975. But once challenges emerged within American public institutions that threatened the capacity of families and churches to pass on their faith to the next generation, born-again Protestants became politically active in ways that caught scholars, pundits, and campaign strategists off-guard. As part of the coalition of conservatives that helped to elect Ronald Reagan and that secured the landmark 1994 victory of a Republican majority in Congress, the Religious Right established itself as one of the Right's core constituencies. So reliable did evangelical Protestants appear that sociologist James Davison Hunter could write, "The association between Protestant orthodoxy and political conservatism is perhaps the most reliable and enduring of all commonplaces concerning [evangelicalism], and not without good reason."[1] The 1993 assessment by political scientist Michael Lienesch was more restrained than Hunter's but equally confident that the Religious Right, despite orga-

---

1. James Davison Hunter, quoted in Michael Lienesch, *Redeeming America: Piety and Politics in the New Christian Right* (Chapel Hill, NC: University of North Carolina Press, 1993), 19.

nizational restructuring and revisions of political strategy, was a permanent presence.[2]

Fifteen years later these assertions sound exaggerated. With Religious Right figures such as Jerry Falwell, Pat Robertson, and Dobson either dead or close to retirement, evangelicals lack clear leaders and institutions to corral their millions. Meanwhile, the baby boomer generation of born-again Protestants does not appear to have the stomach for the culture wars or political partisanship that animated evangelicals as part of the Reagan coalition. Indeed, most younger evangelicals writing about politics or engaged in activism or policy appear to be allergic to conservatism. Evangelicalism's Greatest Generation may have been predictably right of center, but their children increasingly identify with Democrats and the Left.

For social scientists who assumed that religious and political conservatism go hand in hand, the rise of an evangelical Left would appear to upset three decades of political developments and certain theories about the relationship between faith and American politics. But in fact evangelicalism has always espoused a form of religious and moral idealism that is profoundly at odds with political conservatism. As such, the real surprise for American politics may have been the post–World War II generation of evangelicals who formed the fifth column in Reagan's coalition. This is a plausible conclusion given the current spate of evangelical writers who reiterate the need for a faith-based politics and who insist that conservatism is a poor vehicle for such religious activism.

God Is Not a Republican or a Democrat

Jim Wallis is the Left's favorite evangelical. The graying editor of *Sojourners* has been laboring to secure the attention of the Left for the better part of four decades. When the Chicago Declaration was published in 1973, Wallis was on hand as one of the young evangelicals to ratify the statement's call for born-again Protestants to repent of their social and political vices. He had recently graduated from Mich-

2. Lienesch, *Redeeming America*, 260.

igan State University, where he was president of Students for a Democratic Society, and from Trinity Evangelical Divinity School, a seminary where Richard Nixon would have been more popular than George McGovern. In addition to collaborating with other activist evangelicals, Wallis had formed a Christian community in inner-city Washington, D.C., in hopes of breaking down the divisions that plagued American society and its political parties. The community was designed to unite blacks and whites, poor and middle-class, and overcome suburban indifference to the city. Wallis's efforts included a magazine, originally called the *Post-American* and renamed *Sojourners,* to function as a forum for the "holistic" Christianity that he advocated. Unlike Olasky and compassionate conservatives who would eventually come around to a concern for the poor as vital evidence of true faith, Wallis believed the church needed to do more than provide charitable assistance. Christians also needed to identify themselves with the destitute and marginal, because this was the way God had acted throughout history — salvation was God's exalting the humble over the proud, the hungry over the rich, the weak over the strong.

Wallis has written many books, and the ones of more recent vintage appear to be designed more to maintain visibility than to extend an argument about Christian activism abstractly considered. The seed of most of his subsequent books was planted in his very first, *Agenda for Biblical People.* In many respects it was an updated version of the older Protestant Social Gospel that tried to combine evangelical ideals of evangelism with a biblical basis for social activism. Wallis called evangelicals to abandon an understanding of the gospel that only involved personal redemption and preparation for the world to come. The kingdom of God, as proclaimed and inaugurated by Jesus Christ, was the establishment of a new world order:

> The gospel of the kingdom is the central message of the New Testament. It speaks of the inauguration of a whole new order in Jesus Christ and the establishing of a new people whose common life bears witness to that new order in history. The proclamation is not a personal gospel, not a social gospel, not even a gospel of "both," but rather the gospel of a new order and a new people.

Wallis's reason for distinguishing this perspective from the Social Gospel was his own effort to show that the Christian call to repentance questioned all forms of complacency. His was an explicitly radical call to Christian faithfulness. "The call to discipleship always involves a break with established norms and values, with the prevailing assumptions and idolatries of the present order," he wrote. "It is a choice of a path that leads the Christian out of conformity to the world." Various institutions, authorities, and conventions had become forms of idolatry for evangelicals, whereas "[t]he gospel signals the end of the uncontested dominion of the principalities and powers of the world over people's lives."[3]

Evangelical churches had lost a sense of the kingdom, Wallis believed, because of a narrow concern for the salvation of souls. This meant that born-again Protestants had reduced racism to a "social problem," poverty was simply an "economic question," and war and foreign policy were merely "political" issues. The evangelical faith had segregated these social and political realities from a holistic account of salvation that included a believer's relationship to others. For Wallis the kingdom aspect of Christianity was so extensive that anything that "would bind and oppress, all that would hold people captive and prevent them from being what they were created to be, falls within the range of the concern of biblical faith."[4]

Because Wallis began with a coming-of-age story about his views as a teenager and college student, he unintentionally opened himself to the criticism that his understanding of Christianity relied more on his experience than a careful reading of Scripture. He mentioned becoming involved in radicalism on campus, antiwar protests, and the struggle for African American civil rights. What was obvious beyond the realities of racism, poverty, and war was "a cycle of injustice and violence, of exploitation and manipulation, of profit and power, of self-interest and competition, of hate and fear . . . a cycle whose final meaning seemed to be death itself." In these circumstances Wallis turned to the New Testament and realized that "realism, respectabil-

3. Jim Wallis, *Agenda for Biblical People* (New York: Harper & Row, 1976), 3, 20, 21.

4. Wallis, *Agenda for Biblical People,* 16.

ity, and reasonableness," the marks of the contemporary American church, ran directly contrary to the teachings of Jesus. Christianity did not yield a church of "comfort, property, privilege, and position" but instead a community characterized by "abandonment, insecurity, persecution, and exile." This was a reading of Scripture that gave an evangelical helping hand to Students for a Democratic Society.[5]

As much as Wallis captured part of the biblical theme of the church as a pilgrim people, his radical posture did not add up as a program of activism or social reform. If "abandonment, insecurity, persecution, and exile" were the norm for Christians, were these attributes also to characterize the social and political order? Was Wallis's own community in Washington, D.C., typified by upheaval and dislocation? Were securing permits from the city government for heating, plumbing, and refrigeration a form of compromise with the cycle of injustice and exploitation?

Before concluding the book, Wallis attempted to come to terms with the implications of his radical posture. He advocated the creation of Christian communities where believers could offer an alternative to the dominant social structures. Forming communities of this kind was a "revolutionary act" because it liberated people from "their dependence upon the dominant institutions of the world system." The revolution for which Wallis called was non-violent, because violence simply perpetuated the "structures of idolatry and alienation." A revolution might "change the patterns of production and distribution but leave untouched the roots of the human condition." The task of the Christian community was "to renounce the struggle for wealth and power" and to identify with the poor and oppressed. In fact, the primary communion for Christians was "with the poor [in] a community of suffering." Wallis's basis for this conclusion was simple: this is what Jesus would do. But by basing his argument on the teaching and work of Jesus, Wallis used a strategy that inevitably involved a religious revolution not only in the United States but also around the globe. The Christian revolution's aim was "not only to change and reform the economic and political facts and forms of the world" — a fairly tall order in and of itself — "but to seek fundamental

5. Wallis, *Agenda for Biblical People,* 1, 2.

change in the very framework of a world system that needs to be continually examined and tested by the judgment of the Word of God." *Comprehensive, idealistic,* even *utopian* are words that come to mind when reading Wallis's prescriptions. Another is *enduring,* because his was an unattainable project that would give work to a young man for the rest of his life.[6]

In fact, Wallis's call for revolution would be repeated in the pages of *Sojourners* and subsequent books. His challenge to evangelicals would become so routine that it became the basis for a career of pestering born-again Protestants to join the Christian revolution. That career has turned Wallis into an established leader and guardian of the evangelical Left whose blessing or endorsement identifies an author or executive as safely beyond the pale of the Religious Right. At the same time, because of his reputation, Wallis attracts endorsements from politicians and celebrities higher up the punditry food chain than his own standing as the evangelical rival to James Dobson. Even so, Wallis's celebrity has come with the price of losing the radical edge responsible for his reputation.

For instance, in *The Soul of Politics* (1994), a book for which Garry Wills wrote the foreword and Cornel West the preface, Wallis repeated the argument of *Agenda for Biblical People* but did so in a work four times as long. He achieved the lengthier form for his "alternative vision" by recounting episode after episode from his own experience, either in the community in Washington that he had helped to create or through his travels as a person of some eminence. Wallis's hope was to forge a third way between liberalism and conservatism by combining the best of each and injecting the combination with a dose of the Spirit. "Liberalism's best impulse is to care about the disenfranchised and insist that a society is responsible for its people," but it had become hampered by "distant institutions and impersonal bureaucracies." Meanwhile, "Conservatism's best impulse is to stress the need for individual initiative and moral responsibility" but by becoming attached to wealth and power it lacked a "strong ethic of social responsibility" and had abandoned the poor and dispossessed. Wallis's solution to this impasse was to restore "the shattered cov-

---

6. Wallis, *Agenda for Biblical People,* 76, 85, 96.

enant." This required "a fundamental transformation of our ways of thinking, feeling, and acting . . . a change of heart, a revolution of spirit, a conversion of the soul that issues forth in new personal and social behavior."[7]

Lacking in Wallis's later book was the radicalism of his youth. *The Soul of Politics* began with "The world isn't working," and ended with an appeal to hope: "hope is a sign of transformation." Also lacking was much new thinking on Wallis's part. His exhortations were generically political and vaguely Christian. They failed to evaluate critically what was wrong with liberalism's structures or what prevented conservatism from offering a social ethic. Wallis simply found himself unable to work with the Left because of their irreligion and with the Right because of their wealth. The way out of the dilemma was the first-century church as the model for twentieth-century urban industrial social arrangements.[8]

God's Politics: Why the Right Gets It Wrong and the Left Doesn't Get It (2005) deviated little from what Wallis had already argued, except for giving more attention to nonviolence in the context of the Iraq War. The book demonstrated the author's celebrity by carrying endorsements from Bono, Bill Moyers, and Desmond Tutu. It also included a publicity campaign with a bumper-sticker that read, "God is not a Republican or a Democrat," which added triteness to the moral earnestness of the book. Still, Wallis was deadly serious in his opposition to the Bush administration and its foreign policy. He objected to Bush's abuse of executive power, faulty intelligence, dependence on oil, and flawed estimate of national sovereignty. But the president's biggest fault was using faith for partisan ends. For Wallis, "the answer to bad theology is not secularism; it is good theology." Wallis's theological counter to Bush was a strong assertion of nonviolence and "enemy-love." The *Sojourners* editor did not place his ideas in relation to just-war teaching, nor did he explain how an ethic of loving one's enemies could ever accommodate state officials whose responsibility, as the apostle Paul taught, was to bear the sword and punish evildoers. Wallis

7. Jim Wallis, *The Soul of Politics: A Practical and Prophetic Vision for Change* (New York: New Press, 1994), 22, 41.
8. Wallis, *The Soul of Politics*, xv, 240.

simply asserted his view, appealed to his interpretation of Scripture, and leavened his argument with accounts of meetings with public officials and excerpts from editorials and columns he had written.[9]

Wallis's main point was the one he had made three decades earlier — namely, that evangelicals needed to move beyond the fixed political traditions of liberal or conservative, Republican or Democrat, to "prophetic politics." This was the alternative to conservatism, liberalism, and libertarianism. "It is traditional or conservative on issues of family values, sexual integrity and personal responsibility" but "*very* progressive, populist, or even radical on issues like poverty and racial justice." For Wallis this position was more than an ideal. It was also a constituency: voters who "are very strong on issues like marriage, raising kids, and individual ethics, but without being right-wing, reactionary, or mean-spirited or scapegoating against any group of people, such as homosexuals." Wallis's was the pro-life, pro-family, pro-feminist, and pro-poor position. It may have sounded idealistic, but it foreshadowed the themes of Barack Obama's campaign with such notions as the "politics of hope" and an epilogue entitled "we are the ones we've been waiting for." *God's Politics* gave no indication that Wallis had encountered a junior state senator from Illinois, but if pollsters and speechwriters in the Obama campaign had been paying attention they would have sensed that Wallis's generation of evangelical Protestants would not be as reliably conservative as many assumed.

The Repugnance of the Religious Right

If Jim Wallis hopes to call born-again Protestants to their better civil selves, Randall Balmer, a religious historian at Barnard College, apparently hopes to shame evangelicals into repenting from political conservatism. Like Wallis, Balmer attended Trinity Evangelical Divinity School, a seminary in the northern suburbs of Chicago hardly on the front lines of campus activism or at the center of public policy de-

---

9. Jim Wallis, *God's Politics: Why the Right Gets It Wrong and the Left Doesn't Get It* (San Francisco: HarperSanFrancisco, 2005), 149, 150.

bates. Balmer attended Trinity a few years after Wallis and came to his political awakening not through the SDS but through George McGovern. While an undergraduate at Trinity's sister institution, Trinity College, the denominational school of the Evangelical Free Church, Balmer organized a field trip for a select group of his college friends to hear George McGovern at nearby Wheaton College. The general disposition of college students is to avoid attending chapel whenever possible, but the prospect of hearing the Democratic nominee for president sent Balmer and company to attend Wheaton's chapel service without even asking for extra credit.

McGovern's talk seemed to make less of an impression on Balmer than the way that evangelicals at Wheaton reacted to the Democratic nominee. (In fact, a few years later Balmer would serve as an intern for John B. Anderson, a Republican congressman from Rockford, Illinois, and a third-party candidate for president in 1980.) Students at Wheaton had invited McGovern to campus, but the administration tried to rescind the invitation when prominent groups within the college's constituency objected. According to Balmer, the student group refused to relent but did agree to invite Richard Nixon to campus also. The Republican nominee was unable to accept, thus giving McGovern an uncontested shot at the solidly evangelical and predominantly Republican campus. Balmer recalls that the students treated McGovern shabbily. He received "boos, jeers, and catcalls" and some students marched around the auditorium with banners and posters of Nixon while chanting "four more years." This incident stuck in Balmer's mind, and when he later pursued a doctorate in religious studies at Princeton he reflected on what seemed to be American evangelicalism's central mystery: nineteenth-century evangelicals had instigated and supported any number of moral crusades, but their Republican descendants had "forsaken the legacy" of evangelical activism. "What went wrong?"[10]

The same question could be asked of Balmer. His father was a minister in the Evangelical Free Church of America who pastored in a variety of settings in the upper Midwest. This denomination, formed

10. Randall H. Balmer, *Thy Kingdom Come: How the Religious Right Distorts the Faith and Threatens America* (New York: Basic Books, 2006), xxv.

in 1950, was the product of Scandinavian pietiest immigrant churches that had assimilated American evangelical conventions of Bible-onlyism and the conversion experience as the best barometers of genuine faith. A few years before Balmer's enrollment, Trinity Evangelical Divinity School became the seminary outlet for defenders of biblical inerrancy who no longer felt comfortable with the direction of Fuller Seminary in Southern California. The Evangelical Free Church, in other words, had the reputation for being predictably evangelical and solidly middle-class. It was the kind of denomination to produce Illinois Republicans like Anderson, not social justice activists like Jim Wallis. Having grown up in that denomination, Balmer's roots were far closer to Chuck Colson, the National Association of Evangelicals, and Ronald Reagan than they were to Charles Finney or the Women's Christian Temperance Union.

But for evangelical baby boomers like Balmer, the mid-twentieth-century brand of evangelicalism that helped to make Billy Graham a celebrity was too unabashedly American, too willing to identify with the silent majority, and too Republican. In his 2006 book, *Thy Kingdom Come: How the Religious Right Distorts the Faith and Threatens America,* Balmer tried to account for his own emergence as a politically liberal evangelical. In addition to his disdain for the treatment McGovern received from Wheaton College Republicans, Balmer became further disaffected with evangelicalism while a graduate student owing to the scandals of televangelists like Jimmy Swaggart and Jim Bakker. A widely acclaimed book on lesser known evangelical institutions and their subculture, *Mine Eyes Have Seen the Glory,* later adapted for a PBS television series, helped Balmer recover some of his former sympathy for born-again Protestantism as an American folk religion. But evangelicalism's "narrowness, legalism, censoriousness, and misogyny" prevented Balmer from identifying completely. Politics was another reason. "The hard-right stance of the Religious Right," Balmer explained, "represents something less than the best of Christianity." It put Balmer in the uncomfortable position of explaining to incredulous interlocutors that "no, the fact that we love Jesus doesn't mean that we take our marching orders from James Dobson or Karl Rove."[11]

11. Balmer, *Thy Kingdom Come,* xxii, x.

Loving Jesus, not political theory, economic science, or practical circumstances, was responsible for making Balmer a political liberal. He asserted that a sizeable number of liberal evangelicals exist, and their politics stem precisely from an understanding of faith that "compels them to serve as peacemakers, to take action on behalf of those whom Jesus described as 'the least of these,' and to champion the rights of women and minorities." At one point in *Thy Kingdom Come* Balmer created a religio-political catechism almost as if to convince himself that he is truly a liberal and an evangelical. "Am I a feminist?" he asks himself. "Of course I'm a feminist," he answers. "I'm a feminist," he explains, "because Jesus was a feminist, and I've chosen to fashion my life, with God's help, after the example of Jesus and his teachings as recorded in the New Testament." Balmer's catechetical affirmation comes easier to him, of course, because of his own sympathies with liberalism. He resents in equal measure the "hard-right ideologues who have succeeded in turning *liberal* into a term of derision and my fellow liberals who have allowed them to do so." According to Balmer, liberalism deserves credit for everything good in American society, "from Social Security, civil rights, public education, and equality for women to the very existence of the republic itself." He concedes that liberals have been guilty of excess, but "overall, the tradition of liberalism in America is a distinguished one, and I am pleased to number myself both as an evangelical Christian and as a political liberal." The problem for Balmer is that evangelical liberals do not have access to mass media the way the Religious Right does. Nor do they have the resources of corporate wealth at their disposal. The arguments of evangelical liberals also defy sloganeering and do not fit into the partisan "shouting matches" that dominate media coverage. Even so, Balmer believes that many evangelicals regard the Religious Right's agenda as "misguided, even ruinous" both to the nation and ultimately to the Christian religion.[12]

Balmer looks at and finds wanting five specific instances of evangelical activism in *Thy Kingdom Come*. Of the five — abortion, the First Amendment, public education, intelligent design, and the environment — the first is the most provocative. At the heart of his argu-

12. Balmer, *Thy Kingdom Come*, x-xi.

ment about abortion is the contention that because the Bible doesn't condemn the practice, it is a selective article of political faith for the Religious Right — as he puts it, "an odd choice, especially for people who pride themselves on biblical literalism." Balmer claims that "fetishizing the fetus" finds no sustained support from Scripture. The passages typically cited, Deuteronomy 30:19, Psalm 139:13-16, and Luke 1:41-42, are capable of a variety of interpretations. This is Balmer's wedge for pinning selective biblical literalism on the Religious Right. He believes that Scripture's teaching on divorce is much clearer than on abortion. And yet, at roughly the same time that Ronald Reagan, a divorcé, ran successfully for president in 1980, evangelicals dropped conveniently their former stance on divorce and adopted a pro-life position as a litmus test. "The ruse of selective literalism," Balmer writes, allowed born-again Protestants "to dismiss as culturally determined the New Testament prescriptions against divorce and women with covered heads. But they refused to read Paul's apparent condemnations of homosexuality as similarly rooted in . . . the social circumstances of the first century."[13]

If the biblical case for pro-life is based on selective biblical literalism, a better explanation for evangelical opposition to abortion is historical. Balmer asserts that "Leaders of the Religious Right would have us believe that their movement began in direct response to the U.S. Supreme Court's 1973 *Roe v. Wade* decision." This ruling so outraged born-again Protestants that they mobilized politically. But according to Balmer, this account is a myth. It is "a compelling story" to say that "these selfless, courageous leaders of the Religious Right, inspired by the opponents of slavery in the nineteenth century, trudge dutifully into battle in order to defend those innocent unborn children." Nevertheless, it simply "isn't true."[14]

Balmer's evidence for demythologizing the Religious Right is his own encounter with Paul Weyrich at a seminar sponsored by the Ethics and Public Policy Center in Washington, D.C. (Perhaps to maintain credibility with his liberal friends and peers, Balmer explains that he attended this seminar "for reasons I still don't entirely under-

13. Balmer, *Thy Kingdom Come*, 5, 7-8, 9.
14. Balmer, *Thy Kingdom Come*, 12.

stand" and insists that he "didn't realize it at the time" that Ethics and Public Policy was "a Religious Right organization.") At this meeting Weyrich lectured other leaders of the Religious Right that the pivotal event in animating evangelicals politically was the Internal Revenue Service's decision to rescind Bob Jones University's tax-exempt status on grounds that its student policies were racially discriminatory. Ed Dobson, an associate of Jerry Falwell, later confirmed Weyrich's history. According to Balmer, Dobson said that "the Religious New Right did not start because of a concern about abortion." "I sat in a non-smoke-filled back room with the Moral Majority," Dobson added, "and I frankly do not remember abortion ever being mentioned as a reason why we ought to do something." Such admissions led Balmer to conclude that the "abortion myth" is simply a fiction that attributes "noble and altruistic motives" to the formation of the Religious Right when in fact its leaders entered the political arena to protect the tax-exempt status of segregated schools. He argued that linking the anti-abortion movement to the abolitionist crusade is particularly disingenuous; the Religious Right "has no legitimate claim to the mantle of the abolitionist crusaders." Unlike the abolitionists who, according to Balmer, forged "a moral consensus against the abomination of slavery," the Religious Right did just the opposite — they concentrated their efforts "on legal redress rather than [working] to alter the moral climate that would diminish the demand for abortion."[15]

Balmer's reading of abortion is as uncharitable to fellow evangelicals as it is toward American history. For starters, Balmer does not exactly get right the way that slavery ended in America. Abraham Lincoln ended slavery by executive fiat during a war that revealed precisely that a moral consensus on slavery had yet to emerge in the American public. Abolitionists were not exactly pleased by Lincoln's willingness to tolerate slavery to preserve the Union. But Balmer's misreading of the nineteenth century is not nearly as brazen as his attribution of mixed if not duplicitous motives to the Religious Right. Balmer admits that abortion is "lamentable" but thinks, as a "libertarian," that it is a "choice made by the individual and her conscience, not by the state." He also concedes that the Democrats have "botched

15. Balmer, *Thy Kingdom Come*, 16, 17, 24.

the abortion issue," elevating it "to an intrinsic entitlement and . . . [refusing] to acknowledge the moral implications of abortion itself." Still, Balmer does not stop to let his own devotion to Jesus and the Bible point toward a properly Christian position about abortion. His purpose is not to demonstrate what loving Jesus would mean for contemporary American politics; it is apparently to discredit the faithful who followed Jerry Falwell and Karl Rove. Balmer uses one piece of the story about how evangelicals embraced the abortion issue to show that "[p]olitical movements and politicians who seek to clothe themselves in the mantle of religious legitimacy invariably fall prey to self-righteousness, intolerance, and fanaticism." For some reason — perhaps one spelled out by Christ himself when he taught about the problem of removing a speck in an adversary's vision while having a log in one's own eye — Balmer fails to notice that he, like the abolitionists, was exhibiting his own brand of self-righteousness.[16]

The remarkable incongruity between Balmer's professed love for Jesus and his disdain for the Christians of the Religious Right is explicit in the conclusion of *Thy Kingdom Come*. He is relentless in trying to demonstrate how feckless born-again Protestants are in siding with George W. Bush. The legacy of the Religious Right's alliance with the Republican Party for Balmer is as obvious as it is ugly:

> . . . the purpose of all this grasping for power looks something like this: an expansion of tax cuts for the wealthiest Americans, the continued prosecution of a war in the Middle East that has enraged our longtime allies and would not meet even the barest of just-war criteria, and a rejigging of Social Security, the effect of which, most observers agree, would be to fray the social safety net for the poorest among us. . . . Indeed, the chicanery, the bullying, and the flouting of the rule of law that emanates from the nation's capital these days make Richard Nixon look like a fraternity prankster.

Balmer surely has a point worth considering, but he appears to have no sense of politics involving compromise, much less patience for wayward fellow travelers. In fact, the same sort of moral idealism that

16. Balmer, *Thy Kingdom Come*, 19, 21, 33.

Balmer uses to skewer the Right was exactly the perspective that allowed leaders such as Falwell and Robertson to denounce Democrats or secular humanists. The irony of a New York academic who is a priest in the Episcopal Church engaging in rhetorical arguments characteristic of the Moral Majority seems to have passed Balmer by.[17]

It is hard not to conclude that evangelicals, whether on the left or the right, are tempted to bring a Sunday school mindset to the public square. Balmer himself invokes the lessons of his childhood lessons at church. He admits that he has a pin indicating his perfect attendance at Sunday school but thinks he missed the lesson about the followers of Jesus being "obliged to secure even greater economic advantages for the affluent, to deny those Jesus called 'the least of these' a living wage, and to despoil the environment by sacrificing it on the altar of free enterprise. I missed the lesson telling me that I should turn a blind eye to the suffering of others, even those designated as my enemies." Yet Balmer was apparently present for all the Sunday school classes that taught that civil magistrates pursue the same morality in secular society as God requires in the church. Despite Israel's theocratic ways and holy wars in Palestine, the Old Testament for Balmer becomes a model of tolerance and compassion. Despite the New Testament's clear instruction about male ordination, for Balmer it reads like a primer on egalitarianism. In fact, the entire Bible, an ancient book that has little explicit political theory and much teaching about the consequences of sin and the promise of eternal life, becomes in Balmer's hands a textbook on liberal democratic politics. Ironically, Balmer is proof that the evangelical Left can thump the Bible just as hard as the Religious Right when marching into the public square.[18]

Jesus Is My Favorite Philosopher

The perspective represented by Balmer and Wallis, of course, is not new. Balmer may have been enjoying a homey meal with his middle-class Republican family during the Thanksgiving break of 1973, but

17. Balmer, *Thy Kingdom Come,* 170, 172.
18. Balmer, *Thy Kingdom Come,* 175.

Wallis was present for the gathering of evangelicals who issued the Chicago Declaration and gave evidence of liberal-left sentiment among born-again Protestants. It is not clear that the dynamics that informed the Chicago meeting are all that different thirty-five years later. Then young academics and would-be activists took umbrage at the politics of their Nixon-voting parents; today baby-boomer academics and activists take issue with the voting record of their Bush-supporting siblings, friends, and fellow communicants. In other words, the evangelical Left that today would displace the Religious Right has been taking shape for some time. What is novel is that the mainstream political outlets for evangelicals have so rapidly given up on the message and outlook of the Jerry Falwells, Pat Robertsons, and James Dobsons, and adopted instead the idealism that fueled some of the Religious Right's biggest critics. Ironically, then, one of the Religious Right's greatest legacies may be the Religious Left, because what Falwell started by endeavoring to take faith seriously in public is now perpetuated by the likes of Wallis and Balmer.

Proof of the pedigree of the evangelical Left's arguments comes from recent books by the social-justice duo of Tony Campolo and Ron Sider, both of whom teach at Eastern University, a school surrounded uncomfortably by the affluence of Philadelphia's WASPy mainline suburbs. Campolo arguably has been involved in left-of-center social activism the longest of any of the recent born-again spokesmen to emerge as counterweights to the Religious Right. A native of Philadelphia, graduate of Eastern both as an undergraduate and seminarian, and sociologist trained at Temple University, Campolo was first a Baptist pastor in the Philadelphia suburbs before teaching sociology at Eastern. There he established the Evangelical Association for the Promotion of Education, an outlet for college students to work in the inner city among the poor. It was Campolo's way of trying to combine evangelism and social reform. "The more involved they became touching the lives of inner-city kids," Campolo later recalled, "the more zealous they became for Christ."[19]

The activism that Campolo inspired among eager undergradu-

19. Ted Olsen, "Tony Campolo: The Positive Prophet," *Christianity Today* 47 (Jan. 2003), 34.

ates became the trademark of his career. He continued to teach sociology but his popularity derived from his abilities as a communicator. In effect, his popular speaking would combine the biblical exhortations of a preacher and the analysis of a sociologist. But Campolo could also be a loose cannon on the speaker's circuit and he drew crowds sometimes because of provocation. For instance, a popular line in one of his talks goes like this: "I have three things I'd like to say today. First, while you were sleeping last night, 30,000 kids died of starvation or diseases related to malnutrition. Second, most of you don't give a shit. What's worse is that you're more upset with the fact that I said 'shit' than the fact that 30,000 kids died last night." Campolo has clearly grabbed the attention of evangelical audiences thanks to his clever mix of slang, inspiration, and statistics. But whether his one-liners add up to a thoughtful or wise grasp of the United States and its capacity for Campolo's biblical justice is another question.[20]

In fact, Campolo's willingness to arouse audiences with uncomfortable ideas or language is indicative of his habit of rattling cages. In 1985 evangelical leaders conducted an informal heresy trial against Campolo for at least incautious if not heretical statements he made about the deity of Christ in *A Reasonable Faith* (1983). His examiners found that Campolo was chiefly guilty of committing a doctrinal "faux pas" but not heresy, because he was not trying to make normative assertions about Christ. This incident did not push the Eastern professor into a course of greater caution. In 1994 with his wife he gave a highly contested speech about homosexuality in which Campolo distinguished between orientation and practice to argue that orientation itself is not sinful. He also affirmed that for gays and lesbians, living in monogamous relationships would be preferable to sexual license.

A few years later Campolo burnished his reputation for ruffling evangelical political feathers by serving as one of the pastors for Bill Clinton during the Monica Lewinski scandal. And in 2002, when asked to speak at the annual meeting of the National Council of Churches, Campolo remarked that the main problem with liberal Protestantism was not its political sensibilities but its inability to connect the dots between liberalism and the teachings of Jesus:

20. Olsen, "Tony Campolo: The Positive Prophet," 32.

What you have to say about war, about sexism, about economic injustice, there isn't anything here that I disagree with. There's just one problem: you didn't give any indication as to what biblical theology caused you to take these positions. When you leave that off, you leave the rest of us behind. The guy in the pew wants to know, "Is this from the Bible, or is this from the platform of the Democratic Party? Because I've got to tell you, this looks like the Democratic Party platform. . . . We're not interested in what the people in the National Council of Churches think, nor are we interested in what Jerry Falwell thinks. We are interested in what the Bible says.[21]

Although Campolo has been pressing concerns similar to Jim Wallis's longer than the founder of *Sojourners,* only in the last decade has he attracted notoriety outside evangelical networks. The attraction has mainly been for journalists and editors who are looking for born-again Protestants who show that the Religious Right is not truly representative of evangelicals. A good indication of Campolo's status as the left-leaning evangelical who still has his finger on the pulse of youth culture — despite being a retired professor — is his contribution to the *Letters* series by Basic Books. Campolo's *Letters to a Young Evangelical* filled out a roster that among others included Dinesh D'Souza's *Letters to a Young Conservative,* George Weigel's *Letters to a Young Catholic,* Christopher Hitchens's *Letters to a Young Contrarian,* Nadia Comaneci's *Letters to a Young Gymnast,* and Bob Duval's *Letters to a Young Golfer.* Considering the grab bag of topics and authors, Campolo might not be expected to have produced his most expensive pearls of wisdom in his book of letters. Even so, the gems that he decided to bestow had less to do with timeless truths about the human condition or spiritual lessons from an older evangelical than with Campolo's own dissatisfaction with the Religious Right and evangelical support for the Republican Party.

After penning letters about evangelism, speaking in tongues, and beliefs about the end times, Campolo devoted the bulk of his letters to convincing young evangelicals not to be fundamentalists who

21. Olsen, "Tony Campolo: The Positive Prophet," 34.

identify with the Religious Right. Free markets were one temptation that young Christians should avoid. "We say it is immoral to be sucked into the affluent spending habits promoted by the marketing techniques of commercialistic capitalism," Campolo wrote. "We call our fellow Christians to live simply so that the poor of the world might simply live." On abortion Campolo gave modest approval to pro-life arguments but hoped his young correspondent would look at the issue from a larger perspective and embrace government programs, sex education curricula, and even adoption policies (including supporting gay couples adopting unwanted children) that would decrease the frequency of abortions. Campolo's openness to gay adoption foreshadowed a letter on homosexuality in which he urged readers to "work for justice for gay and lesbian people" and to remember that the American ideal of no taxation without representation should prevent laws that bar homosexuals from "representation in the military and government agencies." Campolo included a letter strongly in favor of women's ordination. His reason? His mother. "She had all the gifts to be a great preacher," but fundamentalists prevented women like Mrs. Campolo from "actualizing her God-given gifts and living out her calling from God."[22]

This advice did not sit well with one young evangelical who also happened to be a young conservative. In a piece for *First Things,* Jordan Hylden responded with his own letter to an old evangelical:

> You say that you intend *Letters to a Young Evangelical* to be advice for young Christians. I understand that talking points and rhetoric have their place; that's how politics works. But shouldn't you have spent more time introducing young evangelicals to the riches of the Christian faith? You do give some good advice about the importance of prayer, Scripture reading, evangelism, and accountability groups. . . . All that is good, but even so, I still wondered why you spent so much of your book criticizing Republicans. George Weigel took great care to introduce his readers to the fullness of Catholic Christianity in his *Letters to a Young Catholic,* part of the same series to which your book belongs. You spend a

22. Tony Campolo, *Letters to a Young Evangelical* (New York: Basic Books, 2006), 143, 150-51, 173, 172, 198.

whole chapter talking about global warming and nuclear disarmament, but you never try to help young people understand the Trinity or the Atonement.[23]

Two years after *Letters,* Campolo came out with *Red Letter Christians,* a book that came with President Clinton's endorsement. In the letter from the earlier book, Campolo defined a red letter Christian as an evangelical who wants "to change the world, but *not through political coercion.*" The right method was loving persuasion, not politics: "We want Christians to be political but nonpartisan. We don't want power; we just want to speak truth to power." *Red Letter Christians* did little to extend the arguments of Wallis or Balmer. Campolo simply invoked the idea that Christ has come and inaugurated his kingdom. This provided the platform for Campolo to speak his mind on issues as various as the Iraq War, Palestine, environmentalism, crime, the minimum wage, and political lobbyists. Through it all, Campolo claimed to be above partisanship; he even argued that conservatives and liberals "need each other." Conservatives deserve credit for opposing pornography, "sexually destructive forms of behavior," defending free enterprise, and reinjecting "non-sectarian religion" into public life. But liberals should be praised for women's suffrage and extending civil rights to women and African-Americans. "Neither end of the political spectrum has a corner on the will of God," he concluded. Both sides were necessary to establish a kingdom of "justice for the poor and oppressed."[24]

Ronald J. Sider generally plays the good cop to Campolo's bad one. Both have also established activist outlets away from their home campus at Eastern. Sider's counterpart to Campolo's Evangelical Association for the Promotion of Education is Evangelicals for Social Action, a nonprofit organization that dubs itself a "community of Christians committed to living out their walk with Christ holistically." Aside from the language of community, ESA is one part vehicle for Sider and two parts resource center for persons and congregations who want to live out their faith in matters of social justice and policy. Aside from these similarities, the differences are important. Where

23. Jordan Hylden, "A Letter to Tony Campolo," *First Things,* Feb. 2007, 47.

24. Tony Campolo, *Red Letter Christians: A Citizen's Guide to Faith and Politics* (Ventura, Calif.: Regal Books, 2008), 133, 36, 224.

Campolo's manner is breezy and purposefully provocative, Sider is earnest and has no room for cajoling. Where Campolo's books string together anecdotes and personal asides, Sider treats readers as potential activists who with reasoned instruction might adopt a more faithful form of devotion that will have important consequences for society, the nation, and even the world.

Sider's most recent book, *The Scandal of Evangelical Politics,* exhibits precisely the moral seriousness that renders him, according to Richard John Neuhaus, "a regular scold." This was a sequel to *The Scandal of the Evangelical Conscience* (2005), a book that tried to convict American Christians that their way of life was no different from their unbelieving neighbors. On one level, *The Scandal of Evangelical Politics* also endeavored to convince evangelicals that their political loyalties and activities are as compromised by worldliness as their "lifestyles." But the recent book, almost three times as long as the earlier *Scandal,* was also an attempt at a serious piece of political reflection. As such it may be the most representative of the recent books on evangelicals and American politics for unearthing the particular approach of born-again Protestants to the subjects of power, governance, law, the state, and the market. It is certainly the most earnest.[25]

The Scandal of Evangelical Politics was less interesting for its policy proposals than for its political theory. On the matter of policy, Sider mixed commitments that were standard within the rhetoric of the Religious Right with ideals that stem from the evangelical Left's critique of conservatism. For instance, in his chapter on "Human Rights, Capitalism, and Democracy," Sider enumerated basic civil and political rights such as the right to life, the right to freedom of religion, the right to freedom of speech, the right to a fair trial, and the right to vote. That list would have made perfect sense to Jerry Falwell or James Dobson. But the conservative notion of limited government or its related caution about an expansive state is lacking in Sider's subsequent list of social and economic rights. These include a right to food, a right to productive assets, a right to private property, a right to health care, a right to education, and a right to work. Sider recognizes that basic human rights require a somewhat constrained form of gov-

25. Richard John Neuhaus in *First Things* 4:8, 59.

ernment, and that socio-economic rights often assume a state with powers so broad that human rights are in jeopardy. But in the same way that human rights require the state to have police that will secure these rights, so socio-economic rights may need state intervention, though Sider does assert that socio-economic rights are best satisfied not by the state but by families, churches, and other non-state institutions. He concludes that both human and socio-economic rights are foundational to society because the Bible does not teach that one set is more important or fundamental than the other.

On the sanctity of human life, Sider again sounded a note in harmony with the Religious Right. He did not hesitate to affirm that the Bible and science teach that a fetus is human life and that abortion is a form of murder. "Choosing to end the life of innocent persons is wrong," Sider wrote. "Abortion, therefore, is wrong, except when the physical life of the mother is threatened." He also argued that legislation designed to make abortion illegal and also less attractive involves no violation of the separation of church and state. But Sider does not limit the sanctity of human life simply to abortion. It requires that the protection of human life be extended across the board, even to smoking. "Christians must insist that the sanctity of human life applies to everyone," Sider insisted, "including people seduced by clever cigarette advertising." This meant banning tobacco advertising, prohibiting smoking in public spaces, and educating the public on the dangers of smoking. Unclear in Sider's brief case against tobacco is whether he recognized that by including vices such as smoking under the framework of the sanctity of human life he might actually trivialize the idea of sanctity.[26]

The reason Sider might not be deterred by such an objection is that his purpose is substantially comprehensive. *Scandal of Evangelical Politics* attempts to provide Christians with a biblical framework for public life. This scope shows its weaknesses in Sider's considerations of the state and justice. On the one hand, Sider learned well the lesson of conservative political theorists that the state is only one institution in civil society and that tyranny is the inevitable result of con-

26. Ronald J. Sider, *The Scandal of Evangelical Politics* (Grand Rapids: Baker Books, 2008), 148.

fusing society with the state's reach and purposes. "A vast variety of educational, cultural, and civic institutions flourish with very little dependence on the state," Sider explained. And yet, because the purpose of the state is not simply to restrain and punish evil but also "to foster just relationships and all the other institutions in society," Sider's hope for a comprehensive understanding of justice ran roughshod over the principle of limited government. Consequently, despite either political (e.g., the danger of tyranny) or theological (e.g., the depravity of rulers) objections, Sider was unwilling to abandon the big-government, progressive arguments that early on informed efforts to rouse evangelicals against the status quo of Nixon's America. Sometimes, he explained, the state simply needs to make up for the ineffectiveness of mediating institutions. When families, churches, and voluntary associations cannot restrain "economic injustice" or provide care for the destitute, "the state must act directly to demand patterns of justice and provide vital services." Sider qualified this assertion by claiming that such state intervention should not weaken but rather should restore and strengthen "nonstate institutions." But biblical requirements for justice, especially distributive justice, muddled Sider's attempt to balance the interests of the state and mediating institutions. According to Sider, the Bible demands empowering the weak and the needy, and restoring the marginal and stranger to community. Sometimes a proper mix of state and private activity can achieve distributive justice better than state programs that may create dependency. At the same time, "the biblical understanding of justice demands clear, dramatic change . . . *in every society on this planet*" (emphasis added). The utopian accent is hard to miss. But Sider's appeal to the Bible apparently justifies such idealism.[27]

In fact, the major premise of *The Scandal of Evangelical Politics* is that evangelical political engagement has lacked an adequate political philosophy. For Sider, the basis for Christian political theory is "to submit wholeheartedly to the lordship of Christ." The problem for evangelicals is that they have not developed a comprehensive conception of politics the way that Roman Catholics, Lutherans, and Calvinists have. The other difficulty facing evangelicals is the reality of voicing Chris-

27. Sider, *The Scandal of Evangelical Politics,* 80, 81, 90, 126.

tian convictions within a pluralistic society. Sider admitted that the tradition of natural law holds promise for speaking to a religiously diverse and secular society, but he also argued that natural law has significant weaknesses. Its advocates have not been consistent in defining the good society; for instance, some advocate monarchy, others democracy. Furthermore, modern philosophers, such as David Hume and Immanuel Kant, have registered significant critiques of natural law. Yet arguably the greatest strike against natural law is Christianity itself, according to Sider: "Human sin is so powerful that . . . it obscures and conceals" any moral insight that natural law yields.[28]

This leaves Scripture as the only sure basis for political philosophy. "We should turn primarily to the Bible," Sider wrote, "not to unaided human reason, for a clear understanding of morality, the nature of persons, justice, and family." In other words, the normative framework for politics "properly comes largely from the Bible, not mere philosophical reflection." Sider recognized that such an approach would appear to compromise the realities of a pluralistic society. But because of biblical teaching on the dignity of all people, Christians would "distinguish between what biblical norms should be legislated and what should not." The goal is not a "naked public square free of all religious reasons for political proposals." Instead, it is "an open, pluralistic, and civil public square open to all the different religiously and philosophically grounded arguments and proposals that every citizen and every particular community wish to advance."[29]

Two significant problems haunt Sider's laudable attempt to be self-consciously Christian about political engagement. The first concerns the distinctively Christian aspect of his proposal. If the ideal for Christian citizens is to submit to the Lordship of Christ, and if this ideal needs to accommodate non-Christians, then believers will need to live with the frustration of seeing many aspects of policy and law that do not reflect Christ's rule. After all, the norms governing Christians and the ones they might seek to implement cannot be normative for citizens who have not bent the knee to King Jesus. The desire for a consistently biblical approach to politics must inevitably end up with

28. Sider, *The Scandal of Evangelical Politics*, 27, 37.
29. Sider, *The Scandal of Evangelical Politics*, 39-40.

inconsistency. How much inconsistency Sider is willing to endure is a calculation that *Scandal* did not reveal. But by naming his book *The Scandal of Evangelical Politics,* and arguing that the recent evangelical engagement in politics suffers from inconsistency, Sider implicitly claimed ground that his argument itself will not take captive. His point may be biblical, but it is hard to see how it yields the singularity of religious conviction that he finds wanting among evangelicals.

The second difficulty with Sider's framing of Christian political philosophy is its almost compete silence about the political order of the United States. To be sure, the cover graphic is an American flag that appears to be partially wadded like a sheet of paper. So it is clear that Sider is writing with the United States in mind, and that his intended audience is American evangelicals. But these circumstances make all the more curious Sider's failure to mention the most important aspects of the American political tradition — federalism, republicanism, constitutionalism, limited government, and the separation of powers, for starters. Neither does *The Scandal of Evangelical Politics* refer to any of the notable thinkers or statesmen in the history of the United States, from James Madison and John Adams to Abraham Lincoln and Franklin Delano Roosevelt. So intent is Sider on drawing his political theory from the Bible that the concrete realities of the nation that writes and enforces the corporation laws for his publisher go unnoticed. Of course, Sider has what he believes to be good reasons for examining the teaching of Jesus rather than the reflections of Thomas Jefferson. And for the purpose of creating an explicitly Christian approach to public life, his choice has obvious merit. Even so, Sider does not seem to consider where his efforts will place either him or his audience. In all likelihood, such a biblically based political theory will leave Christians with little meaningful to say to other citizens, legislators, and policy makers who are wrestling with the meaning of the Constitution, the scale of the federal government in relation to local governments and communities, or the legitimate sphere of the United States' interests and responsibilities in matters of foreign policy. That the Bible does not address such matters is not surprising. What is surprising is the idea that a book written millennia ago is capable of addressing the specific challenges of modern statecraft.

Even so, the desire for biblically derived political engagement is the wedge that divides evangelical Protestants from the rest of the American Right. That the Bible itself does not unite American conservatives is one obvious predicament. Roman Catholics and Protestants include different books in the Bible and hold divergent theories for how to interpret Scripture; in addition, Christians, Jews, and Mormons, just for starters, hardly agree about holy writ. But even beyond the surface differences over the contents and interpretation of the Bible, evangelical biblicism — the attempt to derive all truth from Scripture — invariably causes the wheels of the Religious Right to veer from the path of conservatism. If evangelicals do not find in the Bible discussion of the priorities or policies that have animated conservatives — after all, balanced budgets and strong national defense were not at the forefront of Christ's teaching — their attachment to the Right weakens noticeably. The search for all political answers in holy writ may be admirable behavior for believers, but it is marginalizing for citizens or members of a political party. Even worse, deriving one's political philosophy from the Bible is remarkably deceptive, and maybe even hypocritical, if it merely baptizes the Left or the Right as Jesus' politics.

From Right to Center-Left

Judging by the most vocal evangelical Protestant writers on public matters, evangelical political engagement has been a flop. That might sound overly harsh. But from the perspective of political conservatism, it is a plausible assertion. Since the mid-1970s, when Republicans began to court evangelicals, the most prominent born-again writers about religion and politics have moved noticeably from an umbrella of concerns associated with conservatism — such as family values, limited government, free markets, balanced budgets, and strong national defense — to items generally identified with the Left — state-sponsored welfare, justice, egalitarianism, and progressive tax policies. The recent public policy statement from the National Association of Evangelicals to which Ron Sider contributed significantly, "For the Health of the Nation" (2005), testifies to the liberal outlook among evangelical Protestant elites. The policy areas to which evangelicals believe they can make the most Christ-honoring contributions are religious freedom, family life, the sanctity of human life, social and economic justice, human rights, peacemaking, and the environment. These are not wrongheaded ideals — who exactly supports war for its own sake? But aside from the matters of family and abortion, these commitments are decidedly different from those of classical American conservatives.

The cumulative effect of statements like "For the Health of the Nation" and books from authors such as Wallis, Balmer, Campolo, and Sider is a marked shift among evangelical leaders away from anything that might be reasonably described conservative. In fact, the relationship between the Religious Right and American conservatives seems to have made born-again Protestants identify more with the Left than the Right. This is not to say that American conservatism has avoided all change since Reagan's first inaugural. The divisions between paleo- and neo-conservatives in 1986 and 2006 are examples of painful refinements and developments on the Right. At the same time, pointing out the shift among evangelicals should not imply that the move from conservatism to liberalism is inherently wrong or without justification. Nowhere does the Bible say that evangelical Protestants must be conservative — it might even have important things to say about not putting one's hopes in princes or the White House. Instead, the point is that the assumption held by most journalists, academics, and pundits, not to mention the general American public, about born-again Protestants being conservative is seriously flawed. During the last twenty-five years evangelical writers have either overtly criticized or shown complete indifference to political conservatism.[30]

In fact, what has emerged over the course of evangelicalism's alliance with the Right is a reversion to the theological framework of evangelicals a century ago — when they supported the Social Gospel.

---

30. In both cases, six years into the presidency of a Republican whom the media and popular perceptions deemed conservative or even far right, traditionalist or paleo-conservatives regrouped to argue that being conservative was much more an understanding about human nature and civilization than about politics or free markets. See, for instance, the symposium on conservatism in *The Intercollegiate Review* 21:3 (Spring 1986); and the various essays on conservatism in *Modern Age* 47:4 and 48:1 (Fall 2005 and Winter 2006).

Long before "WWJD" bracelets became a popular trinket, the notion of asking "what would Jesus do?" was the slogan that motivated American Protestants to seek the Lordship of Christ over all of life. Charles Sheldon, a turn-of-the-century Congregationalist minister in Topeka, Kansas, popularized the motto with his novel, *In His Steps* (1896), a story about the transformation of a town after the members of one congregation simply asked "what would Jesus do?" before doing anything. Sheldon himself was a theological liberal, educated at institutions in the Northeast that pushed America's mainstream Protestant churches to the theological left. But that did not prevent his novel from being a favorite among conservative evangelicals who have kept the book in print over a century later. The reason has less to do with the merits of plot or character development than with Sheldon's appeal to the basic born-again Protestant motive: trying to follow Jesus.

Even the greatest evangelical politician of the twentieth century, William Jennings Bryan, could not resist Sheldon's logic. To be sure, the three-time Democratic nominee for president did not invoke "what would Jesus do?" in his famous "Cross of Gold" speech before the 1896 Democratic National Convention in Chicago. He did not even mention Jesus or the Bible. But Bryan's political theorizing bore the telltale marks of evangelical political reflection, according to Mark Noll. It drew "upon intuitive conceptions of justice because evangelicals in general have trusted their sanctified common sense more than formal theology, the systematic study of history, or the pronouncements of formal moral philosophy." Not to put too fine a point on it, Noll writes, "Evangelical political reflection is nurtured by a commonsensical biblicism for the same reasons that a 'Bible only' mentality has flourished among evangelicals."[31] For this reason, the appeal of the Bible or simply following the teachings of Jesus for evangelicals should not surprise anyone who understands the history and character of born-again Protestants in America. What may be surprising is that American citizens with such evangelical convictions *ever* identified with political conservatism.

---

31. Mark A. Noll, "The Scandal of Evangelical Political Reflection," in Richard John Neuhaus and George Weigel, eds., *Being a Christian Today* (Washington: Ethics and Public Policy Center, 1991), 70.

SEVEN

Conservatism without Heroism

―――

I n its cover story for February 7, 2005, on the twenty-five most influential evangelicals in the United States, *Time* magazine described Michael Gerson as President George W. Bush's "Spiritual Scribe." Prior to joining the Bush campaign in 1999, Gerson had worked as a writer for Chuck Colson and Bob Dole, as an aide to Indiana Senator Dan Coats, and as a senior policy advisor at the Heritage Foundation. Whether or not these credentials constitute a career deeply linked to either movement conservatism or the Religious Right, Gerson's identity as both an evangelical Protestant and an advisor to several conservative politicians, not to mention writing speeches for the president who straddled the worlds of conservative politics and evangelical faith, established him as one of the representative figures of faith-based conservatism. When in 2007 his book *Heroic Conservatism* was published with HarperOne, it became a benchmark for gauging the place of evangelical Protestantism within the American Right. Gerson's book represented the most mature reflection from within the world of the Religious Right on the nature of conservatism. It was, in effect, evangelicalism's dissertation after twenty-five years of advanced study with political conservatives.

As much as Gerson's book was an apology for an administration under siege from both the Left and the Right, he also tried to define conservatism in a way that would answer the president's critics. Gerson's approach to conservatism was an attempt to combine the best of America's political traditions and the moral convictions of Christianity. In sum, the author was unapologetic in defending the value of religious and moral truths for the task of governance both domestically and internationally. "I believe the security of our country depends on idealism abroad — the promotion of liberty and hope as the alternatives to hatred and bitterness," Gerson wrote. "I believe the unity of our country depends on idealism at home — a determination to care for the weak and vulnerable, and to heal racial divisions by the expansion of opportunity." The Republican Party had a special obligation to carry out this idealism. If not, the GOP would face "severe judgment."[1]

Heroic conservatism, according to Gerson, is a conservatism "committed to the defense of human dignity at home, and the promotion of human rights abroad," one that responds "to attacks on American ideals with confidence in those ideals . . . a conservatism of restless reform, and idealism, and moral conviction." At its root, heroic conservatism takes the Declaration of Independence seriously, not only for American citizens but for all creatures who "bear the Divine image." The fundamental imperative of respecting human dignity leads, then, to an affirmation of the equality of all people as the core of heroic conservatism's political theory. Equality is so basic that Gerson had little trouble using the word *radical* to earmark heroic conservatism; in fact, his commitment to equality was so pronounced that he could not help but present his perspective as radical. "Taking the Declaration of Independence seriously," he writes, "introduces into conservatism a radical belief in the rights of every individual, and a conviction that government must act, when appropriate, to secure those rights when they are assaulted by oppression, poverty, and disease." The breathtaking sweep of such a governing philosophy, Gerson argued, yields "a conservatism elevated by a radical concern for human rights and dignity." Of course, some might wonder if the correct verb was *expand* rather than *elevate*. With this universal mandate, Gerson turned conservatism from a concern for preserving local

---

1. Michael J. Gerson, *Heroic Conservatism: Why Republicans Need to Embrace America's Ideals (And Why The Deserve to Fail If They Don't)* (New York: HarperOne, 2007), 10.

and particular human arrangements into a perpetual state of radical reform — if not revolution.[2]

Yet Gerson showed no discomfort with such radicalism. Conservatism, he admitted, is chiefly a preoccupation with "the accumulated wisdom of humanity — a kind of democracy that gives a vote to the dead — expressed in the institutions and moral ideals which we inherit from the past." But simply following in the path of what is "old and settled" would not do. Gerson objected that conventional conservatism had stressed tradition to the point of becoming "disconnected from a moral vision of human rights." When that happened, conservatism became a "source of injustice." *Heroic* conservatism is the remedy, then, for Republican orthodoxy which casts a skeptical eye on the poor and immigrants, and for "the narrow passions of the Religious Right" which obscure biblical teaching about serving the poor with a moralism that judges "the behavior of our neighbors."[3]

The roots of this new and improved conservatism, according to Gerson, run deep in American and Christian sources. Of the three influences he mentioned, Abraham Lincoln comes first, because he was willing to "risk bloody war rather than abandon the universal moral claims at the heart of the American experiment." Second on Gerson's list of sources was Christianity's doctrine on law and government, "embodied in Roman Catholic social teaching." This tradition combined "a conservative respect for the institutions of family and community" with a "radical, uncompromising concern for the poor and weak." The third source for Gerson was the history of religious reform among American Protestants, an admission that unites him with other evangelicals as diverse as Ralph Reed, Randall Balmer, Jim Wallis, and Chuck Colson. These religiously inspired reformers "pushed for abolition, insisted on the reform of prisons and mental hospitals, and led the struggle for women's rights and civil rights."[4]

Aside from Lincoln, most of the United States' presidents that Gerson mentioned were twentieth-century Democrats, thus inviting

2. Gerson, *Heroic Conservatism*, 265, 270, 271.
3. Gerson, *Heroic Conservatism*, 22, 23.
4. Gerson, *Heroic Conservatism*, 23.

the question of whether heroic conservatism is substantially different from twentieth-century American liberalism. For instance, he highlighted John F. Kennedy and Franklin D. Roosevelt's attribution of human dignity to a belief in God. Gerson praised Harry Truman's foreign policy for advancing the cause of freedom in Europe after World War II, and Lyndon Johnson for implementing the Civil Rights Act and upending formal oppression of blacks in the American South. The only Republican president other than Lincoln to receive favorable mention was the Reagan Democrat of Reagan Democrats, Ronald Reagan, who as the leader of the free world extended the progress of liberty by winning the Cold War.[5]

Gerson's litany of American presidents could lead a reader to wonder why the speechwriter for Bush didn't simply embrace modern liberalism as the embodiment of heroic conservatism. The answer was not terribly thoughtful, but it was to the point. Liberalism, as embodied by the Democratic Party, failed the moral and religious litmus tests. Their commitment to liberty was so thorough that it supported the legalization of abortion. The Democrats, according to Gerson, had become "resolutely secular." In both cases Democratic leaders had abandoned earlier parts of their tradition, articulated by the likes of Hubert Humphrey and William Jennings Bryan, who were committed to protecting human life or regarded politics as "applied Christianity." Gerson's reasoning leaves the impression that but for the Republicans' ability to harness opposition to *Roe v. Wade* and *Abington v. Schempp*, evangelicals might be comfortable with big-government liberalism.[6]

That sense gained plausibility when Gerson tried to justify heroic conservatism as still basically conservative. At one point he considered the objection that his "gallery of heroes," from abolitionists like William Lloyd Garrison to progressives like William Jennings Bryan, is hardly conservative. "In what sense," he asked, "is [heroic conservatism] conservative?" Gerson answered by reworking conservatism, changing it from an understanding of government to a religious and moral conviction. In fact, Gerson objected to traditional-

---

5. Gerson, *Heroic Conservatism*, 11, 19-20.
6. Gerson, *Heroic Conservatism*, 11-12.

ist conservatism precisely for failing to make faith and morality a priority.[7]

Traditional conservatism's problem was its attachment to culture and tradition, according to Gerson. The limitations of traditionalist conservatism became more obvious after the critiques of Leo Strauss, Roman Catholic intellectuals, and reform-minded evangelicals. Gerson explained that Strauss, the great political theorist who inspired neo-conservatism, believed tradition was insufficient to determine right from wrong and that politics ultimately needed reason to correct tradition. Roman Catholics contributed natural law as another source of God-ordained morality that could make up for the limits of culture and tradition. Evangelicals joined the conservative coalition by "contributing a moral vision rooted in faith." (Gerson did not say how evangelicals viewed culture and tradition, likely because they did not theorize about politics.) These critiques of the conservatism that was associated with Russell Kirk and Richard Weaver, and that informed many of the writers and editors for the original *National Review,* did not mean that conservatives and believers were inherently at odds. Indeed, heroic and traditional conservatism overlapped in recognizing the moral character of human nature as the proper basis for political liberty. Both sets of conservatives acknowledged that persons are created to live in community: "We are designed and intended for the noble commitments of family, community, and patriotism — and undermining those duties leaves individuals scattered, lonely, and more susceptible to the false order of totalitarianism." As such, heroic conservatism also upholds limited government. But Gerson's fear of Leviathan had almost no relation to man's need for community. Instead, human depravity dictated that no person or institution could be entrusted with "absolute power."[8]

Despite Gerson's affirmation of limited government, his commitment to a "radical belief in the rights of every individual," coupled with a conviction that "government must act, when appropriate, to secure those rights," quickly overwhelmed any sympathy for traditionalist conservatism. In fact, he had trouble understanding why conserva-

---

7. Gerson, *Heroic Conservatism,* 261.
8. Gerson, *Heroic Conservatism,* 269, 270.

tives had historically been skeptical of big government. Gerson called traditionalism a "world-weary conservatism." "Since, in this view," he explained, "all policy is crippled by unintended consequences, since government is a blunt and ineffective instrument, the best course of action is generally inaction." This position was so incredible to Gerson that it deserved to be mocked: "Conservatives should stand athwart history and yell stop. Don't just stand there; do nothing."[9]

Unlike many of his evangelical peers, Gerson was aware of the diversity within the American Right. That he could tell the difference among traditionalists like M. E. Bradford, neo-conservatives like Leo Strauss, Roman Catholic appeals to natural law, and evangelical Protestant family values showed the effects of working in an administration that tried to satisfy the various constituencies of the Right. But that Gerson was unconvinced by traditionalist affirmations of small government, neo-conservative critiques of the welfare state, or even Roman Catholic teaching on subsidiarity, and still found room to insist on national government as the institution with the responsibility to preserve human dignity and implement the freedom of individuals both in the United States and on planet earth — these elements of Gerson's conservatism suggested an inability to grasp fundamental tensions between his own idealism and the realism that undergirds any position that qualifies as conservative. One of the chief reasons for Gerson's willingness to identify with conservatism, which was at the same time the source of his discomfort with the Right, was his faith. Unlike the skepticism about idealism that characterizes conservatism, firm religious and moral convictions, he believed, inspire and motivate. "Without a belief in right and wrong," Gerson asserted, "without a firm conception of better and worse . . . without a vision of how things ought to be . . . we do not even know what progress might look like." "Muscular action," however, "based on conservative principles, has led to progress, sometimes dramatic progress." In other words, Gerson's faith and moralism could not find a resting place within the many rooms of the Right's intellectual mansion.[10]

9. Gerson, *Heroic Conservatism*, 277.
10. Gerson, *Heroic Conservatism*, 275, 278.

Conservatism Rightly Understood

Asserting that evangelical Protestantism is not politically conservative could be almost as meaningless as saying that Rush Limbaugh is not politically conservative. In each case, the verdict assumes a definition of conservatism that could well be quirky and highly arbitrary. An analogy might be declaring that Irish-American Roman Catholics are not WASPs. Technically, Swedish-American Lutherans, Danish-American pietists, and Swiss-American Anabaptists, along with Irish-American Roman Catholics, should not be classified by the sociological category that used to define the heirs of seventeenth-century colonial Protestants who constituted the so-called Protestant Establishment in the United States. But for cultural politics in the era of race, class, gender, and sexual orientation, making the precise point that Irish-Americans are neither Anglo nor Protestant is to border on preciosity. So what, some might wonder, if evangelicals are not technically conservative? Yet being clear about the character and meaning of American conservatism after World War II is necessary for situating evangelicals on the ideological and cultural spectrum and for readjusting expectations of both evangelicals and conservatives about each other and their place within the American Right.

As mentioned in the introduction, a self-conscious conservative outlook developed between 1950 and 1965 thanks to the contributions of three somewhat diverse groups: traditionalists, libertarians, and anti-communists. Traditionalists like Richard Weaver and Russell Kirk generally took the cultural high ground and argued that civilization precedes politics, and that the permanent things — truth, goodness, and beauty — were more important than policy or power. Libertarians, such as Friedrich Hayek, argued for free markets against state planning. But the libertarian perspective was not simply economic; it also had implications for the nature of true virtue and for the best way of promoting social order. Anti-communists such as Whittaker Chambers overlapped with traditionalists and libertarians by recognizing the pernicious philosophy upon which Soviet communism rested and by acknowledging the worth of human freedom, even in such seemingly mundane matters as economic choices. These three aspects of post–World War II conservatism gave the American

Right a distinct perspective on culture (preserving the heritage of the West), politics (conserving America's traditions of federalism, republicanism, and constitutionalism), and international affairs (support for the free world leavened with a heavy dose of American patriotism). Over time other groups joined conservative ranks. Neo-conservatives — that is, American liberals who grew pessimistic about the abilities of the welfare state but who were committed to America being victorious in the Cold War — emerged in the early 1970s as important conversation partners and sometime allies of the American Right. Finally, evangelicals brought up the rear in the mid- to late-1970s thanks to born-again convictions about traditional morality, hostility to secularism, and the importance of the family.

These historical markers give a feel for the character of late-twentieth-century American conservatism but still do not yield a definition. The granddaddy of all definitions is the one Russell Kirk penned in his groundbreaking book, *The Conservative Mind* (1953), long considered the text that birthed post–World War II American conservatism. There Kirk identified six "canons" of conservative thought. The first was a "belief in a transcendent order, or body of natural law, which rules society as well as conscience." The corollary to this was that politics is simply a manifestation of deeper concerns, both religious and cultural. Kirk's second canon was an "affection for the proliferating variety and mystery of human existence, as opposed to the narrowing uniformity, egalitarianism, and utilitarian aims of most radical systems." This conservative pleasure principle was the source of conservatives' enjoyment of life. The third canon was the "conviction that civilized society requires orders and classes," and so is opposed in principle to the idea or appeal of a classless society. Equality before the law was one thing, but equality of condition was completely another, usually the product of radicals and dreamers. The fourth canon, arguably the shortest, was the "persuasion that freedom and property are closely linked." Without a sphere of private possession, the state invariably controls more and more of human existence. Kirk's fifth canon was a "faith in prescription" or custom and convention, coupled with a distrust of "sophisters, calculators, and economists" who sought to reconstruct society according to abstract ideals. Finally, conservatives recognized that change was not always desirable; "hasty innovation may be a devouring conflagration, rather than a torch of progress." For this reason, a conservative's chief virtue was prudence, which involved taking providence into account when considering social change.[11]

The problem with Kirk's canons of conservative thought was that they were only grudgingly canonical. He warned that conservatives were inherently reluctant to "condense profound and intricate intellectual systems to a few pretentious phrases." Even more, conservatism was "not a fixed and immutable body of dogmata." Instead, it was constantly in flux, seeking to re-express its convictions to time and place. In effect, conservatism was not an ideology but in fact an anti-ideology. This is why Kirk avoided defining conservatism by ideas or doctrines. Instead he used words like "belief," "affection," "conviction," "persuasion," "faith," and "recognition" to point to conservative instincts or disposition. This underscored the point that as much as conservatives emphasized the past, with its wisdom, morality, and social order, conservatism was not an abstract system of ideas imported from an ideal social or political order. It was rather an intuition. Kirk may have been trying to say, as counterintuitive as it sounds, that liberals were the ones who believed ideas have consequences. He believed that liberalism was responsible for intellectual blueprints that would make society and citizens conform to ideals. By contrast, conservatives sensed what is right or true or beautiful and ideally adjusted thought to real circumstances, both good and bad.

This submission to concrete human existence in all of its earthly diversity and messiness explains why some regard conservatism, rightly understood, as based more on memory than desire, and so more defensive than progressive. Fundamentally, the noun *conservatism* depends on the verb *to conserve*. What a conservative tries to conserve, generally speaking, is the good, a hardly surprising self-definition that seemingly skirts what constitutes the good. But holding fast to the good of the past is important for contrasting conservatism with other outlooks on the Left, where the good is something still

11. Russell Kirk, *The Conservative Mind* (1953; Washington, D.C.: Regnery Publishing, seventh rev. ed., 2001), 8-9.

to be grasped or implemented. According to the political theorist Mark Henrie, "the imagined goods of modern progressive or leftist ideologies are conceived to be 'universal' values (such as liberty, equality, and fraternity)." In contrast, "the good and values defended by conservatives are more readily understood as contingent particulars."[12] This is precisely where Gerson stumbles over conservatism. The conservative's recognition of the provisional character of the good supposedly breeds relativism. According to Gerson, traditional conservatism is inherently skeptical and so "impatient with moralism and dismissive of all grand ideals and schemes of reform." The problem, Gerson argues, is that such an acknowledgment of the contingency of the good cannot determine "which traditions are worth preserving, and which should be overturned."[13]

Where a heroic conservative like Gerson goes wrong, from a conservative perspective, is by looking at traditions as all-or-nothing, either-or propositions, as if all traditions, by virtue of their accommodating specific, less desirable aspects of human or social existence, do not still embody some good and so are worth preserving. For Gerson, concrete human goods need a philosophical or moral foundation that transcends time and place. "The ideas of justice and tolerance," he writes, "require at least one absolute truth." For Gerson, that truth is human dignity. Without a moral foundation, conservatism bleeds into skepticism. But according to Henrie, conservatives know of no "single substance knowable as Tradition per se, but rather many historical traditions, great and small, each making a claim for allegiance and conservation on its own particular terms." Henrie adds that "while there may be a Socialist International or a Communist International — one may even speak of a Liberal International — there has never been a Conservative International."[14] The reason is that the aspects of personal, social, and cultural existence that conservatives seek to conserve vary according to time and place. Again, conservatives are driven more by concrete realities than by abstract thought.

12. www.firstprinciplesjournal.com/articles.aspx?article=58theme=weciv&loc=b.
13. Gerson, *Heroic Conservatism*, 273.
14. www.firstprinciplesjournal.com/articles.aspx?article=58theme=weciv&loc=b.

A particularly good illustration of conservatism's concreteness as opposed to liberalism's abstractness is Gerson's political ideal of individual rights. English philosopher Roger Scruton explains helpfully that the guiding principle of liberalism is "an attitude of respect toward the individual existence — an attempt to leave as much moral and political space around every person as is compatible with the demands of social life." Inherent in this understanding of personal liberty, Scruton adds, is a form of egalitarianism, because "by its very nature, the respect which liberalism shows to the individual, it shows to each individual equally." Conservatism, in contrast, is less concerned with the individual (even if modern conservatism has included libertarians, who like conservatives fear the growth, consolidation, and centralization of power in remote and large-scale national structures). Scruton argues that conservatives pay attention to the "long-term effects of social customs and political institutions." "Immediate and consoling prejudices" may conflict with a single person's ability to do whatever he wants, but conservatives "are reluctant to countenance the reform of institutions that seem to promote the happiness of those who submit to them."[15]

Underneath this contrast between conservatism's regard for order and liberalism's advocacy of individual freedom are conflicting dispositions about the nature of human existence. To illustrate this difference, Scruton contrasts Immanuel Kant's understanding of human rights with David Hume's recognition of historical contingency. For the former, the ideal of personal freedom leads to the construction of "a transcendental self, outside nature and outside the 'empirical conditions' of the human agent," governed entirely by reason disconnected from real, earthly attachments and affections. This conception of the rational autonomous self leaves a person unable to act in the real world and completely untethered to "the conditions which distinguish *me*." Hume approached the human situation differently. He rejected the Kantian notion of reasoned autonomy, according to Scruton, because that perspective is "fraught with illusion." For Hume the correct understanding of the self was to see

15. Roger Scruton, *The Meaning of Conservatism* (Chicago: St. Augustine's Press, third rev. ed., 2002), 182, 186.

people "immersed in the contingencies of social life, acting from passions which respond to the changing circumstances of existence."[16]

In sum, according to Scruton, liberalism and conservatism differ fundamentally in their dispositions. The liberal relies upon a transcendental perspective that abstracts individuals from social circumstances and human limitations, while the conservative presumes the inescapable nature of an individual's social, historical, and personal existence. Scruton captures well the conservative disposition when he writes,

> People are born into a web of attachments; they are nurtured and protected by forces the operation of which they could neither consent to nor intend. Their very existence is burdened with a debt of love and gratitude, and it is in responding to that burden that they begin to recognize the power of "ought." This is not the abstract, universal "ought" of liberal theory — or at least, not yet — but the concrete, immediate "ought" of family attachments. It is the "ought" of piety, which recognizes the unquestionable rightness of local, transitory and historically conditioned social bonds. Such an "ought" is essentially discriminatory; it recognizes neither equality nor freedom, but only the absolute claim of the locally given.[17]

By this standard, of course, the ranks of American conservatives thin out considerably. Along the way through Scruton's remark, conservatism loses its chief radio celebrities, many standard-bearers in the GOP, and various columnists and think-tank intellectuals. Even so, the point is not to read Kirk, Henrie, or Scruton as the keepers of an Ivory-Soap conservatism. Rather it is to recognize a disposition about which conservatives themselves seldom theorize. Balanced federal budgets, strong national defense, free markets — these are a long way from the conservative disposition that traditionalist conservatives describe. And yet these attributes of the American Right do tap the conservative regard for the particular and concrete.

What is revealing, however, is that when self-identified evangeli-

16. Scruton, *The Meaning of Conservatism,* 189, 190.
17. Scruton, *The Meaning of Conservatism,* 192.

cal conservatives such as Gerson attempt to theorize their own instincts, they end up running more in the direction of Kant than of
Hume. Time and time again, born-again Protestants fail to see that
the ideals of autonomy and universal human rights that they so often
champion derive more from liberal sources than from conservative
ones. In fact, the evangelical temperament is inherently progressive.
It seeks to implement change and improvement invariably as a cor-
rective to the past's wickedness. Consequently, the evangelicals in the
U.S. have resembled more closely the Enlightenment project of social
transformation than conservative wariness about change and revolution. Another English philosopher, Michael Oakeshott, wrote that to
be conservative is

> to prefer the familiar to the unknown, to prefer the tried to the un-
> tried, fact to mystery, the actual to the possible, the limited to the
> unbounded, the near to the distant, the sufficient to the superabun-
> dant, the convenient to the perfect, present laughter to utopian
> bliss. . . . It is to be equal to one's own fortune, to live at the level of
> one's own means, to be content with the want of greater perfection
> which belongs alike to oneself and one's circumstances.[18]

Could it be that evangelicals' devotion to God and their yearning for
God's kingdom undermine their capacity to nurture real, tangible,
and yet flawed attachments? To answer that question requires some
attention to the born-again Protestant devotion that inspires both the
Religious Right and the evangelical Left.

Socially Conservative, Dispositionally Progressive

The assumption that any American citizen who favors prayer in public
schools or restrictions on abortion is conservative has not done much
good for the body politic, American conservatism, or even the
churches where many worship. To overlook America's political traditions of republicanism, federalism, and constitutionalism in favor of

18. Michael Oakeshott, "On Being Conservative," in *Rationalism in Politics and
Other Essays* (Indianapolis: Liberty Fund, 1991), 408-9.

a referendum-like proposition on a specific form of behavior is to miss the genuine contributions of the American framers and what they believed was necessary to sustain a liberal republic. To reduce American conservatism to what goes on in or comes out of the bedroom, or to equate the Right with small government, is to miss a thick account of human virtue and the good society embedded in millennia of experience of and reflection about human nature, civil society, and political power. Furthermore, to equate Christianity with the second table of the Decalogue — those commandments having to do with love of neighbor — is to do a great disservice (just for starters) to the first table (i.e., the love of God), not to mention the rest of the Old and New Testaments.

Of course, to blame evangelicals for simplistic renderings of America's political traditions would be equally simplistic. Plenty of journalists, policy wonks, and academics also deserve blame — people whose job it is to know better about Protestantism, American conservatism, and the United States government. Even so, from evangelicalism has issued much confusion about the Christian faith and American politics. An important way to cut through some of this disarray is to inspect more carefully the devotion and zeal that characterizes born-again Protestantism. What is the religious disposition of evangelicalism? Why are evangelicals so different from many conservatives? And how does evangelical piety color political reflection and activism?

At the most basic level, the mother of all evangelical convictions is a reverence for the Bible as the divine, and therefore the only reliable, source of truth. For many of the figures featured in this narrative, the ideal source for political reflection, public policy, and the professional lives of public servants is holy writ. A Christian who does not appeal to the Bible is suspect, because ignoring the Bible in public life is what non-Christians do. Of course, evangelicals make all sorts of allowance for public officials, think tanks, and op-ed writers who do not cite chapter and verse from Scripture; they are not theocrats, having imbibed far more of modernity's servings of cultural pluralism and the differentiation between public life and private conviction than those who view evangelical conservatives as manqué mullahs. At the same time, from an evangelical perspective, other sources of truth about the world are suspect. This explains why so few evangelical authors interacted either with the emerging post–World War II American Right or with a range of other political thinkers, from Aristotle and Augustine to Burke and Jefferson. Evangelicals are simply uncomfortable going to authorities other than Scripture; it feels like an act of disloyalty. Less admirable, perhaps, is the assumption that appealing to the Bible wins game, set, and match in a moral debate. Surely Russell Kirk, an average evangelical might think, has no more wisdom than God. For that reason, the question "what would Jesus do?," which is nearly synonymous in evangelical minds with "what does the Bible require?," haunts evangelical Protestants when they venture into the public square.

This conviction, which is both the legacy and an abuse of the Reformation's doctrine of *sola scriptura,* is not without its problems for political participation in a nation where for many citizens the Bible is not authoritative. Making Scripture a standard for public life while also protecting religious liberty is an exceedingly complex feat. Richard John Neuhaus, by no means hostile to evangelicals or even fundamentalists, put the problem of Bible-onlyism well when he wrote that born-again Protestants want

> to enter the political arena making claims on the basis of private truths. The integrity of politics itself requires that such a proposal be resisted. Public decisions must be made by arguments that are public in character. . . . Fundamentalist morality, which is derived from beliefs that cannot be submitted to examination by public reason, is essentially a private morality. If enough people who share that morality are mobilized, it can score victories in the public arena. But every such victory is a setback in the search for a public ethic.[19]

Neuhaus's reference to fundamentalism should not confuse his point, which is equally applicable to evangelicals more generally. Evangelicals may comfort themselves that they are nicer than fundamentalists; but Neuhaus rightly observes that an appeal to the Bible on political

---

19. Richard John Neuhaus, *The Naked Public Square: Religion and Democracy in America* (Grand Rapids: Eerdmans, 1984), 36-37.

matters, whether from Sarah Palin or Jim Wallis, is not essentially different from the attitude of fundamentalism. Appealing to an authority that has no standing within the legal and political institutions of a society is likely going to be as unpersuasive as the fundamentalist pastor's sermon on behalf of prayer and Bible reading in public schools. Born-again Protestants may not feel comfortable with the formal terms of the society they inhabit — a discomfort that explains efforts to retell the American founding as an episode in Christian history — but in the United States, the Bible is not legally authoritative.

The tension between rival authorities — say, between the Bible and the Constitution — underscores a deep ambivalence among evangelicals about the relationship between public and private spheres in society, a second aspect of born-again devotion that undermines conservatism. The appeal to the Bible for political matters demonstrates that evangelicals have trouble distinguishing norms for one sphere of human existence from those for another. This isn't simply a question of separating church and state. At a deeper level it concerns basic realities about the nature of civil society, the separation of the state from social life so that politics does not dominate all human interaction, and the necessity of voluntary associations and private institutions for all areas of human existence outside the state. With the kind of social differentiation that modern civility requires, differing norms must prevail in the variety of spheres citizens inhabit. In the family, one standard rules; at work, another; at church, another; in the neighborhood association, another; in the political party, still another. But the evangelical appeal to the Bible often breeds the desire for one norm that will establish Christ's Lordship over all areas of life. Given the competing rules by which most moderns live, the appeal of one norm to govern human existence is understandable; it comforts and clarifies. But to appeal to the Bible the way evangelicals so often do is to run roughshod over the very social differentiation that not only allows churches in the United States to thrive but also gives parents freedom in rearing children. Yet when evangelicals appeal to the Bible for public life, they blur a bedrock distinction between private and public life in healthy societies.

Discomfort with the distinction between the public and private only increases when evangelicals turn from questions of human and divine authority to the movement and direction of human history — a third factor that differentiates evangelicals and conservatives. No one will be surprised to see born-again Protestants claim that the United States is God's favored nation. They may no longer use the rhetoric of America as the New Israel, but thanks to several centuries of millennial thought, American Protestants instinctively conceive of the United States as the most important contemporary site in the history of salvation. To view America as a Redeemer Nation — or even just as a nation with special obligations before God — is a safe way for Christians to legitimize their political involvement.

The difficulty with a millennialism that attributes such import to any nation is that it misses a fundamental Christian insight, as old as Augustine if not the New Testament, that is equally important to conservatives — namely, the distinction between ultimate and proximate realities. The apostle Paul, speaking for most of the early church, constantly distinguished between the spiritual realm and the one of this world, imploring Christians to look beyond the fortunes of worldly success or defeat and hope for ultimate delivery in the world to come. Augustine relied on such a distinction between the designs of men and the will of God to understand the fall of the Roman Empire and posit that the City of God was more durable than the City of Man. Fundamentalists, supposedly, used to know this distinction between the affairs of the world and those of the spirit, and their otherworldliness was a constant source of criticism: if only they were not so devoted to Jesus' second coming they might take the existing social order more seriously. Of course, questions may be raised about how genuine fundamentalist otherworldliness was. By dissenting from the mainline Protestant view that the United States was inaugurating the kingdom of God, fundamentalists may not have been questioning the idea that America was divinely favored. Instead, they may only have been criticizing an increasingly materialistic and secular nation for abandoning God's kingdom. Even so, by the time that some fundamentalists' heirs — evangelicals — decided to become politically involved, the older Augustinian ambivalence about the ephemerality of worldly affairs receded and born-again Protestants recovered the conviction, basic to the Social Gospel, that doing the work of the nation was carrying out the will of the Lord.

Over the course of the twentieth century, and especially during the Reagan era, older religious sensibilities that prevented the identification of the Lord's work with American affairs evaporated among evangelicals. This is obvious in the degree to which evangelical writers on both the Left and the Right appeal to the social reforms of the Second Great Awakening as exemplary models of political involvement, or in invocations by allegedly conservative evangelicals, such as Ralph Reed and Michael Gerson, of the Social Gospel. These were instances in American history where Protestants were on the front lines of political engagement and reform, when believers were fighting to eradicate evil and exonerate their Lord. Social reforms, from abolitionism to temperance to women's suffrage to Civil Rights, so the appeals go, demonstrate the success of faith-based politics and the importance of evangelicalism to American society. So even if evangelicals are uncomfortable with an older form of postmillennialism that crudely coordinated God's kingdom with the advance of liberal democracy and Western civilization, they implicitly repeat the error by expecting American life to conform to biblical standards. To require the United States to submit to divine will as revealed in holy writ is not simply an instance of reverence for Scripture; it is also the basis of older American Protestant beliefs about the redemptive purpose of Christian America.

The theological legitimacy of identifying the kingdom of God with the United States is an issue for another time (and for plenty of other books). The concern here is simply that evangelicals consistently violate a basic axiom of twentieth-century conservative political theory: namely, *do not immanentize the eschaton.* Evangelical convictions about the Bible as the standard for national affairs, coupled with assumptions about America's special place in the world, run roughshod over this conservative commandment.

Equally troubling is evangelical theological naiveté about human depravity — a fourth source of evangelical discomfort with conservatism. Born-again Protestants invariably understand the personal transformation that comes with conversion as a complete change that reorients the affections and standards of the Christian. Some of the nineteenth-century's most reform-minded evangelicals, such as Charles Finney, even taught a view of Christian devotion known as perfectionism. Influenced primarily by John Wesley's views on entire sanctification, many American evangelicals held that believers could achieve a state where all known sin was absent. Without getting into the doctrinal technicalities, this view of Christian devotion was a long way from the Pauline and Augustinian outlook that saw sin as reaching down to the innermost recesses of the human heart, something so deeply ingrained that it tinged even the good deeds of believers and could only be overcome in death.

But American Protestants at large, with the exception of some Calvinists, Lutherans, and Anglicans, never warmed to the Augustinian view. Far more appealing was the perfectionist model which inspired individual Christians themselves to seek a complete break with sin, and to look for a society populated with such individuals where righteousness prevailed. This is another reason for American evangelicals' instinctive progressivism. Born-again Protestants tend to be fundamentally optimistic about the possibility of eradicating evil.

Most observers would regard evangelical optimism about holiness to be at odds with conservatism, not to mention large swaths of historic Christianity. The conservative affirmation of human imperfectibility has always nurtured suspicion of utopianism or any effort to establish a perfect society. But evangelical enthusiasm for perfection runs directly counter to this conservative sensibility. Wilfred McClay astutely pointed out this tension between evangelicalism and conservatism in remarks about George W. Bush's faith:

> There is not much of . . . original sin, or any other form of Calvinist severity, in the current outlook of the Bush administration. That too is a reflection of the optimistic character of American evangelicalism, and therefore of evangelical conservatism. . . . But conservatism will be like the salt that has lost its savor, if it abandons its most fundamental mission — which is to remind us of what Thomas Sowell called "the constrained vision" of human existence, which sees life as a struggle, with invariably mixed outcomes, full of unintended consequences and tragic dilemmas involving hopelessly fallible people, a world in which the legacy of the past is usually more reliable than the projections of the future.[20]

20. www.eppc.org/publications/pubid.2271/pub_detail.asp.

Evangelicals may be admirable people for their idealism, but that hardly makes them conservative. If Michael Gerson wants to argue that Bush's faith-based activism is conservative, he is entitled to do so. But he will need to rewire the motherboard of the American Right to convince conservatives and Augustinian Christians that human wickedness can be overcome.

The fifth and final attribute of evangelical piety worthy of mention is anti-formalism. This is a feature that feeds born-again Protestant unease with public-private distinctions and creates an inability to recognize that what may be fitting for the private sphere is not proper for public consumption. As long as evangelicalism has existed — most academic historians trace its roots back to the revivals that exploded in the eighteenth century among British North American colonists, the so-called First Great Awakening — born-again Protestantism has put the internal ahead of the external, the heart over the head, the spirit before the body. This has everything to do with evangelical worries about nominal Christianity, the sort of devotion that readily surfaced in the context of state churches. Because the duties of religion were bound up with membership in the political community, church membership could easily become inauthentic or insincere. Revivals were designed to rouse nominal Christians from going through the motions of church attendance and liturgical ceremony. In turn, religious experience became a more reliable indicator of genuine Christianity than external observance; religious feelings became more important than saying the right words (in prayer or doctrine) or performing the right rituals. George Whitefield, the revivalist extraordinaire, captured the logic of evangelicalism's anti-formalism when he defended his own conduct in preaching indiscriminately in any denominational setting, inside church buildings or outside in the markets and fields, despite his own duties as an Anglican priest. "It was best to preach the new birth, and the power of godliness," Whitefield explained, "and not to insist so much on the form: for people would never be brought to one mind as to that; nor did Jesus Christ ever intend it." Of course, sticklers for church polity, the finer points of church doctrine, or the proper order of worship would not see the matter the way Whitefield did. But their concerns for external forms, from the born-again perspective, were tangential to what was at stake in real Christianity.[21]

Evangelical anti-formalism helps to account for one of the odder aspects of the recent culture wars. On the one hand, born-again Protestants are publicly committed to standards of decency and propriety in popular culture and to a basic, no-frills curriculum in education that is sympathetic to the classics of Western civilization. They want cultural and artistic expressions that will nurture and support wholesome values. On the other hand, in worship evangelical Protestants are among the least traditional of Christians. Their most popular services rely upon a soft version of the rock music whose lyrics are devoid of the historic prayers, rites, and creeds that have informed Christian worship, whether Eastern Orthodox, Roman Catholic, or Protestant. In effect, for six days of the week evangelical Protestants are cultural warriors doing battle against artistic deviancy, but on their holy day of rest and worship they are on the opposite side in the so-called worship wars, doing to liturgical norms what their political opponents do to cultural standards. Anti-formalism is an important factor in this glaring inconsistency. In worship, experience is foremost, and liturgical forms, as opposed to contemporary worship music, are incapable of producing the experience so many evangelicals desire. Consequently, while evangelicals are conservative about the most obvious aspects of cultural deviancy, their conservatism has not extended to worship.

A similar inability to see the links between political convictions and legal or political forms hampers evangelical reflection on public life. Born-again Protestants invariably appeal to the Bible in political reflection not simply because of the book's authority, but also because the American political tradition's conventions of federalism, republicanism, and constitutionalism are merely formal arrangements that may be discarded if a better option surfaces. In fact, the absolute truths of Christianity trump most lesser authorities because of the perceived call to implement those truths everywhere in God's creation. Accordingly, evangelicals are largely indifferent to the forms

---

21. Whitefield quoted in Mark A. Noll, *The Rise of Evangelicalism: The Age of Edwards, Whitefield and the Wesleys* (Downers Grove, Ill.: InterVarsity Press, 2003), 25.

that define political life, whether through legislation, policy, or jurisdiction. If a law or policy eliminates a certain vice, evangelicals are less worried about what said law or policy does to the separation of powers established in the Constitution, for instance. To be sure, evangelicals have deep respect for certain basic American ideals, such as the separation of church and state, the one to which they owe the very existence of many of their churches. And as individual evangelicals become involved in the political process and gain experience in the ways of state or federal policy, such indifference to some of those other ideals subsides; it needs to if an evangelical is going to succeed in politics. But for many rank-and-file evangelicals, not to mention their prominent spiritual leaders, anti-formalism haunts their approach to public life.

To take but one example, debates among evangelicals about illegal immigration in the United States revealed that many born-again Protestants considered the matter not on the basis of existing laws, foreign policy, or questions of international trade. Rather, many authors considered illegal immigration solely from the perspective of what Jesus would do: what is the duty of a Christian in carrying out Christ's command to love one's neighbor? As laudable as that conviction may be, it did not help to sort out the various thorny issues involved. When confronted with specific cases requiring legal discernment and political prudence, evangelicals generally disregard questions of procedure or jurisdiction and head straight for the realm of unmediated justice and goodness.

This disparity was particularly evident during the administration in which Michael Gerson served. According to Wilfred McClay, in his 2007 article for *Commentary* on whether conservatism is "finished," the "inherent tension" between evangelical Protestantism and conservatism was palpable. The born-again Protestantism, according to McClay, that "gives American religion much of its distinctive form and energy . . . is a faith of personal and social transformation" that constantly challenges the status quo. Consequently, even while evangelicalism could function as a force for moral conservatism, it was just as likely to be on the side of "moral radicalism, calling into question the justice and equity of the most basic structures of social life." Because evangelicalism does not share traditional conservatism's "preference for stasis, prejudice, and custom," it has always been an awkward presence in the mosaic of American conservatism.[22]

Same As It Ever Was

If evangelicalism and conservatism differ so greatly at the level of basic intuitions about human nature and society, then perhaps the Reagan coalition that sewed born-again Protestants onto the GOP quilt was a fundamental case of smoke and mirrors. Furthermore, if evangelicals and conservatives look at the United States so differently, then journalists and academics were wrong to miss the ways in which an alliance between born-again Protestants and the American Right could easily unravel. These tensions have been easier to detect since 2006, when Republicans lost majorities in both houses of Congress and discomfort with an unpopular "evangelical" and "conservative" president was palpable. In fact, shortly after those elections *Newsweek* reported on the emergence of a war "between the religious right and believers who want to go broader." The piece contrasted the efforts of James Dobson to rally support for legislative bans on same-sex marriage in eight different states and those of a Kansas pastor, Adam Hamilton, who argued for compassion for homosexuals. The Religious Right, according to Hamilton, "had gone too far" and lost focus on "the spirit of Jesus." The world was not black or white but "much more gray." According to *Newsweek's* reporters, a "serious rethinking of the politics of Jesus in America" was underway. Examples like pastor Hamilton and the mid-term election results showed that "a new generation of evangelical believers is pressing beyond the religious right of Jerry Falwell and Pat Robertson, trying to broaden the movement's focus from the familiar wars about sex to include issues of social and economic justice."[23]

A little over a year later, David D. Kirkpatrick reported in the *New York Times* on the "evangelical crackup" — that is, the aftermath of

22. www.commentarymagazine.com/viewarticle.cfm/is-conservatism-finished-10812?page=all.

23. Lisa Miller, "An Evangelical Identity Crisis," *Newsweek*, Nov. 13, 2006, at http://www.newsweek.com/2006/11/12/an-evangelical-identity-crisis.html.

the Religious Right's founding generation's "passing from the scene." The younger generation of pastors, Rick Warren and Bill Hybels, were taking the place of Falwell, Dobson, and Robertson. Hybels, the highly acclaimed founding pastor of Willow Creek Community Church in suburban Chicago, the megachurch of megachurches, told Kirkpatrick, "The Indians are saying to the chiefs, 'We are interested in more than your two or three issues. We are interested in the poor, in racial reconciliation, in global poverty and AIDS, in the plight of women in the developing world." Hybels added that "we have just pounded the drum again and again that, for churches to reach their full redemptive potential, they have to do more than hold services — they have to try to transform their communities." What Kirkpatrick found remarkable about the emergence of Hybels and Warren was that this trend was playing out even among evangelicals in places like Kansas, some distance from the upwardly mobile born-again Protestants of Chicago's suburbs and California's Orange County. According to one pastor in Wichita, Gene Carlson, who left the Republican Party to become an independent, "There is this sense that the personal gospel is what evangelicals believe and the social gospel is what liberal Christians believe, and you know, there is only one gospel that has both social and personal dimensions to it." Another Wichita pastor, Paul Hill, more comfortable with Hybels than with Dobson, told Kirkpatrick that among evangelicals "there is a kind of push back against the Republican Party and a feeling of being used by the Republican political machine." Hill added that "there are going to be a lot of evangelicals willing to vote for a Democrat because there are 40 million people without health insurance and a Democrat is going to do something about that."[24]

Coverage of the leftward drift among evangelicals continued in the summer of 2008, a little less than two months before the big political parties' national conventions, with a story by Pulitzer-prize-winning journalist Frances FitzGerald for the *New Yorker*. FitzGerald interviewed Joel C. Hunter, an evangelical pastor of a large church in Orlando, Florida, and a board member of the National Association of

---

24. David D. Kirkpatrick, "The Evangelical Crackup," *New York Times*, Oct. 27, 2007, at http://www.nytimes.com/2007/10/28/magazine/28Evangelicals-t.html.

Evangelicals. The fact that so many evangelical pastors like Hunter were echoing Hybels and Rick Warren was significant, according to the *New Yorker* story. "We're at a watershed in our history," Hunter told FitzGerald. "What has passed for an 'evangelical' up to now is a stereotype created by the people with the loudest voices." A new constituency of born-again Protestants is emerging, "like the force of a tsunami under the water." E. J. Dionne, a columnist for the *Washington Post,* told FitzGerald that the era of the Religious Right was over. The old convictions that energized evangelicals — the protection of the family, together with the responsibilities and ethic that sustained Christian families — were no longer sufficient for a new generation of evangelicals. According to Hunter, "The younger generation, that's what's driving this thing. We've got a bunch of kids now who are just reminding us, 'Quit playing to the categories. They don't matter. Try to get things done. That's what matters.'" FitzGerald included polling data that measured the size of the tsunami that Hunter intuited. Born-again Protestants aged eighteen to thirty, according to the data, cared more about abortion than their parents but were more tolerant of gay marriage, and more concerned about healthcare, poverty, and the environment. Another poll indicated that 55 percent of college-educated evangelicals called themselves conservative on personal morality but only 34 percent considered themselves economic conservatives, and only 14 percent believed they were conservative about national healthcare and welfare policy. Statistics like that indicated to FitzGerald that the Religious Right's days were numbered.[25]

Of course, the unpopularity of the Bush administration and the Iraq War made identification with conservatism less attractive than it was under Ronald Reagan or even George H. W. Bush. Still, the shift among born-again Protestants from identifying as conservative to a "broader" or more moderate agenda also tapped sentiments within the evangelical soul that have been too often ignored or misunderstood. At the most basic level, how could restoring a traditional social order even within the most powerful nation on God's green earth compare to taking the entire globe captive for Christ? A conservative

25. Frances FitzGerald, "The New Evangelicals," *New Yorker,* June 30, 2008, 31-32, 34.

outlook is not only too narrow or particular for evangelicals; it may also be simply too small. Still, what evangelicals miss is that to resist change, to try to preserve what is good, involves more than simply yelling "stop" in front of the steamroller of progressive dynamism. A conservative's work is never done. But the never-ending task of questioning and resisting change does not appeal to evangelicals who are addicted to changing the world.

The problem, then, isn't vigor, but perception. Born-again Protestantism thrives on change and breeds discontent with existing arrangements, whether personal or social. This impatience is not inherently radical or utopian, but it produces a similar effect, one that is constantly seeking to pattern existing conditions after a higher ideal. Born-again Protestants stress the imperfections of existing conditions and believe that with the right amount of faith and activity the inequalities and injustices can be fixed. In contrast, the conservative outlook seeks to preserve what is good in existing social arrangements because of an assumption that order is better than chaos, that change invariably produces instability, and that programs of perfection have been some of the most destructive in human history. As Ross Douthat, now a columnist for the *New York Times,* wrote of Gerson's heroic conservatism, "it's a stirring vision in its way, but there's little conservative about it." What evangelicals like Gerson, Hybels, Warren, and Hunter advocate is "an imitation of Great Society liberalism, in which noble, high-minded elites like themselves use the levers of government on behalf of 'the poor, the addicted, and children at risk,'" both in the United States and around the world. This was the similarly high-minded activism espoused by young evangelicals in the 1970s, such as Sider, Wallis, and Mouw, and that even surfaced among so-called conservatives such as Ralph Reed and Chuck Colson. Douthat concluded that American conservatism needs less of evangelicalism's moralism and more of the realism that historically characterized the Right — a foreign policy leavened with a sense of limits, and a domestic policy "emphasizing responsibility rather than charity, and respect rather than compassion."[26]

26. Ross Douthat, "The Future of the GOP: What Michael Gerson's *Heroic Conservatism* Gets Wrong," *Slate,* Nov. 26, 2007, at http://www.slate.com/id/2178571.

The inherently antagonistic dispositions of born-again Protestants and conservatives led Jeffrey Hart, longtime senior editor of the *National Review,* to remark that evangelicalism presents American conservatism with a problem. It used to be an assumption among conservatives, Hart wrote, that religion was part and parcel of what it meant to be on the Right. But according to Hart, evangelicalism has undermined that assumption.[27] Recent history seems like the best — and perhaps the only — basis for that assumption. The longer view, both philosophically and historically, leads to a very different conclusion.

27. Jeffrey Hart, *The Making of the American Conservative Mind: The* National Review *and Its Times* (Wilmington, Del.: ISI Books, 2005), 351.

Why Should *Evangelicals Be Conservative?*

———*ᴧᴩᴧ*———

C onservatism is an acquired taste that is often distasteful to those who self-apply the label. Ever since Edmund Burke articulated a philosophy of opposing change in order to conserve the good within existing social arrangements, conservatism has suffered from theory-surplus disorder. If conservatives are supposed to preserve the best of a society's and culture's ways while building on received traditions to accommodate the inevitable problems that come from human failure (or, in Christian theology, the Fall), then theories about how to conserve tradition are oxymoronic. Traditional societies by their very nature conserve their ways without the help of philosophers or statesmen telling them how to do it. Conservatism is inherently opposed to ideology; thinking about how to be traditional, as opposed simply to living with received customs, is an indication that tradition has ended.

This leaves conservatives in the unlikely position, as Georgetown University professor Patrick Deneen recently described it, of holding on to an "ism" that was intended to resist all "isms." For this reason, Deneen asks, "Can the principled stand against a politics based upon the application of universalized principle avoid becoming universalized?" Conservatism, as this question suggests, can only respond to liberal theories about the good society with its own theory. In which case conservatism becomes another ideology, thus attracting lots of ideologues, such as libertarians, neo-conservatives, and —

the subject of this book — evangelical Protestants. And it is precisely ideologues, those who conceive of conservatism as a universal set of principles — much in the way that the French Revolutionaries invoked freedom, equality, and fraternity as they overturned France — who need to acquire a taste for conservatism.[1]

One implication of the tension between conservatism and conservatives is that evangelicals are not unique in failing to understand the contours of the American Right. In other words, they would hardly be the first group of Americans to examine the menu of political theories and opt for one other than conservatism — at least of the Burkean kind. They would not even be the only self-identifying conservatives to be uncomfortable with the traditionalist conservative opposition to ideology. Even if truth in advertising is becoming to those who tout the necessity and value of the Ten Commandments, the American Right has so many variations that evangelical claims to conservatism do not necessarily violate the commandment against bearing false witness. If born-again Protestants are guilty of not being conservative, their fault is more on the order of omission than of commission. Indeed, if it turns out that evangelicals do not want to be conservative, they are no less virtuous, patriotic, or admirable than plenty of other Americans who shrink from conservatism.

This leads to an important question: other than for the sake of consistency, why might evangelicals want to be conservatives of a traditionalist kind? What's in it for them? A couple of essays from proponents of conservatism are worth considering to answer these questions. While they identify attributes of conservatism that are particularly beneficial for evangelicals and the life they hope to conserve, these authors also implicitly pinpoint the weakest link between conservatism and evangelicalism: conservatives regard diversity and heterogeneity as basic to a conservative society, while evangelicals too often see diversity and heterogeneity as a threat not only to themselves but also to the United States and even the world.

---

1. Patrick J. Deneen, "Are You Sure You Want a Revolution?" *The American Conservative*, April 1, 2010, at http://www.amconmag.com/article/2010/apr/01/00016/.

Uniformity May Be Good for Cars, but Not for Persons

Of these two articles on conservatism, Mark Henrie's is arguably the more provocative, since it was written after twelve years of Republican rule in the White House and at the dawn of the Clinton administration. The early 1990s was a time when most American conservatives were celebrating the accomplishments of Reagan's revolution and cowering at the prospect of Democratic social engineering and big government. Even worse, conservatives were generally blaming George H. W. Bush for defeat in the 1992 election because he had abandoned Reagan's conservative agenda. Although Henrie did not credit Bush with being very conservative, he did concede that the defeat of Soviet communism had left American conservatives without a clear opponent that could clarify their position. The problem for conservatives, then, was one of identifying an enemy. Bush's failure in the contest with Clinton was less an indication of the GOP's distance from conservatism than a symptom of the Right's incoherence after the fall of communism.

Henrie argued that conservatives were right to define themselves against big government. Since communism represented the Wal-Mart of big governments known to political history, the instinctive conservative opposition to the ideology of the Soviet Union made complete sense, and it make conservatism laudable. The problem, however, was in the *way* that conservatives opposed communism. By basing their opposition on social contract theory and liberal individualism, conservatives pitted individual rights and liberties against the laws and authority of the state. For Henrie this was a doomed approach. It failed to recognize that the central dynamic of modern politics is the increase of individual rights and personal liberties along with (not in opposition to) the expanding power of the state. In other words, the state has expanded its scope and power at least in part by granting more and more liberties to individuals. The outcome of granting more freedoms to individuals is restraint not upon the state but upon the authority of intermediate institutions and associations such as families, churches, neighborhood associations, private charities, and schools (whether private or public). "The universal and homogenous state has come to be," Henrie writes, "when the ideas of universal liberty and equality are actualized in a democratic polity that protects individual rights and which features a well-regulated, but free, market economy."[2]

The mention of the economic factor in the state's growing authority led Henrie to correct another popular misconception about conservatism. Rather than pitting big government against free markets (an ideal bound up with that of free individuals, unencumbered in making up their purchasing minds or wills), big government and big business exist in a co-dependent relationship in the process of rationalizing society. The organization of human life into economic, legislative, and policy spheres, Henrie argues, destroyed those informal rules and expectations that govern a host of human activities conducted by institutions outside either the logic of the market or the power of the state. From Henrie's perspective, then, the market is as much a threat to the freedom and authority of families, churches, and schools as is the state. Big business exists in a realm "where uniform laws of rational efficiency act to the end of *homogenization*." Henrie adds that the market also contributes to dehumanization by ignoring, just as big government does, the "human goods" of "community, solidarity, and indeed even eccentricity" that persons experience within the non-political and non-economic spheres of life. Conservatism is fundamentally about conserving these human goods through traditional institutions and associations, because its primary concern is the health of the human soul. For Henrie, "Conservatism is always a *personal* affair."[3]

The problem is that such conservatism runs counter to popular common sense. Henrie admits that conservatism generally resists not only the homogenization upon which big government and corporate capitalism depend, but also the efficiency that the modern state and free markets yield. By favoring heterogeneity and decentralization, conservatives appear to defend the indefensible. "Because the liberalism that gives rise to the liberal and homogenous state presents itself as inherently more efficient and more rational than any other ap-

2. Mark C. Henrie, "Rethinking American Conservatism in the 1990s: The Struggle Against Homogenization," *Intercollegiate Review* 28:2 (Spring 1993), 11.

3. Henrie, "Rethinking American Conservatism in the 1990s," 12.

proach to modern society, those who defend traditional social arrangements" are driven into "illogicalities or insincerities." Henrie recognizes this weakness and thinks conservatives need to acknowledge as well that traditional societies will make available fewer of the goods and services that large bureaucratic states and corporations produce.[4]

Nevertheless, a conservative society will have more of the human goods that liberal rational orders neglect, such as strong families, healthy communities, charitable organizations, and perhaps even greater political participation. This was clearly the political philosophy of the American founders, whether federalist or anti-federalist, who limited the federal government and some of whom envisioned an American republic built on the integrity of strong local governments and modest economic ambitions. This outlook played out in the antebellum era when American civil society — about which Alexis de Tocqueville marveled — thrived through a thick network of private and voluntary associations that provided most of the services that the state could not. Henrie recognizes that after liberal philosophy has gained the upper hand and advertised its wares for the better part of 150 years, conservatives will need to pick their moments. But a creative defense of the basic and ordinary customs that prevail in the quotidian aspects of human existence — from the office, factory, and pasture to the kitchen table — is essential to the outlook that prompts conservatives to resist cultural, political, and economic homogeneity.[5]

The second of the two articles worthy of inspection by evangelicals comes from Patrick Deneen. This piece comes on the heels of another Republican defeat, that of John McCain and Sarah Palin. Deneen is particularly vexed by the current reality of conservatism degenerating into an ideology every bit as ideological as the Left. He points out that conservatism arose (with Edmund Burke) as a denunciation of theoretical (read: ideological) approaches to politics, such as the French Revolutionaries' attempt to rationalize and even mechanize traditional French society. Of course, the temptation for conservatism is to respond with a rival theory of politics or the good society.

---

4. Henrie, "Rethinking American Conservatism in the 1990s," 13.
5. Henrie, "Rethinking American Conservatism in the 1990s," 14.

Consequently, over time "political conservatism has stood less for a defense of the principles articulated by Russell Kirk — custom, variety, prudence, imperfectability, community, and restraint of power — and has instead allied itself with national and even international objectives destructive to custom, variety, and community." Deneen observes the irony (and inconsistency) of conservatives demanding "support for the expansion of military and economic power, resource exploitation with little discussion of impact upon future generations, a globalized market, a standardization of law that is increasingly based in Kantian (rather than common-law) reasoning, 'democratization' abroad, federal rather than local allegiances, mobility, and a close affiliation with corporations and the financial industry." At the same time, he faults conservatism for adopting a scorched-earth policy on its own adherents: either follow the program or drop the label.[6]

The reasons for the contemporary difficulties that afflict conservatism are many, but Deneen hypothesizes that an uncritical embrace of nationalism is the culprit, which in turn has fostered neglect of the local, regional, and intermediate aspects of American life. He notes, for instance, that the Pledge of Allegiance, a patriotic rite of the Right, was originally aimed to rid the United States of the particular attachments that supposedly stood in the way of a great nation. "Nationalism was understood to be a necessary step in liberating individuals from local cultures that put limits upon the full expression of a more universal self-understanding, as well as the goals of personal autonomy and upward mobility," Deneen writes. "Thinkers such as Herbert Croly and John Dewey, writing for the appropriately titled *New Republic,* called for a new religiously-tinted devotion to the nation as the source of individual liberation and national greatness." Consequently, while American conservatism was supposed to defend local authorities from nationalizing trends, over the twentieth century the Right embraced nationalism to rival liberalism's proposals for reforming the United States and even the world. According to Deneen,

> If the Left flirted with the idea of a world state, conservatism would counter with fulsome nationalism. If the Left showed signs

6. Deneen, "Are You Sure You Want a Revolution?"

of increasing secularity, conservatism would embrace a civic religion that propounded the idea of America as Redeemer Nation. If the Left became disdainful of the American and Western traditions, conservatism would demand loyalty to the idea of America as articulated in the Declaration and rationalist political philosophy. If the Left moved in the direction of economic socialism, conservatism would embrace the free-market ideology of libertarian economics, despite the fact that thinkers like Friedrich Hayek, Milton Friedman, and James Buchanan rejected the label "conservative." If the Left became increasingly pacifistic, conservatives would respond with a strong assertion of militarism. If the Left's pacifism led it to withdraw from the difficult military challenges presented by tyrants, conservatism would become the Wilsonian defender of a movement toward worldwide democratization.[7]

The result was a form of conservatism distant from the original impulse of resisting radical plans to remake society. Indeed, conservatism has become the opposite of what Russell Kirk described in *The Conservative Mind*. According to Deneen, "custom became economic monoculture (i.e., globalization); variety became nationalism; prudence became Kantian jurisprudence; imperfectability became a religion of secular redemption; community became mobility; and restraint of power became lust for power, particularly control of the national agenda." Ironically, the result has been the "further evisceration of the folkways, traditions, and commitments that an originally conservative disposition arose politically to defend."[8]

As much as Deneen's article raises important questions that extend well beyond the relationship between evangelicalism and conservatism to the very identity of the Right in the United States, it does, with Henrie's, identify a significant stumbling block for born-again Protestants who would be conservative. Conservatism has traditionally resisted uniformity and homogeneity, not because of a sentimental celebration of diversity but because conservatives believe national programs to be incapable of producing the human goods that families, communities, schools, and voluntary associations do. These cul-

---

7. Deneen, "Are You Sure You Want a Revolution?"
8. Deneen, "Are You Sure You Want a Revolution?"

tural goods may not be the same as the grand accomplishments readily produced by large-scale enterprises like nation-states or corporations. But traditional conservatives recognize, as few politicians or business leaders do, that the affairs of states and the capabilities of companies depend on the health of families, communities, schools, and a host of other associations that constitute civil society.

Ironically, while evangelicals also acknowledge the importance of many agencies that fall on the local and provincial (as opposed to the national or cosmopolitan) side of the social spectrum, their piety runs against localism. For born-again Protestants, Christianity is the lone solution to the problems of humanity — from spiritual to familial to political to economic. As such, only as people are converted to evangelical Christianity or as evangelicals themselves assume positions of leadership or authority will social institutions and human associations result in the kind of healthy arrangements that they desire. Thus evangelical faith becomes not a means of preserving the ways and customs of a particular people or community or region, but instead a vehicle for transforming society in ways remarkably similar to the changes that alarmed conservatives like Burke or Hume or Tocqueville. Put simply, evangelicalism is a faith that seeks the conversion of all people and expects a high degree of cultural and moral uniformity among followers of the true religion. Evangelicals, consequently, do not seek to preserve existing institutions, because this would seemingly mean the acceptance of unbelief and immorality. Yet, to become conservative, evangelicals — along with many would-be members of the Right — need to accept and even support the variety of conventions, traditions, and institutions that come from non-evangelical citizens, religious communities, and organizations, because such variety among the "little platoons," as Burke called them, is necessary for a healthy, well-ordered, and free society.

Can Evangelicalism Be Saved?

Even if born-again Protestants trip over traditional conservatism's resistance to political, economic, and cultural centralization and homogenization, it must be said that the very instincts that drew evangelicals into the political fray were fundamentally conservative. During the 1960s and 1970s, the United States experienced a number of significant political transformations — from Civil Rights legislation to Supreme Court rulings on public schools, contraception, and abortion — that edged the country in the direction of greater uniformity and undermined the authority of states, school districts, religious schools, churches, and families. Evangelicals responded positively to conservative complaints about the federal government imposing standards on all Americans set by remote legislators and judges in Washington. They were particularly concerned to protect institutions responsible for passing on their faith to their children — families, churches, and religious schools. As much as it became a cliché, "family values" spoke volumes about the Religious Right. Evangelicals feared that the state was going to impose a national order that established secularity, promoted tolerance for sexual deviancy, and stigmatized traditional religion.

This attachment to the family and the concomitant sense that the family is a basic mechanism for transmitting a way of life is an impulse that, however inadequately theorized, makes many evangelicals potentially conservative. If Roger Scruton is right that conservatism fundamentally senses the "unquestionable rightness of local, transitory and historically conditioned social bonds," if in fact it intuits the concrete, immediate "ought of family attachments," then born-again Protestants, who know the family's import not only for its social or cultural utility but because of the attachments it embodies in and of itself, are inherently conservative. They may not know the difference between Ann Coulter and Ayn Rand, or between Russell Kirk and William F. Buckley Jr. But deep down, their regard for families reflects reverence for local and communal ties that characterizes traditionalist conservatism. As much as it strains credulity, Jerry Falwell's *Listen, America!* echoed Edmund Burke's *Reflections on the French Revolution* because the Virginia fundamentalist sensed, like the British statesman, an effort by political ideologues to refashion society without regard for the customs and beliefs of average citizens.[9]

9. Roger Scruton, *The Meaning of Conservatism* (Chicago: St. Augustine's Press, third rev. ed., 2002), 192.

In fact, had the Religious Right used the language of traditional-ist conservatism, they might have argued a better case for family val-ues. Had they read and interacted more with the American Right that emerged after World War II, their rhetoric and even political tactics might have gained a better hearing than the incredulity they usually encountered (except when pollsters, publishers, advertisers, and poli-ticians understood how many readers, consumers, and voters this constituency supposedly represented). But without a discourse in-formed either by the American political tradition or a moral philoso-phy that drew upon classical and Christian reflection, the Religious Right resorted to the language American Protestants knew best — the patois of civil religion and biblical morality. Consequently, born-again Protestants re-emerged as a forceful electoral constituency armed with beliefs about the United States' Christian identity and mission, and with biblical prohibitions regarding any number of ob-jectionable social practices popularized in the media and condoned in public schools. Their patriotism after the era of the Vietnam War and Watergate could look naive, and their morality pigeonholed them as the nation's scolds. Still, the subtext of the Religious Right's pae-ans to national greatness and public morality tapped the essentially conservative disposition of protecting marriage and the bonds be-tween parents and children.

Figuring out how to negotiate their zealous and totalistic faith with the breadth of convictions among American conservatives would be a challenge for evangelicals, and it could require painful adjust-ments to evangelical attitudes toward the United States. But as awk-ward as the relationship between evangelicals and conservatism has been, it is one from which born-again Protestants could well benefit, because conservatives have the best store of public arguments for de-fending the families, schools, churches, and voluntary associations on which evangelicals depend.

To ease the painful transition from evangelical to conservative politics, American Protestants will want to consider a few recommen-dations.

1. Reconsider the source of American greatness. If the United States is a great nation, does its greatness owe to its religious identity or to its political order? Many traditionalist conservatives are understandably worried that the lack of attention to religion in the Constitution has resulted in an understanding of the United States that is fundamentally hostile to religion. But misgivings about the ways in which the American framers adjusted the older expectations for an established religion do not lead conservatives to feature the United States as fundamentally a Christian nation. They recognize that demographically Americans were (and still are) overwhelmingly Protestant, and that even the founders were God-fearers of varying stripes. But what makes the United States important for conservatives is a form of government that begrudgingly created national structures, left plenty of room for state and local governments, and seemed more concerned to limit the reach of the state than to create a powerful nation.

To be sure, the first American statesmen were divided on the nature of federalism and the best economic arrangements to sustain a federal republic. But these disagreements had little to do with either the morality or the theology of the Christian religion. (Can anyone possibly imagine Thomas Jefferson debating Alexander Hamilton over a biblical case for canals and roads?) Evangelical Protestants would be better served in trying to understand the value of the American order by reading not the pages of the Old or New Testaments but the debates between federalists and anti-federalists, Whigs and Democrats, or Populists and Progressives. Even if subsequent political developments — a civil war, two world wars, and a military-industrial complex to sustain such warfare — have significantly altered the balance of power among the United States' branches of government, reading the Federalist Papers will do more to inform evangelicals about the greatness of their nation than meditating on the Decalogues or the Sermon on the Mount.

1a. Acknowledge that "liberty for all" means legal protection and legitimate status for groups who are not Christian and even oppose Christianity. This may seem obvious, except that when American Protestants speak about a Christian nation, they do not necessarily consider the place of non-Christians in such a polity. This is a real dilemma, since throughout U.S. history the assertion of a privileged place for Protestants made public life complicated not only for nonbelievers but also for other professing Christians, such as Roman Catholics. But whether or not Protestants recognized all the consequences of religious and political liberty for their country, when the federal government decided against religious tests for public office and when the states followed suit and disestablished their churches, they were establishing a principle of freedom that extended to all people no matter what their faith — or lack thereof.

Consequently, in addition to recognizing the tension between a Christian America and religious freedom for non-Christians, evangelicals need to see that political liberties have as much to do with voluntary associations as with individual freedoms. As such, evangelicals should follow political conservatives in trying to protect the privileges and prerogatives of private associations and institutions *even if they disagree with the principles or beliefs to which such organizations are devoted.* A commitment to liberty that recognizes both a place for non-evangelicals in the United States and their freedom of association will also yield a concomitant preservation of the institutions evangelicals cherish and to which they devote their time, energy, and finances. To work for this kind of liberty need not result in a relativistic tolerance of false beliefs. Dividing lines based on beliefs within their appropriate (private) sphere is basic for the freedom of voluntary association. Tolerance within the political sphere only means a recognition of fundamental liberties, not a laissez faire attitude to truth and morality. In fact, the freedom of voluntary association maintains something crucial to evangelical institutions — the ability to proselytize. In other words, freedom of association leaves evangelicals with the best means for trying to convince other Americans to turn from false beliefs or corrupt morals and follow Jesus Christ.

The principle of voluntary association in the private realm also has implications for public institutions, such as public schools. Evangelicals are rightly concerned about ideology in public schools that may encourage children to accept and tolerate behavior or ideas that they and their parents deem harmful or unfaithful. (Imagine pro-gay marriage parents reacting to the news that the local public elementary school has removed *Heather Has Two Mommies* from the library because district officials regard homosexuality to be socially harmful behavior.) What evangelicals fail to see is that the problem of a secular ideology in public schools is similar to the one that non-Protestants encountered when the school day opened with Bible reading and prayer. The point of religious freedom — and its flip side of religious disestablishment — is to avoid institutionalizing ideas or practices that conflict with the beliefs and forms of devotion held by any citizen. As hard as the idea of religious neutrality may be to implement, and as theologically naive as it may be to conceptualize, some effort to remain non-partisan on religious matters in public institutions and spaces where Americans with different and contested beliefs assemble and cooperate is the only sensible policy for a republic that remains open to anyone irrespective of faith or disbelief.

1b. Acknowledge that political solutions do not solve the problems of culture and character formation. A repeated theme in the writings of post–World War II conservatism is that politics is merely a reflection of culture. Russell Kirk articulated this point in his book *The Conservative Mind,* and it continues to inform traditionalist conservative assessments of American life.

Again, this would seem to be an attractive perspective to evangelicals, since so much of born-again Protestant identity is bound up with agencies and institutions that shape faith. It is a perspective, however, at odds with thirty years of political activism geared toward putting a godly man or woman in the White House who will restore Christian values in the nation. In effect, if evangelicals can learn from conservatives the priority of cultural matters over politics, they might back away from their identity as a voting bloc and work harder to build and maintain institutions that strengthen families, neighborhoods, and churches (while of course also attending to the variety of local, state, and federal policies that facilitate such institutions). At the same time, if individual evangelicals sense a calling to public office, they may want to consider using their skills at those levels of government — city, township, county, and state — that are closer to the institutions they want to protect and advance. Political conservatives object to the centralization of American polity at the federal level not only because of the tensions between such consolidation of power and the ideas that brought the American republic into existence. They also value local and state governments because such polities work on a human scale and are more capable than national authorities of addressing the diversity of peoples, places, and convictions.

Bottom line: if evangelicals want their children to grow up to be

Christians, they will likely have better results if they spend time coaching in Little League or leading a troop of Brownies instead of lobbying a member of Congress or giving to the GOP.

2. **Reconsider the source of Christian greatness.** Closely connected to the adjustments that evangelicals will need to make in their understanding of American politics is a similar change of mind about the nature and purpose of Christianity. Ever since Augustine, at least some Christians in the West have understood that the true mark of faithfulness is not evident in outward displays of power, such as those possessed by great empires, from the Roman one that fell on the Bishop of Hippo's watch down to the current American regime. Instead, the Christian religion made its most telling marks in simple, ordinary, and spiritual ways, such as saints gathered for prayer and worship, catechumens learning the church's creed, or the care of widows, orphans, and the otherwise dispossessed. Such an idea of Christianity's greatness meant a diminished estimate of the state, and raised considerably the stakes for the work of the church.

One way of coming to grips with a spiritual (as opposed to worldly) conception of Christianity is to consider the doctrine of the keys of the kingdom. Many American Protestants assume that this teaching is only part of Rome's toolkit. But the Reformers also appealed to Christ's delegation of power to his disciples, refusing to grant special powers to the Apostle Peter or his successors in the Roman church's ministry. The Heidelberg Catechism, for instance, codified the doctrine of the keys in the following manner:

83. Q. What are the keys of the kingdom of heaven?
    A. The preaching of the holy gospel and church discipline. By these two the kingdom of heaven is opened to believers and closed to unbelievers.

84. Q. How is the kingdom of heaven opened and closed by the preaching of the gospel?
    A. According to the command of Christ, the kingdom of heaven is opened when it is proclaimed and publicly testified to each and every believer that God has really forgiven all their sins for the sake of Christ's merits, as often as they by true faith accept

the promise of the gospel. The kingdom of heaven is closed when it is proclaimed and testified to all unbelievers and hypocrites that the wrath of God and eternal condemnation rest on them as long as they do not repent. According to this testimony of the gospel, God will judge both in this life and in the life to come.

85. Q. How is the kingdom of heaven closed and opened by church discipline?

A. According to the command of Christ, people who call themselves Christians but show themselves to be unchristian in doctrine or life are first repeatedly admonished in a brotherly manner. If they do not give up their errors or wickedness, they are reported to the church, that is, to the elders. If they do not heed also their admonitions, they are forbidden the use of the sacraments, and they are excluded by the elders from the Christian congregation, and by God Himself from the kingdom of Christ. They are again received as members of Christ and of the church when they promise and show real amendment.

Of course, plenty of low-church Protestants will have long lists of objections to the implicit clericalism in such teaching, and the point of appealing to this catechism is not to settle these legitimate debates. It is rather to suggest an understanding of Christianity that looks to the ministry of the church in word, sacrament, and discipline as the arena in which the only kingdom of ultimate consequence — that of heaven — is being established and extended. It is also to try to make plausible a Christian, or more precisely an Augustinian, outlook that is less impressed by outward displays of might and greatness that earthly governments cultivate.

This outlook is not inherently conservative politically. But because Christianity at its best lowers the stakes of American politics, it is at least compatible with if not supplemental to an estimate of the United States as more a modest republic than a global superpower. In other words, an American Christian need not worry that the cause of Christ requires American might or victory. At the same time, as one who follows the biblical command to seek the welfare of the city, Christians should be patriotic not because of an overestimation of their country, land, or people, but rather from a proper attachment to neighbors and governors in a particular polity and place.

2a. Acknowledge that spiritual warfare is of greater significance than the culture wars. Harry Emerson Fosdick, the liberal Protestant preacher that fundamentalists and evangelicals knew to be misguided — even wrong — actually argued that political contests were more important than spiritual conflicts in his famous sermon, "Shall the Fundamentalists Win?" He believed that the emerging controversy among Protestants over inerrancy and the Virgin Birth were "peccadillos" and "tiddly-winks" compared to the Turkish slaughter of Armenians. Context is important: caution is of course in order for anyone hoping to defend Scripture's infallibility at a United Nations debate on Turkey's responsibility for the deaths of millions of Armenians. At the same time, the average opponent of Fosdick's preaching might easily be persuaded to rise from studying that inerrant Bible to assist a neighbor enduring persecution. Whether this fundamentalist would pick up and relocate to another land to offer such assistance is another question — and one hardly needing an answer, since Fosdick himself did not move to Asia Minor to aid the Armenians.

Those caveats aside, Fosdick's charge of folly against fundamentalists could readily come back to bite him if a spiritual battle between the legions of heaven and hell were going on at the same time that Turks were imprisoning and executing Armenians. With a reoriented outlook on Christian greatness, or the conservative's sensitivity to what T. S. Eliot called the "permanent things," evangelicals could well find room in their Christian devotion to recognize that most important struggles in this life are not covered in the *New York Times* or by talk-show hosts on the Salem Radio Network. Born-again Protestants might even acknowledge that the bills U.S. legislators sponsor or the battles that American soldiers fight have no direct correlation to spiritual battles with the world, the flesh, and the devil. Such a reminder of the cosmic contest between heaven and hell could lead evangelicals to value political victories, like the ones favored by traditionalist conservatives, that reinforce the authority and integrity of institutions on the front lines of the contest between the City of God and the City of Man.

2b. Understand that Christians are called to be not crusaders but pilgrims. Evangelicals, often with benevolent intentions, have long been busybodies. Going back to the Second Great Awakening, they have organized any number of social or moral crusades. They did this, of course, thinking that the fortunes of the kingdom of God were at stake in the kind of society the United States would be. But while evangelicals were busy establishing a Benevolent Empire, even to the point of creating formal mechanisms for conforming non-evangelical residents to Protestant American ways, other Christians — Roman Catholics, the Orthodox, and ethnic Protestants — were building churches and parochial schools designed to nurture a differently calibrated Christian faith. These Christians did not identify the kingdom of God with America but located it within the church, which had the responsibility for shepherding the spiritual flock from the cradle to the grave. While American evangelicals looked for public institutions to embody Protestant norms, these churchly Christians sometimes resisted the rule of Protestant America in hopes of establishing their own colonies of faith and practice.

In contrast to the evangelical ideal of the earnest Christian as crusader, churchly Christians lived more like pilgrims. As people whose ultimate home was in another world beyond this one, they believed that the American nation was not their home, but only their proximate residence. These Christians may not have done as much to change the nation, though the pursuit of a national and centralized set of institutions to enforce Christian ideals would come back to haunt evangelicals. Still, if the churchly Protestants' calibration of eternal realities was accurate, they may have been more faithful than evangelicals in preparing for and establishing a heavenly kingdom.

Today's evangelicals want many of the same things that these ethnic Christian groups did — strong families, good churches, and healthy schools. If born-again Protestants hope to gain those cultural and religious goods, they need to consider the model of pilgrimage practiced by those older Christian groups and the place that political activism occupied in their faith. Granted, social life in the United States today is overwhelmingly different from nineteenth-century America. Even so, the practices of ethnic groups in the U.S. are fitting ones for believers who are supposed to know that the American nation is not their final resting place, but only a way station to their eternal home.

The Evangelical Dilemma and the Conservative Solution

The need for a different understanding of faith and politics is the cry of the hour if James Davison Hunter's new book is any indication. In *To Change the World: The Irony, Tragedy, and Possibility of Christianity in the Late Modern World* (2010), the University of Virginia sociologist took evangelicals to task for thinking that they can make the world a better place through politics. Hunter conceded that the Religious Right is not alone guilty of this naiveté, and that lots of qualifications generally attend evangelical political activism in the form of leaders reminding followers that politics cannot fix all problems in society. Still, "It is not an exaggeration to say that *the dominant public witness of the Christian churches in America since the early 1980s has been a political witness*," Hunter wrote. He added that this "remains true today . . . particularly among the Evangelicals who, through innumerable parachurch ministries, assert themselves into one political issue after another and into electoral politics as well."[10] Hunter believed such political motivation is completely "mistaken" because cultures do not change through politics, lobbying, or elections; changes in culture actually depend much more on institutions outside the political maelstrom. As Hunter explained in an interview with *Christianity Today*, "Culture is far more profound at the level of imagination than at the level of argument." It is like the difference between weather and climate: "Contemporary politics is like the weather, changing day to day or week to week. But culture, in its most enduring qualities, isn't about the weather at all. It's about the climate. Changes in the climate of culture involve convoluted, contested, and contingent dynamics."[11]

Chuck Colson responded critically to Hunter's argument. In a

10. James Davison Hunter, *To Change the World: The Irony, Tragedy, and Possibility of Christianity in the Late Modern World* (New York: Oxford University Press, 2010), 12-13.

11. "Faithful Presence," interview by Christopher Benson, at http://www.christianitytoday.com/ct/2010/may/16.33.html.

companion piece to Hunter's interview, Colson faulted the sociologist for making plausible a form of quietism or cultural withdrawal that would make believers indifferent to suffering. To Hunter's assertion that Christians turning to law, public policy, and politics is a form of using the "patronage of the state and its coercive power to rule the day," Colson responded, "I doubt he would have said that to Dr. Martin Luther King or to William Wilberforce when they waged long and heroic battles against injustice." For Colson, Hunter's proposal will likely result in "Christians remaining silent in the face of injustice and suffering." Instead of seeking the welfare of the city, if evangelicals follow Hunter they will become "indifferent to its decay and that decay's impact on the life of our neighbors."[12]

In his reply to Colson, Hunter explained that he was not advocating abdication of political responsibilities. Instead, he was trying to frame the problem of religiously inspired politics as a "late-modern form of Constantinianism," and for Hunter a state or political religion is the problem that evangelical leaders like Colson do not recognize. What Hunter advocates is a post-Constantinian outlook that first "disentangles the life of the church from the life of America," and second "decouples the public from the private." As such, politics is just one way to engage the world — and not the most effective one at that. Hunter advocates a "faithful presence" that is public and engaged but non-coercive, and therefore not interested in power. For Christians, this post-Constantinian outlook is "the only way forward."[13]

This book resonates with much of Hunter's argument about politics and evangelical activism. I would add, however, that political conservatism — something that Hunter is not necessarily proposing — is another way forward for born-again Protestants. Since it appropriates the form of government established for the United States in 1789, it is clearly post-Constantinian. But it may not fit Hunter's own categories, because this book suggests that the conservatism Hunter eschews is in fact more varied than the current antagonism between Left and Right might suggest. Traditionalist conservatism represents

---

12. http://www.christianitytoday.com/ct/2010/mayweb-only/29-52.0.html?start=2.

13. http://www.christianitytoday.com/ct/2010/mayweb-only/30-51.0.html.

a better form of politics, one that takes the faith of evangelicals seriously while also acknowledging the diversity of the United States and the significance of its form of government. It is on the side of much of what evangelicals want — strong families with parents determining what is best for their children, alternative forms of education that are not dominated by the state's monopoly on schools, respect for the ideals and institutions that have defined American society, and churches that enjoy freedom of worship, speech, and forms of governance. The stumbling block for evangelicals is that conservatism is not inherently or obviously biblical.

If conservatism's lack of an explicitly Christian foundation is troubling to born-again Protestants, another alternative might be to start from scratch and look for an order — say, Christendom or a religious establishment — capable of achieving what they want. But short of going back to medieval Europe or Christian England, or forward to the modern denominational state, conservatism offers a present-day alternative with plausible outlets in already existing institutions and schools of thought. Evangelicals should kick the tires of conservatism and give it a test drive. The ride, despite the potholes, stop signs, and traffic jams that inevitably come from the sinfulness and variety of human beings and their societies, may be just what they need to traverse the City of Man.

Index